Awakening
Your Child's
Natural
Genius

• • • •

Awakening Your Child's Natural Genius

Enhancing Curiosity, Creativity,
and Learning Ability

Thomas Armstrong, Ph.D.

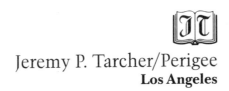

Jeremy P. Tarcher/Perigee
Los Angeles

This book is dedicated to the children of the world—our most valuable natural resource.

Jeremy P. Tarcher/Perigee Books
are published by
The Putnam Publishing Group
200 Madison Avenue
New York, NY 10016

Library of Congress Cataloging-in-Publication Data

Armstrong, Thomas.
  Awakening your child's natural genius : enhancing curiosity, creativity, and learning ability/ Thomas Armstrong. — 1st ed.
    p. cm.
  ISBN 0-87477-623-6 — ISBN 0-87477-608-2 (pbk.)
    1. Education, Preschool—Parent participation.
2. Education—Parent participation. 3. Home and school.
4. Activity programs in education. 5. Learning. I. Title.
LB1140.35.P37A76 1991   90-21074
649 .68—dc20   CIP

PHOTO CREDITS

Frontispiece, Jill Fineberg; page xii, Michael Weisbrot; page 2, Kathryn E. Liston; page 20, Jill Fineberg; page 38, Michael Weisbrot; page 54, Michael Weisbrot; page 74, Jill Fineberg; page 90, Michael Weisbrot; page 106, Michael Weisbrot; page 122, Joe Frost; page 136, Nancy Ellis; page 150, John Schoenwalter; page 164, Jill Fineberg; page 182, Michael Weisbrot, page 196, Michael Weisbrot; page 210, Don Franklin; page 226, Michael Weisbrot; page 240, Nancy Blakey; page 252, Michael Weisbrot.

Copyright © 1991 by Thomas Armstrong

Jeremy P. Tarcher, Inc.
5858 Wilshire Blvd., Suite 200
Los Angeles, CA 90036

To contact the author, write:

Thomas Armstrong, Ph.D.
P.O. Box 548
Cloverdale, CA 95425

Design by Paul Murphy
Jacket design by Tanya Maiboroda
Author photograph by Steven Lee

Manufactured in the United States of America
10 9 8 7 6 5 4 3
First Edition

Contents

Acknowledgments

This book has had its own gradual awakening over the past three years—and there are several natural geniuses who I want to thank for helping me midwife it into existence: Wendy Thomas, former articles editor at *Parenting* magazine who initially hired me to write the "Learning Curves" column that led to the writing of this book; Bruce Raskin, the managing editor at *Parenting* who guided the creation of most of the columns that served as seeds for this book; Rick Benzel, my editor at Jeremy P. Tarcher, Inc. whose enthusiasm for and careful attention to this project inspired me more than words can say; Paul Murphy, for his sensitive design and layout of the book; Jeremy Tarcher, my publisher, for championing the development of talents and abilities in all individuals; Susanne Miller, photo editor at *Mothering* magazine for helping me locate the many gifted photographers whose pictures (most of which have appeared in past issues of *Mothering*) grace this book; Linda Allen, my literary agent who has been there for me throughout the whole process of giving birth to this book; and my wife, Barbara Turner, without whose support I could not have finished the book. Finally, I'd like to thank the many people who gave of their time to be interviewed for this book, as well as the children I've worked with over the years who've helped me understand the nature of the giftedness that lies within the soul of every person.

Foreword

The title of this book makes two assumptions, and I love them both:

1. Your child possesses a *genius* that is asleep, however deeply.
2. Adults still have the ability to guide the attitudes and activities—and therefore the development and destiny—of their youngsters.

I seldom meet parents who doubt the first statement. Most sense that their little ones have big potentials. However, people (who see me as more of an expert than I know myself to be) constantly question me on the second point. They want to know whether today's parents can have *any* control in the face of influences like mass media, peer pressures, and the many distractions offered by life in the Big City which we all inhabit, no matter where we reside.

Since I am not a teacher, therapist, philosopher, nor even a particularly deep thinker, I can only give my opinions as a parent and observer. In that regard, I offer one of my favorite quotes: "Children today are tyrants. They contradict their parents, gobble their food, and tyrannize their teachers." This pronouncement was made by Socrates almost twenty-five-hundred years ago. It suggests that adults have always been a little worried about the upcoming generation.

Today, our challenges are simply different from what they used to be. For example, the increase in dual income families surely limits our opportunities to be hands-on parents. One little girl clarified this for me. She lisped, "My mommy and daddy go to work by Sesame Street and they come home by Dan Rather." Even in homes where this isn't the case, the hectic quality of our lives requires that we become more *conscious* of what we are doing as parents.

In this book, Thomas Armstrong focuses on many essential areas in guiding children's learning that can raise that consciousness. His suggestions will help you encourage and stimulate your children's curiosity and creativity, and at the same time, provide your family with thoroughly enjoyable things to do together.

A couple of years ago, there was a study to determine what caused children to get high scores on the SATs (Scholastic Aptitude Tests). I.Q., social circumstances, and economic status all seemed less important than another subtler factor. The most common denominator researchers found was this: Youngsters who got the highest SAT scores all *regularly* had dinner with their parents. The dinner conversation and the company of adults apparently broadened the children's frame of reference, gave them confidence in the presence of grown-ups, and expanded their vocabularies.

The thoughtful time you spend with your children learning together will really pay off. In this book, you will find that Dr. Armstrong presents hundreds of playful ideas and activities developed in order to guide you toward providing a positive parental influence in your children's lives.

Don't underestimate the value of the effect you exert through your own activities and attitudes. In my own life, my mother was a musician and an orchestra conductor, so I found it natural to do both as I grew up. If your little one sees you reading, it is more likely that your child will cultivate a positive attitude toward reading. Whenever you participate in crafts, sports, science, art, or any other endeavor, you are serving as a role model for your youngsters.

I recently appeared on a panel with my friend, child psychologist Eda LeShan. She shared a story about a distinguished professor she had studied under who once told the class to get paper and pencil ready, for he was going to tell them the three most important elements in child rearing. When they were all breathlessly poised to receive his words of wisdom, he said, *"Example, example, example."*

It *is* a bit of an effort to be consciously aware of providing a good example for your children, but it is worth the effort. After all, kids are still our best source of adults.

I only wish that I had had this book many years ago, when Lambchop was growing up.

SHARI LEWIS

Introduction

And what do we teach our children in school? We teach them that two and two make four, and that Paris is the capital of France. When will we also teach them what they are? We should say to each of them: Do you know what you are? You are a marvel! You are unique. In all of the world there is no other child exactly like you. In the millions of years that have passed there has never been another child like you. . . . You may become a Shakespeare, a Michelangelo, a Beethoven. You have the capacity for anything. Yes, you are a marvel.

PABLO CASALS

This book is about the marvel that is your child. It grew out of a series of articles I wrote for *Parenting* magazine from 1987 to 1990. Although I have been thinking and writing about the natural genius of children for the past eighteen years, my regular column for *Parenting* gave me the opportunity to investigate in depth those conditions in society and in the family that serve to either inhibit or nourish each child's marvelous capacity for learning.

In the title of the book, I refer to your child's *natural genius,* but this book is *not* about how to turn your child into a little prodigy. There are already too many books of this kind that seek to force-feed children with abstract knowledge and artificial learning games far too early in their development. When I refer to the term *natural genius,* I am talking about supporting the intrinsic drive for mastery that is every child's birthright. Parents need to regard this inner spark with a sense of sacredness, cultivating it as one would nurture a growing seed rather than plying it with artificial stimulants.

Parents may wonder whether this book will help motivate

their children to learn more effectively. This, I feel, is the wrong question. I believe children are *already* motivated to learn the basic skills and much more—if only the material is presented to them in a natural and unforced way. As you will see by reading the first chapter, children are programmed by nature to absorb knowledge easily and joyfully when surrounded by a positive learning climate. The problem is that tremendous forces in our culture—and in particular in our educational system—stand in the way of a child's natural learning ability. These barriers include competition, testing, grades, stress, shame, boredom, dull textbooks, bland teachers, student labeling, and educational tracking. A major part of helping children absorb knowledge more effectively, then, involves removing the many externally imposed obstacles to learning. This book will show you how to begin disassembling these roadblocks.

More than this, though, the book will describe how children really learn when they are doing what comes naturally. This book is essentially about how parents can recognize, validate, and work with the positive ingredients that make up every child's life as a learner; ingredients like curiosity, creativity, wonder, intelligence, excitement, exploration, enthusiasm, and passion. It will show you how you can recognize this passion when it occurs in your child, and it will help you to create the right conditions at home and at school so that this zest for learning can grow and prosper throughout your child's life.

While researching the material for this book, I was both disheartened and encouraged by what I saw happening in our schools nationwide. I continued to see much of what I criticized in my previous book, *In Their Own Way*, occurring in the nation's classrooms. The *worksheet wasteland* still lives, and the clamor nationwide for higher test scores threatens to make this condition worse by causing teachers to focus too much attention on test preparation at the expense of real learning. On the other hand while working on this book over the past three years, I've seen many schools take major steps toward significant reform and have observed the presence of innovative educational programs in virtually every state of the union.

It appears that educators now know more than ever about what works in helping children learn, and they are able to implement this knowledge in concrete ways. One of the most consistent research findings is the important role that parents have in educating their children. In program after program where parents are closely involved in their children's learning process, there has been a dramatic improvement in student motivation and achievement. I certainly hope that this book will stimulate parents to become more involved in their children's education at school, and that it also will motivate parents to regard the home as a learning place that is even more vital to their child's educational future than school.

HOW THIS BOOK IS ORGANIZED

The book is divided into five major sections. The first section explores the delicate balance between the three major partners in the drama of learning: the child, the parents, and the school system. The second section examines innovative approaches for helping your child develop an interest in, if not a love for, reading, math, science, and history. It describes exemplary school programs that teach these subjects in nonthreatening and creative ways. While these chapters focus on school learning, parents of preschoolers will find much in them about how children emerge into academics during the early years. The third section explores the important role of free, unstructured play for children, critiques recent toys, surveys methods of music and drawing instruction, and explores the benefits and pitfalls of television and computers in learning.

    Section four focuses on children who don't seem to fit into the assembly-line workbook factories of many school systems, including children who have been labeled *gifted, learning disabled, underachieving,* and *hyperactive*. It offers alternatives for how parents and schools can assess learning progress and organize learning programs so that children don't need to be tracked or labeled but can have their own uniqueness honored in classroom environments that celebrate diversity. The final section spotlights several educational philosophies that have consistently demonstrated their effectiveness in helping children learn: Montessori and Waldorf education, superlearning, and peer teaching.

WHO THIS BOOK IS FOR

This book is intended for all parents who want to help their children become more than simply successful students in school. It is for parents who are interested in assisting their children in realizing their full potential as natural learners in life. This book will be useful to you if you fit into any of the following categories:

- You're searching for ways to support and encourage your child's natural gifts and talents
- You're looking for a creative preschool or elementary school for your child
- You're trying to develop effective strategies for changing your child's school system
- You're struggling with your child's academic difficulties
- You're wondering if you may be pushing your child too hard in his education
- You're feeling that you may not be as involved in your child's education as you ought to be
- You're wanting to develop more positive family learning experiences during school vacations, weekends, evenings, and in the summertime
- You're thinking of homeschooling your child

While this book was written primarily for parents of children aged three through twelve, parents of infants will find much that affirms their baby's instinctual genius, and parents of adolescents will discover activities, ideas, and resources they can use profitably to help their kids make the transition from childhood into adulthood.

In addition, I hope that many teachers and administrators will use the ideas included here to transform schools into more exciting places for learning. I have presented many examples of model programs that school personnel can look to for guidance in structuring their own programs, and hundreds of specific ideas and activities teachers can successfully use in their classrooms to stimulate their students' minds. More than programs and activities, through, I have given a basic philosophy of learning that I hope will filter into schools nationwide so that our country's long bout with educational mediocrity will end.

HOW TO USE THIS BOOK

I have written this book so that it can be used in a number of ways: as a reference manual of ideas, resources, and tools to help children learn more effectively, as a critique of current educational practices, as a practical handbook for how parents can work with their children's natural abilities, and as an inspirational guide to learning. Each chapter includes several basic features designed to provide parents with a comprehensive and multilayered perspective on their children's learning abilities.

The first part of every chapter provides background information, expert opinion, research studies, and other materials that serve to instruct parents about a core issue or idea in the field of learning. This section is followed by a feature entitled What Parents Can Do, which gives practical suggestions for implementing the ideas described in the chapter. Eight of the seventeen chapters in the book also include a feature called Starting Points, which consists of specific activities parents can engage in with their kids right away. Each chapter concludes with a Resources section, which consists of an annotated list of books, pamphlets, periodicals, organizations, and other learning tools and contacts to help you go further in putting together the best support system possible for your child's education. I also have collected quotations, anecdotes, and stories that have inspired me over the years for inclusion in the margins of each chapter. I hope that you will copy down your own favorites and put them up on your refrigerator door or bulletin board to help guide you in awakening your child's natural genius.

There are no age limits for the activities in each Starting Points feature since most of the experiences are open-ended and can be adjusted to the needs of any child. However, to make things a bit easier for parents I've arranged the activities in each Starting Points developmentally, so that the earlier ones can be used more appropriately with preschoolers and the later ones with older school-aged children. Your child's own response to a given activity will tell you whether it's too difficult or too easy for him or her. If it's too easy, the child will likely become bored and want to do something else. If it's too hard, the child may show signs of stress (rebelliousness, agitation, physical complaints, apathy), and the activity should end immediately.

It is *extremely* important to let your child decide whether and to what extent he wishes to become involved in any of the activities of this book. If he completes these activities merely to please you, then you have accomplished little in the way of any real learning. On the other hand, if he shows genuine interest and absorption in some of the activities, then you've probably hit upon experiences that will help awaken his natural genius. I've called these activities *starting points* because I see them not as self-contained exercises, but as opportunities to begin a process of exploration in learning that can lead in a number of creative directions.

That's the spirit in which I'd like you to regard this book: as a launching pad into more creative, exciting, and stimulating learning experiences at home and at school. I hope you will think of this book as a sensible guide to parenting the learning child and as a safe place you can go to whenever you begin to get caught up in the high-paced, test-conscious, worksheet-infested, stress-filled world of academics that entangles so many of our kids. Natural learning is as important to children as breathing, eating, and sleeping. Let's make sure they get all they need.

Part One

◆ ◆ ◆ ◆

The Learning Triad: Child, Home, and School

1. *The Child—Born Genius and Natural Learner*

Your child is a genius. No, you don't need to rush out and have a learning specialist or psychologist test your child in order to verify this. Nor am I saying your child will necessarily score 130 or more on an IQ test. That kind of genius is often just a good test-taker or school-achiever. Your child is a genius in a much broader and deeper sense of the word.

Many people don't realize that the word *genius* actually means "to be born" or "to come into being." In ancient times, all persons were believed to possess a personal genius or attendant spirit that was given to them at birth and that governed their fortunes in life and determined their essential character. In the same way, your child has a light that shines brightly from deep within and represents her own inner wisdom. At each moment in time, your child has the potential to give birth to this creative life.

There is no standardized test you can find that is going to prove the truth of my words. The proof is right before your eyes. Look at your child. Notice his vitality when he's involved in something that engages his interest. Pay attention to the sparkle in his eyes. Observe his ingenuity and excitement. Think

3

Verily I say unto you, except ye be converted and become as little children, ye shall not enter into the kingdom of heaven.

MATTHEW 18:3 (KING JAMES VERSION)

The great man is he who does not lose his child's heart.

MENCIUS

about times when he said or did things that caused you to laugh, or think, or see things in a new way. The new words he made up. The machines he invented with odds and ends around the house. The drawings of strange worlds he created. The song he composed on the spur of the moment. These are the manifestations of your child's natural genius.

Perhaps you have never thought of your child as a genius. If so, this book will show you a side of your child that will delight and inspire you. So much attention these days is focused upon the negative side of children's mental growth with all the concern about falling test scores, learning disabilities, and other educational problems. When educators finally get around to talking about the positive learner, their discussion is often limited to the so-called *gifted* child—a child who usually needs to score in the top 3 or 4 percent on a standardized test.

This book is also for the other 97 percent of kids who *deserve* to be called gifted—who are, in fact, natural geniuses. This book will tell you how you can recognize the genius in your child and nurture that genius at home and school. It will show you how your child is *already* engaged in gifted behaviors in her play, her drawings and music, her language and reasoning capacities, and in many other domains. It will also provide you with ways to gently awaken dimensions of your child's intelligence that lie dormant due to lack of stimulation from the outside world.

But before explaining how to awaken your child's capacities in specific learning areas, I feel I still need to convince some of you that your child is the natural genius I say he is. The rest of this chapter will provide you with a foundation for understanding why all children are endowed with innate giftedness. It will explain how that genius unfolds from infancy to adolescence. It will also show you how to recognize genius and describe what to do when genius is revealed.

CHILDREN: BORN TO BE BRILLIANT

Children are born learners. Were it not so, we would have become extinct long ago. Had the human infant been neurologically wired to respond in a fixed way to the environment, mankind would likely have turned up as some quaint fossil in an antediluvian lake bed. Yet by cosmic chance or higher design, the capacity to adapt, to change, and to *learn* has become part of the human genetic blueprint. Endowed at birth with large portions of the brain uncommitted to any set plan or behavior, the child grows up as a natural learner, capable of responding to the changing demands and currents of life with remarkable flexibility.

Children represent the essence of innovation and ingenuity. According to scientists, the evolution of living things depends upon changes in the children of any given species. Stephen Jay Gould, professor of zoology at Harvard University, indicated that "we evolved by retaining the youthful features of our ancestors, a process known technically as *neotony* (literally, 'holding youth')." Anthropologist Ashley Montagu suggests that children possess specific psychological characteristics that need to be retained into adulthood if our species is to survive. He lists several traits associated with a childlike nature, including sensitivity, curiosity, playfulness, creativity, imagination, a sense of wonder, and the need to learn. Montagu says, "Most adults stop any conscious effort to learn early in their adulthood. This hardening of the mind—psychosclerosis—is a long distance from a child's acceptance and flexibility and open-mindedness."

It appears to be this very openness to new experience that allows children to become the true geniuses of a culture. According to anthropologist Margaret Mead, we live in a *prefigurative* culture where there are few traditions to pass on, and members of the culture must essentially reinvent new ones. Says Mead:

> In this new culture, it will be the child—and not the parent and grandparent, that represents what is to come. Instead of the erect, white-haired elder who, in postfigurative cultures, stood for the past and the future in all their grandeur and continuity, the unborn child, already conceived but still in the womb, must become the symbol of what life will be like."

Interestingly, it is often the adult geniuses of a culture who most closely resemble children in their playful attitudes toward life. Picasso, Miro, and Chagall displayed childlike styles in their painting. James Joyce drew heavily upon childhood memories

In human beings, the density of synapses [connections between brain cells] increases sharply during the first months of life, reaches a maximum at the ages of one to two (roughly 50 percent above the adult mean density), declines between the ages of two and sixteen, and then remains relatively constant until the age of seventy-two. More than one scientist has speculated that the extremely rapid learning of the young child (for example, in the area of language) may reflect an exploitation of the large number of synapses available at that time.

HOWARD GARDNER

Today, nowhere in the world are there elders who know what the children know, no matter how remote and simple the societies are in which the children live.

MARGARET MEAD

If you want to see our way of life, you will see it from the children. It is the children who make our culture, because the children can do something and it will come to stand as something for the old people.

VILLAGER IN
NORTHERN GHANA

in his writing. Einstein called upon fantasies from childhood in creating his theory of relativity. This book is filled with examples of geniuses from all walks of life who looked back to childhood for the source of their inspiration. The true model for geniuslike behavior appears to reside, not in the plodding technical research so typical of adult work life, but in the kinds of creative behaviors that virtually all children display at some point during their young lives.

THE DEVELOPMENTAL STAGES OF GENIUS IN LEARNING

Something profoundly intelligent lies behind the infant's seemingly random movements, the toddler's endless block stacking, the preschooler's dramatic doll or truck play, and the eight-year-old's imaginative drawings. It is the exploratory impulse embedded in a human spirit that is actively exercising its capacity to transform the world. Listen to a child of any age thrill with delight upon discovering a new way of doing something. In the sound of that excitement you can pinpoint the heart of learning: what one Nobel Prize-winning physicist called "the drive in living matter to perfect itself."

The way in which this genius manifests itself will vary depending upon the developmental level of a child. In a baby it may show up in a series of interesting manipulations of a mobile above the crib. For an elementary-school-aged child, it might be displayed in an ingenious project fashioned during a long weekend in the garage or backyard. In an adolescent, it could be found in an artfully created poem hidden away in a diary.

It is important for parents to understand that the face of genius is multifaceted. Children don't have to paint *The Last Supper* or re-create the theory of relativity in order to qualify as natural geniuses. Each developmental stage has its own unique features that lend a specific character to the kinds of intelligent behaviors found there. By knowing what to expect at each stage, you will be more prepared to understand what makes your child a genius at any given age and be more able to respond to his learning needs appropriately.

INFANCY

Beginning at birth, the infant is engaged through all of her senses in an exciting interaction with the world. Every new sight, taste, touch, smell, or sound presents an opportunity for novel investigations.

Jean Piaget, the world-renowned child researcher, conveyed a sense of the infant's delight in exploration while writing about his own infant son Laurent. Piaget had attached a chain to some rattles suspended over his son's crib.

> Laurent, by chance, strikes the chain while sucking his fingers. He grasps it and slowly displaces it while looking at the rattles. He then begins to swing it very gently, which produces a slight movement of the hanging rattles and an as yet faint sound inside them. Laurent then definitely increases by degrees his own movements. He shakes the chain more and more vigorously and laughs uproariously at the result obtained.

Like most infants, Piaget's son rejoices when he makes the environment react to him; when he has an effect on the world.

Notice how your own infant interacts with the sensory world. Pay particular attention to those explosions of excitement that occur in the midst of activity. Inside that enjoyment reside the seeds of genius. What kinds of materials was your child interacting with when she had her great "aha!" experience? What led up to her cry of delight? Infancy is a time when parents need to be especially good observers of genius, for it is often a fleeting phenomenon.

Babies give birth to their creative life in ways as simple as devising a special method of grasping blocks, designing a novel approach to crawling around obstacles, or creating a new set of vowel sounds or melodic tones babbled with unusual intensity. Of particular importance in the life of the infant is the realization that an object hidden from view (for example, a ball behind the sofa) continues to exist. You can tell that this insight has occurred when you see your infant crawl around corners to find lost objects. Such a discovery is to the infant what a first step on the moon or the splitting of an atom is to an adult researcher.

Childhood is the name of the world's immediate future; of such, and such alone, is the promise of the kingdom of man.

WALTER DE LA MARE

The child's true constructive energy, a dynamic power, has remained unnoticed for thousands of years. Just as men have trodden the earth, and later tilled its surface, without thought for the immense wealth hidden in its depths, so the men of our day make progress after progress in civilized life, without noticing the treasures that lie hidden in the psychic world of infancy.

MARIA MONTESSORI

No Columbus, no Marco Polo has ever seen stranger and more fascinating and thoroughly absorbing sights than the child that learns to perceive, to taste, to smell, to touch, to hear and see, and to use his body, his senses, and his mind. No wonder that the child shows an insatiable curiosity. He has the whole world to discover.

ERNEST SCHACTEL

TODDLERHOOD

With the advent of walking at around one year of age, the infant has a whole new vista opened up for him and begins what might be called a regular love affair with life. "The world is the junior toddler's oyster," says psychoanalyst Margaret Mahler. Intoxicated with his newfound capabilities, the toddler embodies youthful persistence as he tests his legs against what the world has to offer. He'll take a tumble on the floor and cry intensely one moment, yet the next instant he'll be up and running with renewed fervor as if nothing had happened. Having the powers of upright locomotion expands his world immeasurably as he is able to explore nooks and crannies of the home that were inaccessible to him during infancy (much to a parent's chagrin!). His genius manifests itself in psychomotor feats of all kinds while he tests his body against the demands of the world.

Parents should exercise care in childproofing their household against such spirited assaults. But they also need to provide plenty of opportunities for this physical intelligence to express itself through recreational, musical, artistic, and building experiences. Some parents attempt to take advantage of their toddlers' flexibility and resilience by enrolling them in intensive gymnastics courses or teach-your-baby-to-read programs designed to maximize their potential for genius early in life. These programs exploit the natural genius of early childhood and place pressures on kids to adapt to adult ways much too soon in their development. Rather than courses or kits, kids need freedom during this time to explore the world in their own way—through blocks, trucks, modeling clay and dough, paints, and other messy, motoric, and manual experiences.

PRESCHOOL YEARS

The child's extraordinary openness to new learning can further be seen in the subsequent growth of language. During the second and third years of life, the child virtually explodes into language, moving from a few dozen utterances at eighteen months to over a thousand-word vocabulary by the age of three and a half (though this will vary quite a bit from child to child, and it's important to remember that one of the world's greatest geniuses—Albert Einstein—did not begin to speak until he was almost four!). Russian writer Kornei Chukovsky regarded all children aged two to five as linguistic geniuses because they had such an amazing capacity to create innovative metaphors in their spoken language.

These are truly the magical years of childhood, when the child is young enough to regard the world with fairy-tale eyes, yet old enough to communicate her archetypal experiences to others through language and other forms of symbolic play. Children begin to draw, paint, sculpt with clay, build with blocks, dramatize, and in other ways play out their fanciful experiences of life. They see the world animistically, as imbued with emotion and intention. Their senses often fuse sight, sound, taste, and touch in a synaesthetic blend of multimodal perceptions, where colors can be *heard* and sounds can be *tasted*.

Parents should be especially attentive to the creative things preschool kids say and do, and take care not to dismiss their children's perceptions as nonsense or fantasy. The roots of metaphor, aesthetic feeling, imagination, and artistic creativity all lie deeply embedded in this fertile period of the child's development. By acknowledging the validity of the child's world-making activities during this time of life, a parent can help to preserve these all too often ignored dimensions of the child's natural genius.

Father talks just like Santa Claus . . . boom, boom, boom! As dark as night . . . ! But we talk light, like the daytime . . . bim, bim, bim.

FOUR-YEAR-OLD CHILD

ELEMENTARY SCHOOL YEARS

Somewhere between the ages of five and seven, another explosion in learning takes place, this time in relationship to culture. Whereas previously the child frequently identified himself with his surroundings, he now becomes an independently contributing member of the society around him. He begins to move beyond his family circle in establishing reciprocal relationships with peers, teachers, and other members of the wider community. These are the years of "industry vs. inferiority," according to psychoanalyst Erik Erikson, when the child's concerns are "to make things and make them well and even perfectly"—through hobbies, sports, and schoolwork. The seven-year-old

When she was eight [Anna Pavlova] was taken as a special Christmas treat to see a performance of The Sleeping Beauty *by the Imperial Russian Ballet. She wrote later: "I was spellbound. I gazed and gazed, and wild plans began to circulate in my brain. It was the second act and the corps de ballet were waltzing together. 'Anna,' said my mother, amazed at my excitement, 'wouldn't you like to join these people and dance with them?' 'No' I replied without hesitation, 'I would rather dance by myself like the lovely Sleeping Beauty. One day I will and in this very theatre.' My mother laughed, but I was lost in my dream and did not heed her. At eight years old I had found the one unchanging ambition of my life.'*

R. S. AND C. M.
ILLINGWORTH

will spend hours in his room playing out cosmic battles with his space action figures. The eight-year-old, motivated to learn all he can about his newly acquired bicycle, will study books and catalogs tirelessly and in a short time know all there is to know about each part. The ten-year-old will stay up late at night trying to finish a school project on time. Freud once said that civilization itself—with all of its monuments, institutions, and intellectual history—can be traced back to these industrious years.

However, parents should be careful not to push too hard for genius in the products made by children at this age—even if those products do reflect special brilliance. For it is at this time that many children turn off their natural genius precisely because they sense themselves being judged by the things they make and thus develop a deep sense of inferiority. It is also at this age that the child enters fully into formal education, where her learning behaviors are evaluated through grades and standardized testing. She may be labeled *gifted* and have her genius restricted to test-taking abilities only, or she may be identified as having some sort of learning problem and totally lose faith in her own inner capacities.

Parents need to recognize and value children's abilities and accomplishments during the elementary school years in a nonjudgmental way. Interests formed during this time can often become the basis for later career and avocational pursuits. Through gentle support, parents can encourage these inclinations and ensure that their children will discover their rightful place in the world.

ADOLESCENCE

Finally, in adolescence, the child bursts into an entirely new mode of consciousness with its own incessant demands for identity, truth, and mastery of the adult world. Carl Jung, describing his personal awakening into this state of mind as a twelve-year-old, wrote: "I was taking the long road to school, when suddenly for a single moment I had the overwhelming impression of having just emerged from a dense cloud. I knew all at once; now I am *myself*."

A fresh quality of intellect settles in on the adolescent endowing him with the capability to think in a totally new way. For the first time he is able to perceive ideals, envision alternate realities, and gain access to abstract logical insights. Jean Piaget regarded what he called the "formal operational thinking" of the young adolescent as the high point of an individual's intellectual life. Many of the world's greatest mathematical discoveries, in fact, were made by teenagers.

The emotional world also reasserts itself as the adolescent develops a unique brand of intensity that manifests in a special kind of passion for life. The object of this passion, of course, is often another human being. But such vitality can also attach itself with equal facility to rock music, computers, a religious organization, a political or social cause, or a set of romance novels.

Genius has a way of manifesting at this age in a parent's blind spot, with the youngster loving and perfecting exactly those things that a parent despises. It's important to recognize that adolescents push against parents precisely to define better their own identity, so the task for parents at this time is to honor adolescent brilliance at a respectful distance—allowing it space to expand in its own way while at the same time providing boundaries within which it can mature into the refined competence of adulthood.

As an adolescent, Richard Wagner heard a famous singer in Fidelio *and was greatly moved. He wrote the singer a letter in which he dedicated his life to music, delivered it to her hotel room, and then "ran out into the street, quite mad."*

JOSEPH WALTERS AND
HOWARD GARDNER

THE BUMPY ROAD TO NATURAL GENIUS

As seen in the developmental descriptions above, children are *always* expressing their natural genius as they strive for mastery from birth to adulthood. What drives them to learn in this way seems to be an innate thirst for knowledge and an inner quest for competence. The process of acquiring knowledge, however, is not always fire and light. There are often long periods of stagnation, times of regression, and turbulent periods when tantrums, doldrums, and rebellions seem to reign supreme over the natural brilliance that resides within every child. Sometimes these negative responses to learning are due to deep-seated problems that require professional help. However, when they occur as a part of the normal processes of growing up they

The child is potential future. . . . The [archetypal] "child" paves the way for a future change of personality. In the individuation process it anticipates the figure that comes from the synthesis of conscious and unconscious elements in the personality. It is therefore a symbol which unites the opposites; a mediator; a bringer of healing; that is, one who makes whole.

CARL JUNG

often represent the dark before the dawn, so to speak, presaging a major transformation in consciousness.

It is important for parents to recognize that when kids are sullen or angry, it may be because they are moving through the bumps and potholes of a labyrinthian learning process. What parents need to do at such times is to have a patient, watchful attitude that sets clear limits for behavior. But they also need to hold an image of genius for their children; to recognize that their kids are actively striving to emerge from their struggles in triumphant fashion.

TWO STEPS FORWARD, ONE STEP BACK

Jean Piaget has given us a model that describes how this kind of learning roller-coaster works. According to Piaget, all learning involves an interaction between two processes, assimilation and accommodation. At any age, the child takes in or assimilates a wealth of information from the environment and attempts to make sense out of it through accommodating or adjusting his own perspective to fit incoming data. Through this process he essentially invents the world or creates inner pictures—Piaget called them *schemes*—of how things work. These schemes allow the child to make sense of what he sees going on around him.

When things are going well there is equilibrium between these two processes of assimilation and accommodation. However, when the information the child attempts to assimilate conflicts with what he believes to be true about the world, there is a disturbance in the balance of the system.

A story that illustrates this concerns a child who was attending church for the first time and listened to the organ play the sound of bells during the service. She cried out "ice cream man!" loudly to her parents and was surprised when they responded with expressions of shock and embarrassment.

This little girl was used to hearing the sound of the ice cream truck passing by her street every day that summer tinkling its bells and announcing its presence to every hungry child within earshot. She had created a scheme or mini-worldview concerning this delicious experience and regularly assimilated the sound of bells to her ice cream scheme. This way of picturing the world worked for her all summer long whenever the ice cream man came by. However, her attempt to assimilate the sound of the church bells to her ice cream scheme failed miserably. Quickly and somewhat painfully, the child learned that all bells do not mean that ice cream is on the way. She had to accommodate her existing perspective to include the new information.

PEAK LEARNING EXPERIENCES

The above example illustrates what occurs all the time during the child's creative young life. Kids give birth to little hypotheses about how the world works, test them against reality, and modify them as they receive feedback from the world. Sometimes the shifts that children need to make are relatively simple, even if somewhat disturbing. At other times, however, children go through major changes in perspective. The equivalent of a miniature scientific revolution takes place inside them. These experiences are the real peaks in the incredible journey of the natural genius.

Such major shifts in ways of thinking about the world often have an ecstatic quality about them. Sometimes the memory of these peak learning experiences can last a lifetime. In one study of childhood recollections conducted at Manchester College, Oxford, England, a fifty-year-old female vividly remembered being a child of three or four learning about the properties of space for the first time.

> We were walking home along the pavement. I became spontaneously aware that each step I took decreased the way between me and my destination by precisely the same amount as it increased the distance between me and my point of departure. I had no sufficient command of language to tell anyone. It was perhaps the most thrilling and significant thing that has ever happened to me. There was something there to do with perfection, a perfect conjunction of increasing and decreasing. I see now it cannot be communicated—the perfection of it.

A developmental psychologist would perhaps regard this insight as the beginning of the child's entry into a new stage of

In the monasteries of Tibet, we are told, there are men who deliberately attempt by training to recover and develop in themselves the outlook of a child, and who, by means of the power thus obtained, can set at naught what we westerners are accustomed to regard as fundamental laws of physiology and psychology.

GEORGE GRODDECK

Grown men may learn from very little children for the hearts of little children are pure and, therefore, the Great spirit may show to them many things which older people miss.

BLACK ELK

cognitive awareness in which she begins to understand that there are logical relationships between concrete objects. To the child, however, the idea emerges as a miraculous discovery. She had made a marvelously fresh observation and radically changed her view of the world. Such an insight is not unlike the *beginner's mind* of Zen Buddhism where thought and perception are undimmed by weighty presuppositions.

Parents may wonder how often these peak experiences occur in their children's lives. The answer is: every day. There are micro peak experiences that happen in a flash and whose only evidence may be a passing sparkle in a child's eyes. There are also gigantic peak experiences that may be preceded by months of stagnation or regression, when a child who has been unable to talk or read suddenly amazes everyone with his newly acquired abilities.

Peak experiences may be particularly evident at critical junctures in the life of a child—during so-called sensitive periods when the child's mind is ripe for new learning. According to Italian physician and educator Maria Montessori, during a sensitive period "all is life and enthusiasm. Every effort marks an increase in power." She referred to a child's absorption in the environment during these times as "the great work," regarding it with an almost religious sense of awe.

In one case, Montessori observed a three-year-old girl intent on placing cylinders of different widths into their respective containers—like corks in a bottle. So focused was the little girl's attention that she remained undisturbed even while Montessori tested her concentration by picking her up in her chair and placing her on a small table. The girl moved the materials onto her knees and continued working without missing a beat. Montessori observed:

> Then she stopped as if coming out of a dream and smiled happily. Her eyes shone brightly and she looked about. She had not even noticed what we had done to disturb her. . . . Similar events kept recurring, and everytime children emerged from such an experience, they were like individuals who had rested. They were filled with life, and resembled those who have experienced some great joy.

GOING WITH THE FLOW

The *great work* that Montessori referred to is similar to a concept developed by Mihaly Csikszentmihalyi, professor of psychology at the University of Chicago. Like Piaget, Csikszentmihalyi (pronounced chick-sent-meh-hi-yee), argues that real learning involves a balance between self and environment. A challenge from the world that requires too much from an individual can cause anxiety and block learning and enjoyment. On the other hand, a task that requires too little from a person can result in that individual experiencing boredom. However, when a learner is faced with challenges that match his or her personal capacities, then something very special can happen, something that Csikszentmihalyi calls *flow*. During an experience of flow, time seems to stand still while the learner focuses intently, and enjoyably, upon the task at hand.

Csikszentmihalyi says that children have frequent experiences of flow. Parents can help set the stage for a flow experience in learning by providing a learning environment that is neither too stressful for a child nor too easy. The next chapter will provide further details for how to structure your home so that it becomes a positive learning environment that allows your child's natural genius to unfold.

One never learns to understand truly anything but what one loves.

GOETHE

Children are not only philosophers; they are cosmologists, they're inventors of myths, of religions.

JOHN HOLT

★ WHAT PARENTS CAN DO ★

Natural learning is a child's birthright. The child's drive to learn is the outcome of a multimillion-year-old process through which nature has attempted to develop the best means of adapting to change. Consequently, it is not something that ought to be tampered with or artificially manipulated. Instead, parents should seek to fully acknowledge the child's exploratory impulse and develop ways of allowing it to be expressed in the world. Here are some ways for you to do this.

Understand that most real learning takes place in the context of everyday life. Virtually all important learning that children do

Children are the most learning-hungry beings in the world.

ASHLEY MONTAGU

Your Children are not your children. They are the sons and daughters of Life's longing for itself. They come through you but not from you. And though they are with you yet they belong not to you.

KAHLIL GIBRAN

is incidental in nature. It happens while we're trying to teach them something else. After all, kids learn one of the most complex skills in the world—their own native language—simply by absorbing the loose bits of dialogue they casually retrieve from the environment and playing around in different ways with the words they hear.

Natural learning does not happen in a structured step-by-step manner, but through a sequence of stops and starts, periods of stagnation and recovery, times of forgetting and times of discovery, and ultimately in the often unexpected insights that change the child's world. So look for natural learning to happen, not just in the isolated exercises and activities in this book or any other book or program, but through the events of life—talking, playing, working, singing, building, problem solving, and through many other real-life activities that provide the context children need in order to become competent in the world.

Value learning for its own sake. The feelings of joy and competence that a child experiences in mastering a new subject or skill are the real rewards in learning. Yet, all too often parents and teachers insist on using rewards of different kinds (praise, food, stickers, grades) to tempt children into performing different learning tasks. These reinforcements serve only to convey to kids the message that learning is not worth pursuing in its own right.

In research conducted by social psychologist Teresa Amabile and her colleagues at Brandeis University, children who were promised a reward if they completed a task (telling a story or creating a collage) performed less creatively than kids who engaged in the activities without the expectation of reward. The message to parents is clear: Toss out the carrot and stick, and start believing in your child's inherent desire to learn.

Look for flow experiences in your child's daily life. Parents can recognize many flow events by looking for signs of zestful absorption in their children's work and play experiences. Be aware of times when your child is intensely focused on a particular project, game, or other activity: vigorously building a tree house, energetically mastering a lay-up on the basketball court, or carefully writing a science fiction story over a period of several days. Unless he needs to attend to important family responsibilities, it's important to let him remain undisturbed at such times so he can complete his *great work*. Notice whether there is a refreshed, joyful, or relaxed expression on your child's face after he has completed the activity. This may also tell you that he has had an important learning experience that has touched his natural genius.

Honor your child's choices in learning. Anyone who has worked with children for a length of time soon discovers how difficult it is to make children learn something against their will. Threats of punishment, behavior modification, or even out-and-out pleading may work in the short run, but ultimately, kids do not learn much when something is imposed on them from without. They may retain the learning long enough to spit it out on a multiple-choice exam or parrot it back to you in rote fashion. However, when kids perceive that such externally imposed learning is no longer needed for their survival, they will conveniently forget all about it. That's why it is especially important for parents and teachers to use the activites in this book with the full cooperation of their children. Allow yourself to be led by your child's own interest and enthusiasm in a subject, rather than moving her from one activity to another freight-train style.

The child, the ordinary man, and the creative artist are all moved by a flash of self-identification in the same way, but there is no doubt that the child is moved more often and that these flashes illuminate his whole being with a more penetrating light.

SIR KENNETH CLARK

RESOURCES

Armstrong, Thomas. *The Radiant Child*. Wheaton, IL: Quest, 1985. Describes peak experiences in the lives of children.

Csikszentmihalyi, Mihaly. *Flow: The Psychology of Optimal Experience*. New York: Harper and Row, 1990. Describes the mechanisms through which individuals become absorbed in learning experiences.

Holt, John. *Learning All the Time*. New York: Addison-Wesley, 1989. Discusses the many ways in which children are constantly learning about the world around them.

Montagu, Ashley. *Growing Young*. New York: McGraw-Hill, 1983. Explores the importance of retaining childlike qualities into adulthood as a primary means of furthering the evolution of the human race.

Montessori, Maria. *The Secret of Childhood*. New York: Ballantine, 1972. Includes Montessori's descriptions of the sensitive periods in a child's development.

Pearce, Joseph Chilton. *Magical Child*. New York: Bantam, 1980. Details nature's plan for the development of children.

Organizations

Association for Childhood Education International, 11141 Georgia Ave., Suite 200, Wheaton, MD 20902; (202) 363-6963. Nonprofit association committed to the well-being of children in the home, school, and community. Publishes a journal, *Childhood Education*, a newsletter, and booklets on a variety of educational themes.

Gesell Institute of Child Development, 310 Prospect St., New Haven, CT 06511; (203) 777-3481. One of the oldest and most respected child-development research institutes in the country. Books available through the institute include *The Child from Five to Ten, Don't Push Your Preschooler,* and *Gesell Institute's Child from One to Six.*

National Association for the Education of Young Children, 1834 Connecticut Ave. NW, Washington, DC 20009; (202) 232-8777. Dedicated to improving the quality of education for children from infancy to age eight. Publishes brochures and booklets on a variety of topics and publishes a monthly journal, *Young Child*.

2. *The Home—True Center of Learning*

No child is an island. The natural genius I talked about in the first chapter finds its truest expression in a social setting and can be powerfully affected, for good or ill, by other people. A newborn elephant and the fallow deer are able to run with the herd shortly after birth. By the age of six weeks, the baby seal swims the high seas without assistance. Yet human infants remain totally dependent upon their mothers or surrogates until at least nine months after birth, and even then require several more years of assistance before achieving total independence.

Evolutionary wisdom seems to have extended our dependence on others past birth in order to provide maximum adaptability to changing circumstances. With large portions of the human infant's brain uncommitted to any specific task or skill, this prolonged period of reliance upon others provides the child's delicate neurological system with extra time to come to grips with whatever sort of environment is placed around him. Instead of being thrown out into a cold world to sink or swim based on inborn characteristics, as is the case with more primitive life forms, children can thrive under a wide variety of

The child becoming incarnate is a spiritual embryo which needs its own special environment. Just as a physical embryo needs its mother's womb in which to grow, so the spiritual embryo needs to be protected by an external environment that is warm with love and rich in nourishment, where everything is disposed to welcome, and nothing to harm it.

MARIA MONTESSORI

Children are given to us—on loan—for a very short period of time. They come to us like packets of flower seeds, with no pictures on the cover and no guarantees. We do not know what they will look like, act like, or have the potential to become. Our job, like the gardener's, is to meet their needs as best we can: to give proper nourishment, love, attention, and caring, and to hope for the best.

KATHARINE KERSEY

circumstances as long as experienced adults are there to help adjust those conditions to their specific needs.

Through sensitive adult intervention, the child's headlong encounter with the world is buffeted and his airborne fancies are brought to a safe landing on soft soil. Thus, the two-year-old about to touch the kitchen stove learns the meaning of *hot* without having to suffer possibly life-threatening burns. The preschooler tangled in an argument with a friend develops appropriate strategies for resolving conflict. The elementary-aged child confused about a school project discovers new ways of organizing her work. And the adolescent, depressed over a social rejection, finds a sympathetic ear. Trusted adults provide a safe and protected space for children within which they can explore the world provisionally before going their own way as mature individuals.

One of my favorite films, Ingmar Bergman's *Fanny and Alexander*, presents stunning images of how families both succeed and fail in their efforts to provide children with this kind of nurturing space. Growing up in a prosperous theatrical family at the turn of the century, ten-year-old Alexander Ekdahl takes us into a world peopled with mischievous uncles and family ghosts, a wicked stepfather, and a kindly grandmother. We see the family matrix in all of its bright colors—snake-dancing its way through the sprawling family mansion during joyous holiday celebrations, practicing plays in its own family theater, and sharing speeches and tributes during large family dinners.

Later we see the dull colors as well when Alexander and his sister are packed off to the ascetic and cruel world of their stepfather, where they are physically and emotionally abused. Alexander often does little more than look and listen during the boisterous and sometimes traumatic activities of the elders around him. However, by the end of the film he seems to have learned a lot. In the final scene, Alexander crawls into the lap of his maternal grandmother and falls asleep while she reads to him lines from Swedish playwright August Strindberg's *A Dream Play*: "Anything can happen, anything is possible and likely . . ."

These cinematic images reflect something profound about families and learning: that kids acquire knowledge imperceptibly by subconsciously looking, listening, feeling, and responding to the adults around them. This kind of learning is quite different from the organized lessons and lectures of school life, where knowledge is made explicit. At home, children seem to pick up tacit attitudes, beliefs, and behaviors simply by being in the presence of adults who model these learnings in complex and often richly subtle ways. In one sense, elders are like mirrors for a child, reflecting back the child's own developing sense of self. On another level, however, parents and other adults serve as windows into uncharted worlds, pointing the way and showing the children, just as Alexander's grandmother did, what might truly be possible in life.

POSITIVE FAMILY CLIMATES

The family serves as the social vehicle through which a child's natural genius can be activated and realized in the world. It does this by providing an atmosphere that nourishes children's inner gifts and talents. There are specific features present in all positive family climates that help to accomplish this goal, including the cultivation of active learning, positive values, nurturing relationships, and self-esteem.

Active learning. In contrast to the old-fashioned dictum that children are to be seen and not heard, kids in positive families are seen *and* heard doing all sorts of marvelously creative things. They're busy running, playacting, building, drawing, conversing, writing, experimenting, reading, exploring, wondering, laughing, and in many other ways vigorously interacting with the world. The adults in these families are often an integral part of their children's exploratory activities, helping to guide them in practical ways toward a realization of their objectives.

Learning in a positive family climate is not of the look-it-up-in-the-encyclopedia variety where the buck gets passed to a remote and abstract authority. It's a hands-on, everybody-learns-together encounter with the nitty-gritty world of real objects and situations. Dad is down on his hands and knees next to the bathtub helping his young son blow the largest possible soap bubbles. Grandma is in the den with a group of kids leading a storytelling session. Mother is out in the garage helping sister put the finishing touches on a handcrafted table. The healthy family learns through a vital interaction with new experiences. It turns the ordinary into the extraordinary by seeing the creative possibilities inherent within everyday life.

Positive values. Parents in positive families help their children form healthy values that serve as guideposts to natural genius. They introduce their kids to the heroes, saints, and leaders who are the moral bedrock of civilization. They talk about qualities like compassion, courage, conviction, integrity, and wisdom in terms that kids can easily understand. They use everyday incidents, especially family conflicts, to illustrate the importance of having a strong personal value system. Above all, they model positive values in their own lives by practicing honesty, consistency, and fairness, however imperfectly, in their interactions with their children.

Nurturing relationships. Nourishing social contacts form an essential part of positive family climates. From birth on, children learn that it is not only safe to be with other people, but stimulating, inspiring, and enlightening as well. People in positive family environments are always teaching and learning from each other. Siblings help each other with learning tasks. Adults teach kids. Kids teach adults. Learning is not just a one-way street in these families. It's a complex mesh of crisscrossing communications. Parents also connect the family in meaningful ways with the outside world by bringing the world to the family (there is often a constant flow of friends and relations coming over to visit) and by taking the family into the world through frequent travels and adventures.

Self-esteem. While social learning is important in positive families, so too is respect for the individual. Parents in these families help cultivate self-esteem by providing frequent opportunities for self-expression and self-actualization. Privacy needs of family members are honored. Praise is used not as a behav-

If the family were a container, it would be a nest, an enduring nest, loosely woven, expansive, and open. . . . If the family were a building, it would be an old but solid structure that contains human history, and appeals to those who see the carved moldings under all the plaster, the wide plank floors under the linoleum, the possibilities.

LETTY COTTIN POGREBIN

ioral pellet to reward acceptable performance but as a natural outcome of joy at seeing an individual realize his potential. Regular time is taken in these families to acknowledge and validate each person's inner experience. All family members have a chance to talk about or demonstrate special abilities and accomplishments and to feel affirmed by their achievements as well as by their very existence.

The impact of growing up in the kind of atmosphere I've described above appears to be far-reaching in determining whether a child will realize his natural genius. For example, in interviews with over seventy creative individuals from a wide range of disciplines, Vera John-Steiner, professor of psychology at the University of New Mexico, discovered that a positive family climate in childhood seemed instrumental in promoting creative and productive behaviors in adulthood. John-Steiner commented:

> Many of those whom I interviewed described an intense and joyful intellectual life that characterized their parents' homes: frequently recalled were family activities focused on nature or the writing of magazines and staging of plays. They also remembered the intense discussions around their dinner tables and that their parents encouraged their own participation and their independence of thought.

A similar project conducted by Benjamin Bloom and his colleagues at the University of Chicago came to many of the same conclusions. This landmark study of 120 gifted pianists, sculptors, athletes, mathematicians, and neurologists concluded: "Parents (or other family members) in pursuing their own interests, created situations that intrigued, interested, or involved the child. The parents responded to this interest favorably, by allowing the child to participate or by arranging special opportunities specifically for the child. Thus, the child's interest was rewarded or encouraged." One three-year-old future pianist, for example, enjoyed going around the house tapping out rhythms on all the furniture. His parents' reaction was to purchase a toy drum.

The observations of such research are not limited to individuals destined for public greatness. All children can benefit

In those days young people, unless invited to speak, were seen and not heard. But as soon as father considered us old enough to have opinions, we were given full scope to express them, no matter how adolescent.

MARGARET SANGER

from these conclusions. Positive family climates, as described above, create conditions that promote the latent genius residing within every child.

Blessed be the hand that prepares a pleasure for a child, for there is no saying when and where it may bloom forth.

DOUGLAS JERROLD

What the mother sings to the cradle goes all the way down to the coffin.

HENRY WARD BEECHER

TURNING POINTS IN LEARNING

When parents consciously acknowledge their children's natural genius, they can activate special learning moments that serve as turning points in their children's lives. David Feldman, professor of psychology at Tufts University, has coined the term *crystallizing experience* to refer to a learning event in childhood (or later) that sets into motion a decision to follow a specific career path or undertake some other major life project. A study of some of the great figures of the past and present reveals that parents and other relatives figured prominently in facilitating such crystallizing experiences.

For violin great Yehudi Menuhin, the crystallizing experience came when his parents took him to see the San Francisco Symphony Orchestra as a three-year-old. This experience so enthralled him that he asked to be given a violin as well as lessons with the orchestra's principal violinist. His parents provided both. In Albert Einstein's case, the turning point was when his father presented him with a simple scientific instrument that evoked his curiosity. "A wonder of such nature I experienced as a child of 4 or 5 when my father showed me a compass," recalled Einstein. "That this needle behaved in such a determined way did not at all fit into the nature of events. . . . I can still remember—or at least believe I can remember—that this experience made a deep and lasting impression upon me." In each instance, family members provided simple resources, seemingly innocent in themselves, that had a powerful emotional impact upon these creative individuals, pulling them along a path of development that ultimately led to their major life accomplishments.

What have been the crystallizing experiences in your own life? Think of a special moment spent with a significant adult in your past that might have been instrumental in determining the course of your life's work or in shaping a special interest. Perhaps it was a toy you were given, or a book, a song, or a tool that opened a new world for you.

Similarly, there are potential triggers to your child's self-development. Usually, they are not the same things that inspired you as a child. Each child will have his own unique entryway into the miraculous. However, by being alert to the possibilities of such an event, and through sharing resources with your child that you feel might interest him, you can make it more likely that such an experience will occur in your child's life.

NEGATIVE FAMILY PATTERNS

Just as positive family climates can generate crystallizing experiences that activate potentials, negative family climates can produce what I call *paralyzing experiences*—incidences of shame, humiliation, and stress that shut down potentials and freeze up a child's inborn capacity to learn. In such a family, a musical child's rhythmical furniture tapping might well be punished as disruptive instead of encouraged with music lessons or an instrument. In a negative family climate, an anxious mother might control a young learner's first attempts to ride a bike by filling her with fear of failure instead of the joys of accomplishment. In such a family, the parents may interfere with the process of learning to read through constant correction so that the child's mind essentially jams and he learns to avoid all books.

I've identified three basic family types that serve to inhibit a child's natural desire to learn: the dysfunctional family, the fast-track family, and the disadvantaged family.

THE DYSFUNCTIONAL FAMILY

In millions of families across the nation, one or both parents are crippled by emotional problems including alcoholism, drug dependence, food disorders, chronic rage, anxiety, and depression. These individual problems tend to reverberate throughout the entire family system, causing stress and dysfunctional behavior in every member.

Most children are curious, they want to know; but their eager inquiry is dulled by our pontifical assertions, our superior impatience and our casual brushing aside of their curiosity. We do not encourage their inquiry, for we are rather apprehensive of what may be asked of us; we do not foster their discontent, for we ourselves have ceased to question.

KRISHNAMURTI

A child, too, can never grasp the fact that the same mother who cooks so well, is so concerned about his cough, and helps so kindly with his homework, in some circumstances has no more feeling than a wall for his hidden inner world.

ALICE MILLER

If there is anything that we wish to change in the child, we should first examine it and see whether it is not something that could better be changed in ourselves.

CARL JUNG

According to family therapists John Bradshaw and Virginia Satir, dysfunctional families have certain basic rules that guide their attitudes toward learning and growing, including: the need to be in control at all times; the need to be perfect; the need to blame others when things don't work out: and the denial of the ability to freely think, feel, perceive, choose, and imagine as one wishes. Virginia Satir points out that "in troubled families, people's bodies and faces tell of their plight. Bodies are either stiff and tight, or slouchy. Faces look sullen, or sad, or blank like masks. Eyes look down and past people. Ears obviously don't hear. Voices are either harsh and strident or barely audible."

In these shame-based families, a child's vitality and spontaneity are all too often crushed under a barrage of insults, put-downs, and pressures, or they shrivel away through sheer neglect. Living in such conditions, children have little room to explore, discover, make mistakes, and do the many other things that go along with being a natural genius. Most of these kids don't even have enough privacy at home to think about the world and experience their own sense of self.

Dysfunctional families need, above all, to seek professional assistance from licensed counselors. They also can benefit greatly from participation in twelve-step programs based on the Alcoholics Anonymous model as well through involvement with parent education programs. As the self-esteem of the adults in these dysfunctional families improves, the imbalances in the family system can be righted and the children can begin to reclaim their own sense of self and recover their natural impulses to learn.

THE FAST-TRACK FAMILY

Many parents, otherwise free from mental illness or addictive behaviors, simply do not seem to have much time for their kids because of their own busy lives. Often highly successful in their professions, these parents spend so much time trying to get ahead in their careers that they neglect their kids or give only token time (sometimes referred to as *quality time*) to their children's learning needs. When they do focus on their kids' educational lives, their concern is usually in terms of discovering how to get *them* on the fast track to success as well. Consequently, fast-track families often pressure their kids to learn academic tasks before they're ready for them. They buy teach-your-baby-to-read programs and look for ways to speed up the learning process in older kids.

As a result, children in fast-track families often suffer stress symptoms, including headaches, nervousness, tight muscles, depression, and apathy. Because they are not allowed time for the natural unfolding of their inner genius, these kids can also develop learning and attention problems. Many of these children burn out or give up emotionally by the time they reach adolescence. They develop a cynical attitude toward life, despair of reaching the level of accomplishment their parents achieved or decide that the world owes them a living.

Fast-track families need to learn to let up on their kids academically, allow them the space to learn in their own way, nourish their emotional lives, and start spending *real* quality time with them in open-ended activities that don't necessarily have specific educational objectives but nurture a deep love of learning.

Today's child has become the unwilling, unintended victim of overwhelming stress— the stress borne of rapid, bewildering social change and constantly rising expectations.

DAVID ELKIND

THE DISADVANTAGED FAMILY

There are also families who, usually through no fault of their own, find themselves at the lower end of the socioeconomic ladder. They spend so much of their time struggling to pay the rent, buy food, and deal with other basic survival needs, that there is no room left for the development of their children's learning abilities. The very fact of their poverty often creates a tremendous stress that further depresses a child's natural genius. Adult illiteracy in the family makes it less likely that the kids will develop their own literacy skills. In addition, problems such as malnutrition, poor prenatal care, drug abuse, and other factors commonly associated with a poverty lifestyle can damage the child's brain right from the start of life, thereby limiting her potential to become the genius she was meant to be.

The real need of this kind of family is for appropriate economic assistance so that they can be freed of financial worries.

In addition, prenatal care, Head Start programs, adult literacy classes, and other medical, educational, and psychological assistance for the disadvantaged can help provide them with the tools they require to properly educate their kids.

Many families will have features of more than one of the family types listed above. In addition, most families will have a combination of positive and negative features. There is no ideal family except on television reruns and within our imaginations. Every family has to deal with the dark and light sides of being human. However, by thinking about the qualities present in both positive and negative family climates, you can begin to consider what kind of changes you'd like to make in your home to provide the very best conditions for unleashing your child's natural genius.

In general, only a child who feels safe dares to grow forward healthily. His safety needs must be gratified. He can't be pushed ahead, because the ungratified safety needs will remain forever underground, always calling for satisfaction.

ABRAHAM MASLOW

★ WHAT PARENTS CAN DO ★

Home is really the child's first and most important school. It's where he will learn perhaps 95 percent of the things he will take with him into life, including feelings of self-respect, emotional maturity, responsibility, and practical know-how. Many kids will also learn reading, writing, and arithmetic skills at home. Some parents have decided that the home is so important to their children's education that they are taking their kids out of public or private schools and homeschooling them full time (see the Resources section at the end of this chapter for books on the homeschooling movement). For most parents in today's busy world, however, homeschooling is impractical. Yet, you can still regard your home as a learning place or school away from school that will prepare your children for life. Here are some suggestions to guide you in your efforts.

Regard your house as a learning center. Since children do most of their real learning at home, not at school, each room in your house should be considered a classroom of sorts, where natural instruction can take place regularly. The dining room might be considered a place for lively discussion during meals; the kitchen a tasting room for measuring, calculating, and reading recipes; the living room a center of family games and activities; the bedroom a place of quiet play and study; the garage an area for building things; and the backyard a focus for physical exercise and recreation.

Resist the temptation to purchase workbooks, textbooks, and other commercially made school supplies. Instead, create opportunities for regular family times together in each area of the house where learning can occur naturally. You might select a specific day of the week, say every Wednesday, to try out a new recipe together in the kitchen. You might make the evening meal a time when everybody gets a chance to talk about his or her accomplishments during the day. You may also want to think about making some changes in the structure of individual rooms. To allow more privacy in a bedroom for reading and writing, for example, try placing a room divider in a strategic location. You also might want to purchase specific resources that can help develop a certain learning area, such as art supplies for the family room or a set of computer games for the study.

Use the extended family and the community as learning resources. Historically, much of a child's upbringing was carried out by an extended family of relatives and the wider community of families in a village or town. Today, with nuclear families and single-parent families the rule, parents have an even greater need to look beyond themselves for help in educating their kids.

Grandparents, aunts and uncles, and family friends can often be instrumental in opening children up to a different perspective. German poet and statesman Johann Wolfgang von Goethe wrote about the tremendous impact his grandmother made in his life when she brought him a puppet theater shortly before she died. Similarly, an uncle of Albert Einstein presented the adolescent boy with a geometry book that provoked him to higher studies. These relatives helped to stimulate crystallizing experiences in the lives of these great thinkers. What sorts of resources might your child's relatives provide?

There are no perfect parents! What's important is that you keep moving in the direction of good parenting. If you remain honest about where you are, your children's trust in you will increase. They care about truth, not perfection, and it is an impossible job for a human to play God. Yet many parents saddle themselves with this terrible responsibility.

VIRGINIA SATIR

The wider community should be considered, as well, in looking for individuals to positively influence your child in learning. Margaret Mead reported that during her frequent moves as a child, "wherever we were living, mother would find someone who was a good craftsman to teach us." Through this informal neighborhood apprenticeship program, Mead learned woodcarving, basketry, carpentry, weaving, and many other skills. Community centers and local colleges are often good sources of information for finding skilled individuals to teach your child. Check the community activities listings in your newspaper, or go to a library and ask to see catalogs of schools in your area for listings of events and courses as well as phone numbers and addresses of people to contact. Even if a course or activity is not appropriate for your child, you may be able to work out an apprenticeship or tutorial arrangement with a teacher at nominal cost.

Do not pressure your kids to learn. Children today are under a great deal of pressure to grow up too fast, too soon. As a result they develop a fear of failure, an absorption in measuring up to the unrealistic expectations of others, and a host of stress symptoms. David Elkind, professor of psychology at Tufts University, has dubbed this cultural tendency *the hurried child syndrome,* and advises parents to let children be children while they're young, allowing them to enjoy stress-free, spontaneous play activities that they regulate themselves.

We have learned a great deal in the past twenty years about the importance of early intervention in influencing a child's chances for success in life. We've also been exposed to a wide range of techniques, activities, and resources for enriching children's lives. The temptation is great, even among those parents who are not part of a fast-track family, to unleash this knowledge upon kids in mega-doses to force a positive mega-effect.

However, here, as elsewhere, the motto *less is more* seems to apply. Children often do their best learning without adult supervision during unstructured playtime. It is often only when they make their own choices about what they wish to learn and how they want to learn it that their motivation and achievement levels go way up. Parents should realize that they can usually better help their kids by simply listening to them, respecting their lives, and allowing them the freedom to explore new ideas and subjects on their own, rather than by piling on another French lesson or computer class.

Share your work life with your children. For thousands of years, most children were educated by learning a craft or trade directly from a family member. Nowadays, many children have little sense of what their parents actually do to support the family. Yet a parent's occupation can be a source of instruction and inspiration to a child, if only the parent is willing to share his or her involvement in some tangible way.

World-renowned linguist Noam Chomsky reported that his own interest in language emerged almost incidentally from helping his father at work: "I sort of grew up with the study of language. As a child I became interested because my father was working on medieval Hebrew grammar, and I used to read his proofs when I was twelve or thirteen or so." In the same way, the sculptor Robert Engman was inspired while watching his stepfather work as a blacksmith, and started to make his own structures.

Invite your child to your place of work and let her see what you do to earn the family income. Find something that she can do there that will provide her with a sense of meaningful involvement. If possible, take your child on business trips and arrange for her to attend some of the meetings. Finally, bring work home with you and look for simple ways in which your child can become engaged. If nothing else, your child will be inspired by your own enthusiasm and absorption in your work.

Get excited about learning. Learning is contagious: Those who don't have it catch it from those who do. It seems that we have been conditioned to think that learning must involve strain and hard effort. Yet a look at the life of young children suggests otherwise—they seem to do most of their learning easily, naturally, and with much accompanying glee.

Unfortunately, if a child is in a household where adults suffer from *psychosclerosis,* or hardening of the mind, then that child is likely to become afflicted with this hidden handicap as well. Keep your mind open, explore new hobbies, read widely, try something new every day, and above all, share your excitement with your children. This enthusiasm, more than anything you try to teach them, will have the greatest impact upon their lives.

RESOURCES

Berends, Polly Berrien. *Whole Child/Whole Parent: A Spiritual and Practical Guide to Parenthood* (rev. ed.). New York: Harper and Row, 1983. Sensitively written guide touching upon the deeper emotional dimensions of parenthood and family life. Includes list of appropriate books and toys.

Bradshaw, John. *Bradshaw On: The Family.* Deerfield Beach, FL: Health Communications Inc., 1988. Describes dysfunctional family systems and explains how parents can heal themselves and their families of addictive behaviors and emotional trauma. Based on the popular PBS series.

Briggs, Dorothy Corkille. *Your Child's Self-Esteem.* Garden City, NY: Doubleday, 1975. Excellent manual for parents on respecting the child's feeling life. Filled with valuable advice and examples showing parents how to interact with children in such a way as to affirm their ultimate worth.

Children's Television Workshop. *Parents' Guide to Raising Kids Who Love to Learn.* New York: Prentice Hall, 1989. Sensible guide to learning at home and at school.

Dinkmeyer, Don and Gary D. McKay. *The Parent's Handbook,* Circle Pines, MN: American Guidance Service, (Publisher's Building, Circle Pines, MN 55014) 1989. Practical workbook based on the author's S.T.E.P. program (Systematic Training for Effective Parenting) includes suggestions for creating family meetings, using logical consequences, and improving communication with children.

Elkind, David. *The Hurried Child.* Reading, MA: Addison-Wesley, 1981. Describes the stress today's child must cope with and offers some practical suggestions in alleviating these pressures.

Hausner, Lee. *Children of Paradise: Successful Parenting for Prosperous Families.* Los Angeles: Jeremy P. Tarcher, 1990. Explores the pitfalls and possibilities of parenting in an affluent or fast-track family.

Holt, John. *Teach Your Own: A New and Hopeful Path for Parents and Educators.* New York: Dell, 1986. A description of the homeschooling movement with practical advice on dealing with legal issues, creating a curriculum, and providing social experiences for the homeschooled child.

Pedersen, Anne, and Peggy O'Mara. (Eds.) *Schooling at Home: Parents, Kids, and Learning.* Santa Fe, NM: John Muir Publications (P.O. Box 613, Santa Fe, NM 87504), 1990. Anthology of articles, most of which were previously published in *Mothering Magazine,* on the process of homeschooling children. Includes several general articles on the nature of learning.

Satir, Virginia. *The New Peoplemaking.* Mountain View, CA: Science and Behavior Books, 1988. Wonderful book on transforming dysfunctional families into harmonious systems.

Periodicals

Mothering Magazine, P.O. Box 8410, Santa Fe, NM 87504. Includes regular sections "The Child's World" and "Ways of Learning." Quarterly.

Parenting Magazine, P.O. Box 52424, Boulder, CO 80321-2424. Features frequent articles on education, plus regular column, "The Learning Curve." Published ten times a year.

Organizations

Family Resource Coalition, 230 N. Michigan Ave., Room 1625, Chicago, IL 60601; (312) 726-4750. Network of support groups designed to strengthen the family bond. Provides books and other printed materials.

Holt Associates, 2269 Massachusetts Ave., Cambridge, MA 02140; (617) 864-3100. Founded by John Holt, this organization promotes homeschooling, publishes a monthly newsletter called *Growing Without Schooling,* and runs a mail-order service that sells books and learning resources.

National Homeschool Association (NHA), P.O. Box 58746, Seattle, WA 98138; (206) 432-1544. Nonprofit organization formed to support the homeschooling movement on a national level. Provides networking and resource referral services; publishes a quarterly newsletter.

National Parenting Center, P.O. Box 10748, Canoga Park, CA 91309; (900) 246-6667, $1.95 for the first minute and 95¢ for each additional minute. Interactive telecommunications resource center providing expert advice on a wide range of parent concerns from birth through adolescence.

Parent Effectiveness Training Inc., 531 Stevens, Solana Beach, CA 92075; (619) 481-8121. Promotes excellent *no-lose* parenting techniques relevant to the learning process, including active listening, resolving power struggles, and sending *I messages*.

3. *The School—Bridge or Barricade to Life?*

During my years as a public school teacher, I often had the feeling that I lived in two worlds. One world was the official school domain, with its academic curriculum, instructional materials, testing devices, disciplinary codes, furniture arrangements, teaching techniques, and educational theories. The other world was real life, with all its complexities, ambiguities, uncertainties, ecstasies, and agonies. I was expected to teach as if the official school world was the only reality, yet real life kept erupting through the cracks of my carefully prepared lessons plans.

The real world came out in the joyful laughter of two girls as they read to each other from a Dr. Seuss book. It made itself known in the animated whispering of three boys in the back of the room as a Native American arrowhead passed from hand to hand. It exploded in the angry shouts of a third-grader disappointed over the failure of a science experiment. It emerged in a thousand other spontaneous events during my busy classroom schedule. The kids were full of life. They brought it with them every day to school. Yet administrators seemed not to

*A child educated
only at school is an
uneducated child.*

GEORGE SANTAYANA

*Soap and schooling are not as
sudden as a massacre, but are
more deadly in the long run.*

MARK TWAIN

have anticipated this vitality in their curriculum, and as often as not, the child's own personal reality had to remain outside the classroom door until the final school bell.

In the summer of my sixth year a great expectation arose within me; something overwhelming was pending. I was up each morning at dawn, rushed to the top of Dorchester Hill, a treeless knoll of grass and boulders, to await the sun, my heart pounding. A kind of numinous expectancy loomed everywhere about and within me. A precise shift of brain function was afoot; my biological system was preparing to shift my awareness from the pre-logical operations of the child to the operational logic of later childhood, and an awesome new dimension of life was ready to unfold. Instead, I was put in school that fall. All year I sat at that desk, stunned, wondering at such a fate, thinking over and over: Something was supposed to happen, and it wasn't this.

JOSEPH CHILTON PEARCE

EDUCATION FOR REAL LIFE

This impression characterizes for me the crucial dilemma of modern education—that schools today are in danger of becoming fundamentally split off from their original mission of transmitting culture from one generation to the next. It wasn't always like this. As mentioned in the previous chapter, for thousands of years (and still in many parts of the globe), children received instruction through real-life experiences and by being in the presence of knowledgeable adults (usually relatives) who regularly practiced the skills of the culture. Traditionally, kids learned hunting by going on expeditions with trained hunters. They learned to weave through practicing this craft under the direct supervision of experienced weavers.

Nowadays, however, society has appointed a select group of individuals called *teachers* and put them in special buildings called *schools* for the purpose of educating children across a wide range of disciplines, from reading and history to citizenship and hygiene. Add to this dichotomy the fact that children spend much of their time in school engaged in activities that have little to do with culturally valued skills (test-taking, waiting in line, raising hands, filling in worksheets, dozing) and it becomes clear that contemporary culture runs the risk of not properly carrying out its time-honored task of educating its young.

Of course, schools do fulfill at least part of their function in helping children adapt to the culture around them. Studies suggest that individuals who have attended school outperform those who have not in a number of areas, including the use of specialized information-processing strategies like *chunking* (splitting up information into smaller bundles of knowledge that can be remembered more easily), the application of certain reasoning skills, and the use of language in a self-reflective way. More importantly, children learn specific notational systems such as reading, writing, and arithmetic—skills that are necessary for minimal functioning in a literate society.

However, schools often fail to address a much broader range of competencies and learning domains that are naturally expressed in the course of everyday life. "Schooling is coming to look increasingly isolated from the rest of what we do," says Lauren Resnick, former president of the American Educational Research Association. Resnick points out that learning outside of school typically emphasizes socially shared experiences, active use of tools of the trade, and direct application of knowledge to specific situations or contexts. She cites numerous studies documenting ways in which individuals employ highly refined methods of carrying out occupational tasks, from navigating the high seas to interpreting X rays in a medical laboratory, without the use of formal school skills. School learning, on the other hand, tends to focus more on individual experience, pure mental activity, and generalized forms of knowledge.

Now what I want is Facts. Teach these boys and girls nothing but Facts. Facts alone are wanted in life. Plant nothing else, and root out everything else. . . . In this life, we want nothing but Facts, sir; nothing but Facts!

SCHOOLTEACHER
MR. GRADGRIND IN
CHARLES DICKENS'S
HARD TIMES

◆　◆　◆　◆

Real-Life Learning Versus Conventional School Learning

Real-Life	*Conventional School*
Learning takes place *directly* through interaction with experiences and objects in their natural context.	Learning takes place *indirectly* through talking, thinking, reading, and writing *about* experiences and objects.
Emphasis is placed upon using tools to accomplish practical tasks that have tangible results.	Emphasis is placed upon abstract thinking processes that are more or less invisible.
Skills and competencies are mastered within the context of a meaningful activity.	Skills are broken up into discrete segments and taught apart from any connection with a meaningful activity.

Real-Life	Conventional School
Children receive immediate feedback from the environment and use it to adjust their performance accordingly.	Children often have to wait days, weeks, or months for feedback and by then often forget its connection to the original performance.
Success or failure is determined by a child's actual performance in a concrete situation.	Success or failure is determined by a child's accumulation of test scores, course credits, and/or grades.
Learners determine their own rate of speed in mastering a skill.	Learners have their learning rate determined by a school district's timetables for an entire group of students.
Learners pool their experiences and competencies together to accomplish common goals.	Learners work in isolation and compete against each other.
Mastering a skill provides its own intrinsic rewards.	Students learn in order to please other people or to receive external rewards or avoid punishment.
Teachers are selected by virtue of their practical competence and experience in specific areas.	Teachers are selected through having graduated from teachers' colleges and having acquired general teaching skills.
Learning embraces a broad spectrum of areas, including verbal, logical, musical, artistic, physical, social, political, spiritual, and moral domains.	Learning is generally limited to logical and verbal domains.

The chief reason for going to school is to get the impression fixed for life that there is a book side to everything.

ROBERT FROST

◆　◆　◆　◆

In one of the largest studies of schools ever conducted, classroom life appeared under the researcher's microscope looking like a poor substitute for the richness and variety of real life. This massive research effort, entitled "A Study in Schooling" and funded by over a dozen major foundations, went into a thousand classrooms nationwide and discovered that nearly 70 percent of what went on during instruction time was talk, usually teacher to student. The next most widely observed activity involved students working independently on written assignments ("Much of this work was in the form of responding to directives in workbooks or on worksheets"). Finally, the study noted that "the amount of time spent in any other kind of activity (e.g., role playing, small group planning and problem solving, constructing models) was minuscule." In other words, the activities that are most characteristic of real-life learning are among those least represented in the majority of school programs.

Most kids spend a high percentage of their roughly 13,000 schoolhours from kindergarten through high school graduation focusing on tasks bearing little relationship to real-life activities. Textbooks still structure from 75 to 90 percent of all classroom instruction. And while average citizens as well as educators and policy-makers understand that something is clearly wrong with the way we run our schools, reform efforts often focus on the wrong issues: bigger course loads, tougher graduation requirements, and longer school days.

These recommendations neglect to address the fact that it may not be greater *quantity* that is needed, but rather a better *quality* of instruction in the schools. John Goodlad, director of the monumental school study described above, summarized the observations of classrooms in the research project by saying: "Shared laughter, overt enthusiasm, or angry outbursts were rarely observed. Less than 3% of classroom time was devoted to praise, abrasive comments, expressions of joy or humor, or somewhat unbridled outbursts such as 'wow' or 'great.'" The American educational system is in danger not because the school day is too short or because there is not enough mathematics in the curriculum, but because our classrooms have become emotional wastelands. The schools must become centers of passion and purpose for children before the crisis in education is truly addressed. Only then will we be able to begin bridging the gap between the sterility of the official school world and the vitality of real life.

If an unfriendly foreign power had attempted to impose on America the mediocre educational performance that exists today, we might well have viewed it as an act of war.

NATIONAL COMMISSION ON EXCELLENCE IN EDUCATION

Let us reform our schools, and we shall find little reform needed in our prisons.

JOHN RUSKIN

What is desired is that the teacher cease being a lecturer; satisfied with transmitting ready-made solutions; his role should rather be that of a mentor stimulating initiative and research.

JEAN PIAGET

POSITIVE SCHOOL PROGRAMS

Constructive change in the direction of real-life learning is already occurring at several different levels within the teaching profession. Recently, both of the nation's major teachers unions formulated plans to implement innovative programs in the schools. The National Education Association endorsed the creation of special learning laboratories that would allow teachers working with administrators and parents to "redefine not only what we teach, but how we teach." These special programs are experimenting with more flexible scheduling (finding alternatives for the forty-five-minute school period), developing more cooperative ways of grouping kids than through tracking them by ability, and initiating other creative methods of organizing school instruction and classroom management.

Similarly, the American Federation of Teachers proposed a plan that would enable over a thousand school districts to set up teams of six or more teachers that would be free to attempt widespread, radical experimentation in their schools. According to AFT president Albert Shanker, teachers in these "schools within schools" could decide to remain with the same group of children for several years, spend more time on selected subjects, and use teaching methods such as videotape and computers rather than the more traditional approaches of lecture and textbooks. Such efforts are paving the way for public schools to become more relevant to the demands of a changing society.

On the level of the individual school, numerous examples exist of teachers practicing real-life education in their classrooms. The Oliver Springs Elementary School in Tennessee, for example, has an outdoor educational lab that covers twenty-seven acres. The lab includes an outdoor theater, a bluebird trail, a plant trail, physical fitness trails, and a weather station, where kids can gain hands-on experience in mastering environmental issues. The Underwood School in Raleigh, North Carolina, provides over a hundred electives for students, ranging from studying architecture in the community to putting on dramatic performances where kids learn how to operate lights and apply makeup as well as sing, dance, and act.

At South Medford High School in Massachusetts, seniors must complete a final project demonstrating practical knowledge of a given subject matter. Students have staged benefit rock concerts for the hungry, written novels, built riverboats, choreographed dance performances, produced TV commercials, and set up laser beams as part of this program. These schools, among many other fine examples described elsewhere in this book, serve as models for what can be achieved when communities decide that it's important for their children's sake to make school serve as a learning bridge to the outside world.

✯ WHAT PARENTS CAN DO ✯

How can you tell if your child's school is life-affirming or reflects, instead, the official school worldview? The best way of determining this is through visiting the school and observing your child's classroom. You should plan a visit at the beginning of each school year, and consider additional visits during the middle and end of the year or whenever an issue arises that may significantly affect your child's school career. Call the school first to schedule an appointment. Every school should be willing to allow parent observation at some point during the year, and a failure to permit this may be a warning sign that the school is too rigid to allow real life into its corridors. If you encounter resistance, contact the school principal and discuss your concerns.

HOW TO EVALUATE YOUR CHILD'S SCHOOL

When you visit your child's classroom and speak with the teacher and other school officials, here are some questions to consider.

- ◆ Is the classroom stocked with real-life materials (for example, animals, plants, computers, building materials, interesting books, art supplies, telescopes, and machines), or does it contain little else besides textbooks and worksheets?

A teacher who can arouse a feeling for one single good action, for one single good poem, accomplishes more than he who fills our memory with rows on rows of natural objects, classified with name and form.

GOETHE

Teaching is more difficult than learning because what teaching calls for is this: to let learn. The real teacher, in fact, lets nothing else be learned than—learning. His conduct, therefore, often produces the impression that we properly learn nothing from him, if by "learning" we now suddenly understand merely the procurement of useful information.

MARTIN HEIDEGGER

A teacher affects eternity; he can never tell where his influence stops.

HENRY ADAMS

◆ Are kids doing things in class that seem to be preparing them for real life (building, problem-solving, designing, experimenting, communicating, planning), or are they engaged in irrelevant paper-and-pencil tasks they will forget as soon as they leave school?

◆ Does the teacher seem to be actively involved in stimulating children's thinking through dialogue, open-ended questions, multimedia presentations, and hands-on experiences, or does he or she spend time lecturing *at* the students and requiring them to perform mindless academic tasks?

◆ Do school officials treat children as active explorers of knowledge, or do they have a *mug-jug* philosophy of learning where the teacher as *jug* pours knowledge into the empty *mug* of the student?

◆ Do teachers regard children as intrinsically motivated and seek to draw out their inner impulse to learn, or do they use behavior modification techniques (happy-face stickers, toys, food, and special privileges) in order to prod them into performing school tasks?

◆ Does the school provide activities that involve children in the community (bringing in community members to teach and speak, sending kids out into the community to perform real tasks), or are kids isolated in their classrooms from the complexities of the real world?

◆ Does your child bring home skills and products that he can put to use right away in his daily life, or does he instantly forget what he's learned at school and throw away most of what he produces there?

If you consistently find your child's school described more in the first part of these questions than in the second part, you can relax in the knowledge that your child is probably in very good hands. However, if the school seems to fit in more with the latter part of each question (teacher-centered, worksheet-oriented, behavior modification-ridden), then you may have cause for concern and should consider taking steps to improve the quality of your child's school life.

TIPS FOR CREATING CHANGE IN THE SCHOOLS

The process of changing a school from a paper-and-pencil factory to a garden of real-life possibilities is not easy. Textbook
manufacturers, test-makers, and parents, teachers, and administrators set in their old-fashioned academic ways help to
preserve the status quo against even the most spirited reform
efforts. However, change *does* occur, even in rigid institutions. It
usually happens when a grass-roots movement, spearheaded
by parents and teachers, grows in a school and transforms it
from the inside out. Here are some pointers for helping to
create your own local educational revolution.

Inform yourself. There is a wealth of information available indicating what works and what does not work in promoting effective learning in children. As you read through this book, for
example, you'll discover that much research has demonstrated
the effectiveness of hands-on math and science activities in educating children, while there is little evidence to show that
workbooks and ditto sheets help children master these subjects. Several books, programs, and organizations are cited at
the ends of the math and science chapters (chapters 5 and 6)
that support these conclusions. If you find your child's school
still using antiquated methods of teaching math and science,
you should obtain some of these resources and consider sharing them with the school.

Similarly, every chapter in this book concludes with a listing of resources that support quality learning experiences. Go
to bookstores and libraries and buy, borrow, or duplicate some
of this material, and write to relevant organizations for more
information. Educate yourself and stay up-to-date on educational innovations. This sends a message to school officials that
you are serious about change in the schools and that you have
solid research and expert testimony to back up your opinions.

Work cooperatively. Don't charge aggressively into a school
meeting demanding reforms. This will rarely produce results.
Teachers and administrators are wary of pushy parents and
have developed a number of strategies for dealing with them

*The essential weakness of
the old and traditional
education was not just that
it emphasized the necessity for
provision of definite subject
matter and activities. These
things are necessities for
anything that can rightly
be called education. The
weakness and evil was that
the imagination of educators
did not go beyond provision
of a fixed and rigid
environment of subject
matter, one drawn moreover
from sources altogether too
remote from the experiences
of their pupils.*

JOHN DEWEY

Our research shows that, of all the places teenagers hang out, the school is the one place they least wish to be. Moreover, when they are in school, the classroom is the one place they most strongly wish to avoid. They far prefer the cafeteria, the library, or the hallways.

MIHALY
CSIKSZENTMIHALYI

(changing the school structure is not one of them). More likely, you will be told politely that everything is being done to help your child, and nothing will really change.

If you want to make a difference in how your child's school is run, you need to be perceived as an ally and not an enemy. Avoid becoming a thorn in the side of the classroom teacher or school principal. Focus on the positive and seek ways in which teachers and administrators can expand on what they are already doing right. Begin any interaction with a teacher or administrator by talking about something constructive you've seen happening in the school. Only after you have created a good rapport should you begin sharing your concerns.

Volunteer for school activities. Studies suggest that parent participation in the schools almost invariably produces student gains in achievement and motivation. It also gives you the opportunity to share your own vision of education by practicing it in the classroom. Offer to speak to your child's class about your profession, a special hobby, or a recent trip you have taken. Encourage your friends to do the same. Volunteer to take kids on field trips to interesting places where people are engaged in real-life activities—for example, banks, museums, factories, restaurants, or farms. Help to organize special school activities such as a talent show, a science fair, or art exhibit where children's abilities can be displayed.

If you have time available on a regular basis, offer to be a classroom aide. You might teach reading or math groups using hands-on materials, or conduct special mini-courses in an area of your own expertise such as cooking, chess, art, photography, video, or computers. Some parents have gotten so involved in the school program that they have decided to become part-time or full-time teachers themselves. Any role you decide to take on in your child's school, however small, will help bridge the gap between home and school.

Get involved in school politics. The most direct way of influencing educational change is to become part of a policy-making body at your child's school. Join the local parent-teacher organization and become a member of any PTA committee having to do with teaching methods (call the school and ask how to contact your local PTA representative). In addition, many schools have steering committees or advisory groups (consisting of parents, teachers, and administrators) that make recommendations on important school issues such as curriculum, discipline, and how certain funds are to be used. You can find out about these groups by contacting the principal at your child's school.

Some parents have decided to create their own independent advocacy groups to push for specific programs or policies (for example, in the area of special education). You can start your own group by networking with other parents through existing parent or school organizations or by advertising your concerns in local newspapers. Some areas of the country have special parenting newspapers or newsletters where groups of this kind can be announced.

Finally, you can meet with school board members to present your case for reform, support school board candidates who share your perspectives, or even run for the school board yourself and have a major impact upon school policy decisions. Contact the superintendent's office of the school district for information about your local school board. Keep in mind that while there's strength in unity, there's also a lot you can accomplish working alone. One study conducted by the Institute for Responsive Education indicated that individual contacts with school board members often got a better response than group presentations.

However you decide to become involved in your child's school, remember to think positively and to work constructively toward change. Many parents have come up to me after talks and lectures completely frustrated with a school's mishandling of their children's potentials. Most of these parents lacked a solid game plan for dealing with the schools. On the other hand, many parents have shared with me their success stories. These parents usually had a specific strategy for change that they themselves initiated—a committee they started, a volunteer activity they became involved with, a letter-writing campaign they created—to help cultivate better schooling for their children. That old Chinese proverb, "A journey of a thousand

Whatever you can do or dream you can, begin it. Boldness has genius, power, and magic in it. Begin it now.

GOETHE

miles begins with a single step," certainly fits here. Start with a single concrete action, do it tomorrow, and watch your child's school start to transform itself from a worksheet wasteland that blocks curiosity and creativity into an active learning center that serves as a bridge to the real world.

RESOURCES

Albert, Linda. *Coping with Kids and School*. New York: Dutton, 1984. Answers common questions parents have about the schools and provides tips and resources for taking an active role in your child's education.

Goodlad, John. *A Place Called School*. New York: McGraw-Hill, 1984. Highly readable account of the monumental "A Study in Schooling" project described in this chapter.

Holt, John. *How Children Fail* (rev. ed.). New York: Dell, 1982. One of the best books available to explore the distinctions between real-life learning and school learning. See also Holt's *How Children Learn*.

Leonard, George. *Education and Ecstasy and the Great School Reform Hoax*. Berkeley, CA: North Atlantic Books, 1987. Utopian visions of what the schools can be, as well as criticisms of recent reform efforts.

Oakes, Jeannie and Martin Lipton. *Making the Best of Schools: A Handbook for Parents, Teachers, and Policymakers*. New Haven, CT: Yale University Press, 1990. Practical guide emphasizing active learning, heterogenous (mixed-ability level) grouping, and positive strategies for parent participation in school learning.

Smith, Frank. *Insult to Intelligence: The Bureaucratic Invasion of Our Classrooms*. New York: Arbor House, 1986. Stinging indictment of the widely practiced worksheet approach to classroom learning.

Weston, Susan Perkins. *Choosing a School for Your Child*. Washington, D.C.: U.S. Department of Education Office of Educational Research and Improvement, 1989. A thirty-six-page booklet guiding parents in exploring different educational options, asking the right questions before and during school visits, and selecting the school that meets their child's specific needs. Single copies are available for free by writing: Consumer Information Center, Department 567V, Pueblo, CO 81009.

Periodicals

Education Week, 4301 Connecticut Ave. NW, Room 250, Washington, DC 20008; (202) 686-0800. Newspaper written for educators, but a valuable resource for parents who want to be regularly informed of the most recent developments in education from kindergarten through high school. Published weekly during the school year.

Learning, Springhouse Corp., 1111 Bethlehem Pike, Springhouse, PA 19477; (215) 646-8700. Designed for elementary school teachers, this magazine of classroom teaching ideas can be enjoyed by concerned parents as well.

Organizations

Home and School Institute, Special Projects, 1201 16th St. NW, Room 228, Washington, DC 20036; (202) 466-3633. Provides activities and curricula that parents can use to stimulate their children's learning at home, including the book *MegaSkills*® (Houghton Mifflin, 1988) by Institute president Dorothy Rich. A series of MegaSkills® workshops for parents, now in twenty-five states, is also available.

Institute for Responsive Education, 704 Commonwealth Ave., Boston, MA 02215; (617) 353-3309. Dedicated to fostering greater parental involvement in the schools, especially among poor and minority parents in urban areas. Distributes books, pamphlets, and other publications reporting on successful parent-school programs.

National Coalition for Parent Involvement in Education, 119 N. Payne St., Alexandria, VA 22314; (703) 683-6232. Clearinghouse for information about parent-school participation programs.

National Committee for Citizens in Education, 10840 Little Patuxent Parkway, Suite 301, Columbia, MD 21044; (301) 997-9300. Excellent source of information for nuts-and-bolts issues in the schools, including parents' rights. Operates toll-free hotline for parents (1-800-NETWORK).

National Congress of Parents and Teachers, 700 North Rush, Chicago, IL 60611; (312) 787-0977. National headquarters for the 28,000 local PTA chapters around the country. Publishes educational materials for parents (including several free pamphlets) on a wide range of learning topics.

National School Volunteer Program, 601 Whythe St., Suite 200, Alexandria, VA 22314; (703) 836-4880. Brings together community resources with schools to promote balanced educational programs. Distributes several publications designed to help create more effective school volunteers.

Part Two

. . . .

Academics
the
Natural
Way

4. *The Whole-Language Road to Literacy*

One of the great miracles of human development is the child's ability to master the language of his culture. Scholars still do not completely understand how a child can learn to speak in such a short period of time with little or no direct instruction. World-renowned cognitive psychologist Jerome Bruner reflected on this achievement when he said: "The acquisition of language has always been a puzzling phenomenon. How can human beings learn so complex a system of rules for producing and comprehending messages so quickly, so well, with such subtle flexibility of use, a system of rules so complex that we who concern ourselves with language can scarcely decide how to describe it?"

The answer, of course, is that children have a natural genius for language. Massachusetts Institute of Technology professor Noam Chomsky suggests that the child has an *innate* capacity to generate complex linguistic structures through experimentation and play. However, the child does not develop this creative ability unless there are proper support systems in place during the early years. The devastating effects of environmental deprivation can be observed in the case of Genie, a young

Beginning with the age of two, every child becomes for a short period of time a linguistic genius. . . . There is no trace left in the eight-year-old of this creativity with words, since the need for it has passed; by this age the child already has fully mastered the basic principles of his native language. If his former talent for word invention and construction had not abandoned him, he would, even by the age of ten, eclipse any of us with his suppleness and brilliance of speech.

KORNEI CHUKOVSKY

A parent is a child's first tutor in unraveling the fascinating puzzle of written language. A parent is a child's one enduring source of faith that somehow, sooner or later, he or she will become a good reader.

THE REPORT OF THE
COMMISSION ON READING

girl who was abused by her parents and isolated from the world for the first ten years of her life. Robbed of the opportunity to use language during this time, she never developed the ability to go beyond simple one-word statements, having apparently lost that precious opportunity to cultivate the syntactic structures necessary for communicating in whole sentences.

The natural linguistic genius of the child requires parental guidance and stimulation in order to be fully realized. In the earliest years, it demands parents who talk *with* their children, not *at* them. According to Paula Menyuk and her colleagues at Boston University, parents who listen to their babies' babbling, make responsive comments, and continue dialoguing in this talk-response way make a greater impact on their children's language skills than do parents who simply carry on one-way communication. Similarly for preschool kids, research suggests that parents who read to their children, write notes to them, and in other ways carry on interactive forms of literacy can have a tremendous influence in determining the children's later ability to read and write. Once children reach school age, teachers become increasingly important in determining their progress in literacy skills. However, the parent continues to be a major ally to the child in developing fluency with the spoken and written language.

The rest of this chapter will explain what you can do at home to support the natural unfolding of your child's genius for language, as well as show you how you can make sure that your child receives the best possible reading and writing instruction at school. In order to understand better the range of issues surrounding these questions, however, we must first look at what has been done over the past three decades to cultivate children's literacy skills at home and at school.

THE CONTROVERSY OVER PHONICS

In 1955, educator Rudolf Flesch sounded a clarion call in classrooms and homes across America that is still ringing in our ears today. In his book *Why Johnny Can't Read*, he advocated the use of intensive phonics instruction as the answer to the nation's reading woes. Flesch accused the schools of using a *look-say* approach to reading instruction that required children to memorize thousands of single words. This method had failed to produce results, according to Flesch. The remedy was simple: Teach children the individual sounds or *phonemes* of the English language and show them how to blend these sounds together to create words. To get parents started, *Why Johnny Can't Read* included fifty pages of phonetically organized word lists to be used in systematic drilling of children.

Flesch's cry for educational reform had an amazing effect during the next thirty years. Phonics became a kind of rallying cry for millions of parents who put it right up there with God, Mom, and apple pie as a sacred American institution. By 1971, an extensive review of reading research and practice revealed that phonics books and exercises were being widely used in U.S. elementary schools. In 1972, phonics-related skills were added to the achievement tests being employed to assess reading progress among the nation's young. Throughout the 1970s and 1980s, phonics instruction continued to grow, becoming a part of almost every major reading instruction program published in the United States.

Yet the payoff that Flesch expected through this increased emphasis on phonics seems not to have materialized. According to statistics taken from the National Assessment of Educational Progress, a federally mandated nationwide testing program, no growth in reading achievement took place among nine- and thirteen-year-olds from 1980 to 1984; in 1986, test results even dropped among certain age groups. Currently, the United States is 49th in literacy out of the 159 members of the United Nations. Every year, 2.3 million graduating seniors and other adults join the ranks of the functionally illiterate and semiliterate in the United States, a group consisting of over 60 million Americans. It's clear that the phonics approach to reading instruction has not been the cure-all that Flesch hoped it would be.

Although the reasons for such widespread illiteracy are complex and multifaceted, it seems valid to suggest that today Johnny can't read, in part, precisely *because* he has been "phonickst" to death. Recent studies indicate that kids are spending an inordinate amount of time in the classroom filling out phonics

Clarence [Darrow] had great difficulty with grammar. No matter how hard he struggled . . . the parts of speech, especially the verb, remained a veiled mystery to him. His teachers and parents kept telling him that he would never be able to write or speak unless he learned grammar. At first, with despair in his heart, he believed them, but gradually a suspicion grew that perhaps they might be wrong. Finally, in the middle of a severe lecture on his grammatical shortcomings, he interrupted the teacher and said through his tears, "When I have something to say, I can always say it!"

MIRIAM GURKO

I have no patience with the stupidity of the average teacher of grammar who wastes precious years in hammering rules into children's heads. For it is not by learning rules that we acquire the powers of speaking a language, but by daily intercourse with those accustomed to express themselves with exactness and refinement and by copious reading of the best authors.

ERASMUS

worksheets and engaging in other skill-and-drill tasks that have little to do with the actual process of reading and comprehending a book. One federally commissioned report on reading indicated that children spend an average of only seven or eight minutes per day in elementary school classrooms actually reading books silently. Over 70 percent of their reading instruction time is given over to what has been described as *seatwork*. According to the reading commission, "Most of this time is spent on workbooks and skill sheets. . . . In the course of a school year, it would not be uncommon for a child in the elementary grades to bring home 1,000 workbook pages and skill sheets completed during reading period."

Most of these worksheets require students to do little actual reading. Instead, the process of reading has been cut up into hundreds of discrete skills, many of them phonics-related: "Draw a line from the picture of the apple to the sound it makes." "Fill in the blank with the proper short vowel sound (p__g)." "Put a circle around the object that begins with the 'th' sound." As one boy commented upon finishing a worksheet, "There! I didn't understand that, but I got it done!" Such a disconnected approach to reading threatens to turn our kids into paper-pushing bureaucrats and assembly-line robots instead of clear-thinking readers.

EMERGING INTO LITERACY

Perhaps the biggest problem with the phonics controversy is that it has created a huge polarization among parents and teachers who have divided themselves into either *phonics* or *whole-word* camps. The truth is that both of these approaches are inadequate by themselves as methods. Each approach fails to address a deeper perspective concerning the child's development of language. The newer and broader picture suggests that the child emerges into literacy by actively speaking, reading, and writing in the context of real life, not through filling out phonics worksheets or memorizing words.

Furthermore, the process of emergence begins much earlier than previously thought. Recent studies in literacy development suggest that children as young as two years recognize what a story is when they're being read to, and understand that adults get the story in some way from the pages of a book (although children this young think the story comes from the pictures and not the printed text). They also begin to form attachments to specific books. When bedtime rolls around, they simply *must* have their "bear book" or their "truck book." Around the age of three or four, children begin to make particular connections to the printed text in a book, understanding that a line of text is read from left to right and top to bottom, and that the story moves from page to page and has a beginning and an ending.

At this age, many children also begin reading print around them, such as brand names on cereal boxes or the words on traffic signs or billboards, with widely varying degrees of accuracy. They'll sit down and "read" a book using their own words to tell the story. And they'll do it in an appropriate manner using the right intonations, breaking points, and inflections. This suggests that they have mastered many of the underlying skills of literate behavior. They also create their own "books" consisting of page after page of scribbles, or compose simple notes and messages to family members in symbols that begin to resemble letters.

Over time, these skills serve as the foundation for reading and writing behavior as the child seeks meaningful ways of communicating with others and making sense out of the literate world around her. As Nigel Hall, senior lecturer in educational studies at Manchester Polytechnic in Manchester, England, puts it, "Most children will arrive at school knowing something about what written language is, how it works, and what it is used for." Parents and teachers need to acknowledge this fundamental base of knowledge that many young children already possess concerning reading and writing skills and provide educational structures that will allow this understanding to continue to grow into full-blown literacy.

SCHOOLS AND READING

Regrettably, many kindergarten and first-grade classroom teachers treat young children as if they were illiterate, and impose

There, perched on a cot I pretended to read. My eyes followed the black signs without skipping a single one and I told myself a story aloud.

JEAN PAUL SARTRE

It was in that tree that I learned to read, filled with the passion that can only come to the bookish, grasping, very young . . . bewildered by almost all of what I read, sweating in the attempt to understand a world of adults I fled from in real life but desperately wanted to join in books.

LILLIAN HELLMAN

on them what are called readiness activities. These pre-reading skills consist of worksheets and workbooks where students must discriminate between different kinds of geometric symbols or pictures in preparation for their exposure to letters. Then they start to learn phonics skills, a process that begins with initial consonant sounds ("buh" for *b*, "tuh" for *t*, and so on) and continues through several hundred specific rules and skills during the elementary grades. For some students the process ends only in junior or senior high school, where remedial texts continue to include phonics activities—despite the recommendation of one reading panel that phonics instruction be completed by second grade.

The books that kids actually read during these years parallel the banality of the accompanying worksheets. If a phonics approach is being emphasized, the text might read: "The fat cat sat on the mat. The rat sat on the hat." If a whole-word approach is being used, the reading material is likely to consist of a tightly controlled vocabulary in a dull basal reader with lines such as: "The dog ran to the boy. The boy ran to the dog. The dog and boy ran to the girl." Add to this the fact that screening tests place many students in lower reading groups during the primary grades, where the emphasis is placed on their *inability* to read, and it's no wonder that so many kids begin to tune out reading not long after they start school.

THE WHOLE-LANGUAGE ROAD TO LITERACY

Instead of focusing on boring texts, reading groups, and sequential phonics skills, teachers should be helping children develop the literate behaviors they came into school already starting to know how to use. Luckily, some schools are doing this using a philosophy known as *whole language*. Originally developed in New Zealand some twenty-five years ago, this approach has gained increasing support among classroom teachers in this country over the past decade. Fueled in part by recent psycholinguistic research describing the child's natural develop-

Once, far back in my childhood, when I had barely learned to read, I felt an intense emotion and set down a few words, half-rhymed but strange to me, different from everyday language. . . . I had no way at all of judging my first composition, which I took to my parents. . . . My father took it absentmindedly, read it absentmindedly and returned it to me absentmindedly saying, "where did you copy this from?" Then he went on talking to my mother in a lowered voice about his important and remote affairs. That, I seem to remember, was how my first poem was born.

PABLO NERUDA

ment of language, whole-language classrooms teach reading, writing, spelling, handwriting, and grammar as one seamless process of communication. Instead of dividing up reading or writing into separate skills, whole-language teachers emphasize the total experience of being literate.

The whole-language approach to reading instruction should not be confused with the whole-word method, which focuses on memorization of sight words and the use of basal readers. Instead, whole language engages all aspects of a child's drive to communicate. Children spend their time, not hunched over worksheets, but actively involved in reading and writing about things that passionately concern them. They read *real* books—classic children's literature, adventure stories, poetry, how-to-do-it books, current events—not artificially contrived textbooks that lack controversy, conflict, and character development. Kids learn about language by *using* it every day in meaningful ways rather than by completing disconnected assignments bearing little relationship to real-life activities.

In the kindergarten classrooms at PS 192 in New York City, for example, words are everywhere—on the windows, doors, floors, and chalkboards. Every child has his or her own special collection of favorite words, such as *helicopter* and *television*—words far too difficult to be used in a typical basal reader or phonics program but easily mastered by children when the words arise from their own personal interests and concerns. Kids dictate stories to the teacher and have them bound into little books that they can then read along with trade books in the classroom library.

Instead of filling out worksheets and reading standard textbooks, children in a second-grade classroom at Crocker Farms Elementary School in Amherst, Massachusetts, study the life and work of Emily Dickinson. Students read her poetry, study biographies, visit her home (she was an Amherst resident) and then write about their experiences. "At any particular time," says their teacher, Susan Benedict, "it became impossible to decide if we were studying oral language, reading, writing . . . or social studies. . . . At each step along the way there was time: time to talk, time to observe, time to question, time to investigate one topic, time to think, time to read, time to write."

*Dreams, books, are each a
   world; and books, we know
Are a substantial world,
   both pure and good.
Round these, with tendrils
   strong as flesh and blood,
Our pastime and our
   happiness will grow.*

WILLIAM WORDSWORTH

There is a tradition that when a Jewish child was introduced to study, he was given a slate covered with honey. As he licked the honey, the alphabet appeared. So the child learned to associate learning with sweetness.

TAMMY ORVELL

Perhaps it is only in childhood that books have any deep influence on our lives. . . . In childhood all books are books of divination, telling us about the future, and like the fortune-teller who sees a long journey in the cards or death by water, they influence the future. I suppose that is why books excited us so much. What do we ever get nowadays from reading to equal the excitement and the revelation of those first fourteen years?

GRAHAM GREENE

Providing children with the time and resources to explore reading and writing in meaningful ways appears to pay off in improved achievement levels. By the end of the year at PS 192, all 225 kindergartners could read their own dictated stories as well as simple examples of children's literature. Some were even reading on a second-grade level. Similarly, one year after implementing a whole-language program in the Portland, Oregon, public school system, administrators reported significantly higher reading achievement levels compared to the previous five years when phonics-oriented reading programs were used. Perhaps the most powerful argument in favor of the whole-language approach comes from New Zealand, where this method has been in place on a national level for several years. New Zealand currently ranks first in literacy among all nations of the world.

Whole-language learning should not be considered an alternative to phonics instruction. Phonics is actually incorporated into its method. In the whole-language approach to literacy, phonics is taught in the context of meaningful activities, not as a disconnected set of skills. For example, when the students at PS 192 were read the children's book *Pickle, Pickle, Pickle Juice* by Patty Wolcott, they had the opportunity to identify the repeating *P* sound in the title and talk about other words that began with that sound, including the names of classmates.

Children in whole-language classrooms are encouraged to invent their own spellings as they write, since this appears to help them discover phonetic rules in a natural way. The child who spells *monster* "MTR," for example, indicates he knows something about consonant sounds at the beginning, middle, and end of the word. Similarly, in reading, the errors that children make often actually help them learn more about word patterns. The child who reads "putt" for *put* is using a phonetic pattern he learned from his acquaintance with other words, such as *but, cut* and *rut*. Ultimately, though, phonics is only one part of a much larger framework in the whole-language classroom that includes listening, thinking, sharing, dramatic reading, cooperating, investigating, choral reading, writing, editing, and silent reading. Put in this perspective, the intensive phonics instruction that Rudolf Flesch proclaimed would save a nation from illiteracy in the 1950s seems impoverished by comparison.

★ WHAT PARENTS CAN DO ★

The implications of the whole-language method for parents are clear. According to this approach, parents should not try to *teach* their children to read or write, as many popular books have attempted to suggest over the past twenty years. Instead, they should cultivate their own literate behaviors and speak, read, and write with children in natural ways.

Denny Taylor, a University of New Hampshire researcher, investigated literacy as it spontaneously occurred in several families of children who were successful readers and writers in school. She discovered that these families practiced literacy skills daily: Parents and children alike kept calendars and telephone logs; they left notes for each other taped to bulletin boards and doors; they read to each other and expressed strong feelings in print. They didn't sit down to learn reading or writing "in thirty minutes a day." Their reading and writing activities were woven into the fabric of everyday life. The following suggestions, therefore, are not intended to be methods you should use to teach your children reading and writing, but rather ways in which you can enrich the quality of your family's life to promote literacy among all its members.

FOR THE PRESCHOOL CHILD

(Most of the following suggestions are also appropriate for school-aged children.)

Read to your child on a regular basis. Studies of children who entered first grade already reading indicate that their parents *invariably* read to them, right from infancy. Select a regular time during the day—just before bedtime is a good choice—and share with your child some of the best children's literature available. Hearing a wide variety of books read over a long

Literature is my Utopia. Here I am not disenfranchised. No barrier of the senses shuts me out from the sweet, gracious discourse of my book friends. They talk to me without embarrassment or awkwardness.

HELEN KELLER

Reading and what it can contribute to one's life is not something that pertains only to the ego and the conscious mind; it is also deeply rooted in the unconscious. Those who retain all through life a deep commitment to literacy harbor in their unconscious some residue of their earlier conviction that reading is an art permitting access to magic worlds, although very few of them are aware that they subconsciously believe this to be so.

BRUNO BETTELHEIM

period of time will sensitize your child to the rich and diverse sounds of language. This sensitivity to the flow of words can become internalized, creating an inner voice in your child that will assist him or her immeasurably in later reading and writing activities. The resources section at the end of this chapter includes several books for parents on selecting children's literature.

Choose beginning reading books that are multisensory. For many children just beginning to read, letters and words appear strange and confusing, even when there are not too many on a page. The first aim of parents should be to help children develop a book-positive attitude, not to get their kids simply to read the words placed in front of them. Consequently, look for beginning reading books that are children-friendly and that have features even nonreaders can enjoy. These include touch-and-feel books, scratch-and-sniff books, pop-up books, books that come equipped with computerized musical keyboards, and books with unique and intriguing illustrations. These books help bridge the gap between symbol systems children are familiar with (spatial, musical, kinesthetic) and the more mysterious symbol system of the English language.

Integrate reading with other activities. A child's ability to understand and enjoy reading depends in large part upon the connection of this skill to individual experience. Children need to see that reading is a part of life and not an isolated activity remote from their own personal concerns. Dramatize books that you read to your child by putting on little family plays or puppet shows. When a child experiences the joy of role-playing Toad in *Wind in the Willows* or Little Red Riding Hood, then the subsequent reading of these stories takes on a new depth. Similarly, drawing a story or fashioning favorite characters out of clay helps to connect the material to the child's own vivid imagination.

Create a print-rich environment in the home. Young children's minds are what psychologists have described as field-sensitive—they respond to and take in, often unconsciously, whatever happens to be in their immediate environment. If there are no printed words around the home, then when the child finally encounters words in the outside world, they can appear strange and even threatening. Make sure you have words visible around the house and read them out loud from time to time in your child's presence. (However, avoid putting your own labels on objects around the house; to many children this appears to be a contrived attempt to get them to read.) Naturally occurring examples of print include lists on chalkboards, messages on buttons and T-shirts, posters, brand names and texts on food packages, furniture labels, magazine and book covers, captions on pictures, names on a mailbox, and trademarks on appliances. Point out words to your child when you're out in the community as well, including those found on signs, billboards, and store windows.

Supply your child with a variety of writing tools. A major part of becoming literate involves practicing the behaviors of literate people. Kids are great imitators, and even if they don't know the alphabet, they can still engage in exploratory play activities leading to literacy if they have the tools to do so. You can help your child gain access to the world of literacy by providing some of the following resources: pencils, crayons, pens, paper of different sizes, finger paint, a stamp set, a label maker, some plastic or wooden letters, and a typewriter. You may want to supply your child with a special basket or box where she can have easy and regular access to writing tools. Answer your child's questions about letters and words, but take care not to impose your own agenda on her free play. Out of the scribbles and jumbled letters, meaningful text will eventually begin to emerge.

FOR THE SCHOOL-AGED CHILD

Provide access to books and other reading materials. Too many children in this country think only of textbooks and basal readers when they think of books. It's natural, then, that they are often turned off to literacy. But if you provide your child with real books that speak to his most driving personal concerns and passions, then you've helped to create a lifelong reader.

My father said that, as I could read, I had better learn to write. This was not nearly so pleasant.

AGATHA CHRISTIE

I cannot remember a time when I was not in love with [books]—with the books themselves, cover and binding and the paper they were printed on, with their smell and their weight and with their possession in my arms, captured and earned off to myself. Still illiterate, I was ready for them, committed to all the reading I could give them.

EUDORA WELTY

If I were asked to name the chief event in my life, I should say my father's library. In fact, sometimes I think I have never strayed outside that library.

JORGE LUIS BORGES

Try to recognize which subjects interest your child, then take him regularly to the public library or bookstores and encourage him to create his own personal library.

Give him gift subscriptions to children's magazines such as *Ranger Rick, Ebony Jr.*, and *Cricket* and enroll him in a children's book club where he can choose his favorite books. In addition, allow him access to your own library and to the many other forms of reading matter around the house, including catalogs, magazines and newspapers, reference works, schedules, maps, telephone books, sheet music, and even junk mail. The more your child understands that reading can help him find things out and get things done, the more his love of the printed word will grow.

Model reading during the course of each day. A lot of parents insist that their children become good readers yet hardly take time in their own lives to enjoy a book. Many children never have the opportunity to see their parents or other significant adults practicing reading skills in meaningful ways. So make sure to nurture your own love of reading. Join a book club. Subscribe to magazines and newspapers in areas of interest. Create a daily family reading time, when every family member reads quietly for thirty minutes, perhaps taking turns afterwards to share what was particularly enjoyable. When your child sees you engaged in reading material that actively absorbs your own interest and attention, she can't help but be powerfully influenced by your example.

Encourage the use of writing skills as part of daily life. Instead of having writing take place only during homework time, develop concrete ways in which your child can put his writing skills into practice. Suggest that he write letters to friends and relatives. Find out if your school or community has a pen pal program he can join that will connect him with other English-speaking kids his age from around the world. Encourage him to write notes to you when there's something he wants to get done or when he has a complaint. Let him have his own bulletin board or even a graffiti board in his bedroom for freestyle writing and drawing. Put up a family message board or create a suggestion box to which each member can contribute.

Let him know he can keep a personal journal or diary of his private thoughts. Purchase a word processor, particularly if handwriting is difficult or laborious for him, and spend time together learning how to get the most out of it (schools are increasingly including word processing as part of their language skills programs). In each of these ways, you can stimulate your child's natural impulse to write by helping him to see it as a tool for the expression of his deepest feelings and needs.

I can't emphasize too strongly the importance of letting your children, whether preschool or school-aged, develop their literacy skills naturally, in their own way and at their own pace. There are great pressures on children these days, from school and home alike, to read and write at earlier and earlier ages. Yet research suggests that pushing children to read or write before their time causes stresses that ultimately prove to be self-defeating. While some children may become readers and writers as early as four or five, others may not emerge as fully literate individuals until eight, nine, or even later.

Sadly, our culture seems to expect kids to begin reading by the end of first grade or be considered reading-disabled. This is nonsense. As long as parents provide a literacy-positive environment (reading aloud to kids from an early age, valuing books in the home, using reading and writing skills in meaningful ways, answering children's questions carefully), then their child's eventual emergence into literacy is assured. That doesn't mean the child will read as fast or as perfectly as the parents want, or that she will read the books her parents desire. But it does mean that in time the child will find her own way in the world of literacy and will be able to use words to enrich her life.

At the Cole School, where they had community singing every morning the teacher noticed that Jack [London] remained silent. She asked him why. He replied that she did not know how to sing, that she would spoil his voice because she flatted. The teacher dispatched him to the principal to be punished. The principal sent him back with a note saying that he could be excused, but that he would have to write a composition each morning for the fifteen minutes of singing. Jack ascribed his ability to write a thousand words every morning to the habit formed in this class.

IRVING STONE

✎ STARTING POINTS ✎

Word collections. Provide your child with a recipe box, a pack of blank three-by-five-inch index cards, and a set of alphabetized dividers. Let him know that you will write down for him any word he wishes to learn how to read (or let him do the writing while you provide the spelling). After he has collected a number of special words, he may want to begin creating his own sentences or stories from them.

Rubber stampede. Buy your child a nontoxic water-soluble ink pad and a set of rubber stamps featuring the letters of the alphabet. Let her create her own messages, signs, and composition. Show her how she can take one letter and repeat it across a page to make an art design. Include stamps with images so that she can create combined word and picture compositions.

Word pictures. Write down words that look like what they mean. Examples might include *tall* written in thin, high letters; *sun* with rays of light emanating from it; *dog* with the stem of the *d* looking like an ear and the stem of the *g* turned into a tail; and *yellow* written with a yellow crayon. After showing your child some examples, ask him to create his own favorite word pictures or write down some words for him to illustrate.

Found poetry. Collect a number of old magazines, newspapers, junk-mail circulars, catalogs, and other printed material. Suggest to your child that she search for favorite words in all this material to create her own special poem or story. Provide her with a large piece of construction paper, some glue, and scissors so that she can cut out individual words and paste them onto the sheet. Don't establish any constraints on how she can do this (it's okay to place words vertically, diagonally, or in any other order). Younger kids may want to include pictures.

The great dictator. Have your child talk to you about whatever happens to be on his mind while you write down or type everything he says. If he has nothing in particular to report, suggest that he tell a story, express an opinion, deliver a funny joke, explain how to do something practical, or describe an incident that occurred to him recently. After you have written or typed down this narrative, go over it with your child to make sure that it's accurate. You might want to copy it over in a more finished

Proust wrote on and on and his teachers thought his compositions disorganized.

VICTOR AND
MILDRED GOERTZEL

form or let your child do this. If your child is willing, see if he can read the material back to you on his own (you can provide assistance whenever requested). Then put the dictated material into a three-ring binder or folder so that your child can re-read it whenever he wishes. He may also want to illustrate his narrative with pictures on a separate sheet of paper.

Word clusters. This activity is helpful for older school-aged children who are interested in writing stories, poetry, reports, or other material but can't seem to get started. Suggest that the child write down the subject or main idea of the composition in the middle of a sheet of paper using as few words as possible (one to four words works best). Have her circle this central thought. Then ask her to write down all the different ideas that pop into her head related to that central subject. Each idea should be placed somewhere around the main idea, circled, and connected to the central thought with a line. These ideas in turn may give birth to related ideas, and these new words should likewise be written down, circled, and connected to the secondary thoughts. Eventually, the page should be filled with a web of words that begins to reveal the depth and breadth of a potential written work. Let your child use this *mind-map* as a resource of ideas in writing a more linear composition. She may want to create several word clusters before actually starting to write.

Sensory reading. If your child is having difficulty understanding what he's reading, suggest that he explore the material through his other senses. Ask him to close his eyes and visualize the content of the material, seeing the faces of characters, scenery, and any other images that occur to him (he may also hear sounds, feel movement, and smell or taste things as he does this). It might also help if he briefly sketches what he visualizes on a sheet of paper. You might also suggest that he act out the passage in a little role-play that you and your child spontaneously create. Finally, go back to the reading material and read it together, talking about how the material relates to the experiences he's just had.

Family newspaper. Create a weekly or monthly newsletter that contains contributions from every member of the family. Suggestions for contributions: drawings, poems, stories, opinions on current events, memories, recipes, how-to-do-it instructions, lists, advice, reflections, personal feelings, and family news of the week. You can type the material and have it duplicated or use a desktop publishing program to produce it. Hand it out at a time when the whole family is gathered together so that members can read their contributions out loud if they wish.

Letter writing. Have a regular time during the week when the family sits down to write letters. Provide plenty of paper, writing implements, envelopes, and stamps for the whole family. You might want to supply your child with personalized stationery or let her create her own letterhead. People to write to include friends, relatives, pen pals, and celebrities. Have some postcards on hand for requesting catalogs, free samples, or information from companies and organizations. Your child might also want to simply write letters that will never be sent—for example, to her dog, a favorite character in a book, or an imaginary playmate. Show your child a model of how letters are typically written, but help with punctuation and spelling only when asked.

Personal diary. Purchase a diary, blank book, notebook, or other personal journal for your child to record his private thoughts (you may want to let him choose his own notebook). Suggestions for things to record include dreams, ideas, personal feelings, poems, drawings, the day's activities, and special memories. Let him know that everything he writes will be private unless he chooses to share something. (A diary with a lock may be appropriate for those who need special reassurance.)

RESOURCES

Aston-Warner, Sylvia. *Teacher.* New York: Bantam, 1964. Describes Ashton-Warner's method of *organic reading*—creating reading vocabularies based on a child's personal concerns and interests. A pioneering work.

Becoming a Nation of Readers. Washington, D.C.: U.S. Government Printing Office, 1986. The final report of the 1985 federally funded Commission on Reading. Includes recommendations for teachers on improving the quality of reading instruction in school and for parents on helping children with reading at home. To order, send $4.50 to: Becoming a Nation of Readers, P.O. Box 2774, Station A, Champaign, IL 61820-8774.

Bettelheim, Bruno, and Karen Zelan. *On Learning to Read: The Child's Fascination with Meaning.* New York: Knopf, 1982. Attacks the banality of many basal readers used in classrooms and explores the subconscious meanings of typical reading errors.

Bissex, Glenda L. *Gnys at Work: A Child Learns to Write and Read.* Cambridge, MA: Harvard University Press, 1980. Fascinating study of a child's spontaneous exploration of word structure and meaning.

Graves, Donald, and Virginia Stuart. *Write from the Start: Tapping Your Child's Natural Writing Ability.* New York: NAL, 1987. Describes the process through which children learn to write spontaneously from their own desire to make sense out of the world and to communicate to others.

Gross, Jacquelyn. *Make Your Child a Lifelong Reader.* Los Angeles: Jeremy P. Tarcher, 1986. Many excellent suggestions for stimulating literacy in the home. Includes names and addresses of major book clubs and children's magazines, organized by age (under six, six through eleven, and twelve through sixteen).

Hodges, Richard E. *Learning to Spell.* National Council of Teachers of English, 1111 Kenyon Rd., Urbana, IL 61801. Practical booklet describing recent research in spelling instruction. Provides forty activities to encourage active spelling exploration.

Larrick, Nancy. *A Parent's Guide to Children's Reading.* Philadelphia: The Westminster Press, 1982. One of the oldest and best guides to choosing books for kids. Includes directions for building a home library.

McGuire, Jack. *Creative Storytelling: Choosing, Inventing, and Sharing Tales for Children.* New York: McGraw-Hill, 1985. Useful for parents who want to go beyond simply reading stories to their children at bedtime.

Stillman, Peter R. *Families Writing.* Cincinnati, OH: Writer's Digest Books, 1989. Over sixty activities to help families record special moments, share stories, preserve family traditions, and work through conflicts.

Trelease, Jim. *The New Read-Aloud Handbook.* New York: Penguin, 1989. Explains why reading out loud to children helps prepare them for life. Includes annotated treasury of more than 300 favorite children's novels, anthologies, picture books, and other stories.

Wiener, Harvey S. *Talk with Your Child: How to Develop Reading and Language Skills Through Conversation at Home.* New York: Viking, 1988. Explores the fundamental importance of meaningful dialogue between parent and child in providing a solid basis for later literacy skills. Tells how to ask good questions and how to talk to children about books, TV, and their own personal lives.

Organizations

Great Books Foundation, 40 E. Huron St., Chicago, IL 60611; (312) 332-5870 or (800) 222-5870. The Junior Great Books program trains volunteers and teachers to guide children through readings of classic children's literature.

Heinemann Educational Books, Inc., 70 Court St., Portsmouth, NH 03801; (603) 431-7894 or (800) 541-2086. The best single source of books on whole-language education. Write or call for free catalog.

International Reading Association, Dept. TE, Box 8139, Newark, DE 19714; (302) 731-1600. Dedicated to improving the quality of reading instruction at all levels. Disseminates information on the latest research in reading. Publishes *Magazines for Children,* a listing of 123 periodicals for kids with descriptions, cost, age levels, and ordering information.

National Association for the Preservation and Perpetuation of Storytelling, P.O. Box 309, Jonesborough, TN 37659. Provides books on the art of storytelling, recordings of accomplished storytellers, and information about story-telling events around the country.

Reading Is Fundamental Inc. (RIF), P.O. Box 23444, Washington, DC 20026; (202) 287-3220. Sponsors grass-roots reading motivation programs for over 2 million children nationwide.

Teachers and Writers Collaborative, 5 Union Square W, New York, NY 10003; (212) 691-6590. Publishes books on the teaching of writing in the schools. Write for free catalog.

5. *Math for the Real World*

Children are natural mathematicians. Watch a young child skipping along the sidewalk carefully stepping on every other square or touching every third fence post. Notice a group of kids arguing about a baseball score during a sandlot game. Children seem to have an inherent drive to search for patterns and regularity in life, and mathematics serves as a way of helping them find order in their universe.

The elementary mathematical ideas that we take for granted as adults—numbers, arithmetic operations, simple geometry—are for the young child a rich garden of possibilities. Jean Piaget relates, for example, one account of a mathematician friend who recalled his first momentous encounter with number theory at the age of four or five years.

> He was seated on the ground in his garden and he was counting pebbles. Now to count these pebbles he put them in a row and he counted them one, two, three up to ten. Then he finished counting them and started to count them in the other direction. He began by the end and once again found he had ten. He found this marvelous. . . . So he put them in a circle and counted them that way and found ten once again.

I suspect that many children would learn arithmetic, and learn it better, if it were illegal.

JOHN HOLT

[Blaise] Pascal . . . used to mark with charcoal the walls of his playroom, seeking a means of making a circle perfectly round and a triangle whose sides and angles were all equal. He discovered these things for himself and then began to seek the relationship which existed between them. He did not know any mathematical terms and so he made up his own. . . . Using these names he made axioms and finally developed perfect demonstrations . . . until he had come to the thirty-second proposition of Euclid.

C. M. COX

He had unlocked the hidden secret within numbers: their capacity to serve as a stable tool for rendering an account of the contents of the real world.

For children, the universe is alive with these kinds of logical-mathematical discoveries. In many cases, the child makes these investigations on his own. However, children still need significant adults in their lives to guide them in their explorations. Without exposure to logical thinking and the presence of curious adults who themselves are pattern-seekers, the child's natural genius for math often remains dormant.

PARENTS AND MATH PHOBIA

The seeds of mathematical genius lie fallow in too many households across the country precisely because parents have long ago turned off their own logical-mathematical potentials. Many parents shut down these abilities because of their own negative childhood experiences. They may remember being bored with flash cards, rote memorization of arithmetic facts, and endless math problems to solve. They may recollect times when they were mystified by the new math, algebra, or other seemingly irrelevant subjects. They may recall being paralyzed with anxiety over having to walk up to the blackboard in front of the class and give the "right answer" to a stern-faced teacher.

Sheila Tobias, author of *Overcoming Math Anxiety*, talks about the math phobic individual: "These are the people who typically get clammy fingers when it comes time to figure out the tip at a restaurant, who turn down promotions rather than deal with quantitative information, who change college majors to avoid a math requirement." Tobias points out that the root of the problem involves the fear of making mistakes and looking stupid in front of other people.

Many adults repress these traumas and grow up thinking they are simply nonmathematical. Their own parents may have even subtly reinforced these conclusions by pointing out, "Mom's side of the family never could add very well," or "Girls aren't able to do math as well as boys."

Our culture itself seems to provide a certain immunity

from mathematical ignorance. "There's a general cultural attitude toward math that sees it as a cold mechanical subject, only for scientists and engineers or for nerds, and we 'regular' people don't have to bother with it," says John Allan Paulos, professor of mathematics at Temple University and author of *Innumeracy: Mathematical Illiteracy and Its Consequences*. Statements such as "I can't balance my checkbook" and "I'm just not a logical person" offer adults a way to avoid looking at the childhood roots of their math frustration. Failing to see how they were conditioned to hate mathematics, they tend to pass their dislike on to their children.

SCHOOLS AND MATH

The result of growing up in a math-phobic society has been continued mathematical illiteracy in a new generation of students. Several recent studies support this view in delivering devastating reports on the state of innumeracy among our nation's young. In one evaluation given by the National Assessment of Educational Progress, 69 percent of thirteen-year-olds were unable to solve a simple problem that involved finding the perimeter of a rectangle ten feet long and six feet wide. A related study reported that over half of the nation's seventeen-year-olds were able to function only at a junior high level in math and fewer than one in fifteen could cope with problems at a high school level that took several steps to solve or that included algebra or geometry.

These statistics suggest a generation woefully unprepared for the challenges ahead, considering that 60 percent of the majors in the average university require a level of mathematics up to beginning calculus and 75 percent of the jobs in the marketplace demand a knowledge of simple algebra and geometry.

It appears many of these students have learned to become afraid of math in the same way their parents did: through negative school experiences. "Math is taught in a rigid authoritarian manner," says John Allan Paulos. "There's too much emphasis on computation, as if it represented all of mathematics. If children were required to diagram sentences for twelve years,

I went to several p_ schools, beginning a_ of six. The very first was u dame's school at Wimbledon, but my father, as an educational expert, would not let me stay there long. He found me crying one day at the difficulty of the twenty-three-times tables. . . . Also, they made me do mental arithmetic to a metronome! I once wetted myself with nervousness under this torture.

ROBERT GRAVES

The teacher pretended that algebra was a perfectly natural affair, to be taken for granted, whereas I didn't even know what numbers were. . . . Mathematics classes became sheer terror and torture to me. I was so intimidated by my incomprehension that I did not dare to ask any questions.

CARL JUNG

it wouldn't be a surprise if kids were turned off to English." Dr. Paulos suggests that many other practical areas need to be incorporated into the standard math curriculum, including the ability to estimate, compare magnitudes, interpret data, and understand the function of numbers in everyday life.

"If you look at what we use math for as adults," argues Ray Whinnem, principal of Martin Elementary School and mathematics coordinator for the Manchester City Schools in Manchester, Connecticut, "ninety percent of it involves estimation and mental computation: Do I have enough money for pizza? How far is it to the next gas station?" Yet, according to a recent report by the Mathematical Sciences Education board, most math instruction consists of talking by teachers and memorizing by students, even though these are the strategies found to be least effective in promoting mathematical understanding.

"Parents need to see that math isn't arithmetic worksheets with smiley faces on them," says Marilyn Burns, author of *The I Hate Mathematics! Book.*

> The ability to repeat rote procedures is not what's most important. Not only can a calculator do it much better, but what are you going to do with those numbers once you have a decision to make? If you're figuring out how much wallpaper you need, you'd better overestimate because if you come up short, you might have a hard time finding that pattern again in the stores.

Schools, Burns argues, need to develop better ways of helping children use mathematics as a means of solving real-life problems instead of wasting their time with isolated and irrelevant math drills.

INNOVATIVE SCHOOL PROGRAMS

Increasingly, educators are waking up to the need for these kinds of reforms. Recently, the state Department of Education in California rejected 145 out of 150 math textbooks submitted to them for adoption in the state's schools because they focused too heavily on the rules of mathematics and not enough on the practical side. California schools are now putting more empha-

Industry spends as much on remedial mathematics education for employees as is spent on mathematics education in schools, colleges, and universities. In addition, 60 percent of college mathematics enrollments are in courses ordinarily taught in high school. This massive repetition is grossly inefficient, wasting resources that could be used better to improve rather than to repeat mathematics education.

NATIONAL RESEARCH COUNCIL

sis upon problem solving, estimation, geometry, probability, and hands-on approaches to math education.

Similarly in Connecticut, principal Ray Whinnem reports:

We weren't happy with performance on conceptual and problem-solving parts of national standardized tests so we threw out the texts and are teaching elementary school mathematics with concrete materials and teacher-made worksheets. Now our kids are doing much better on national and state tests and when we hear from parents, it is to find out how to get their kids into our program.

Whinnem goes on the public-address system every Friday morning at his elementary school to present the math trivia question of the week: What's the average score of an NFL game? How many home runs were hit in the National League last year? What percentage of Americans say their favorite color is red? Trivial though they may seem, these questions form part of the school's innovative curriculum designed to help students become expert problem-solvers in the world of mathematics. Students in the Manchester elementary schools work with concrete materials instead of textbooks, use calculators instead of worksheets, and engage in practical activities in geometry, logic, classification, and probability, instead of using their math time simply to memorize arithmetic procedures and number facts.

In one activity at Martin Elementary School, students use twenty one-inch tiles to build a rectangle four tiles wide and five tiles tall. Through this activity, they graphically learn traditional arithmetic skills like multiplication ($4 \times 5 = 20$) and division ($20 \div 5 = 4$), as well as geometric concepts such as perimeter and area. Kids can also use the tiles to explore logical patterns. (A red tile followed by two white tiles and another red tile would lead to what kind of color sequence in the placement of additional tiles?). Principal Whinnem points out that many primary teachers use similar math manipulatives, "yet once a child gets to a certain level, usually third grade, most teachers stop using them." Whinnem recommends that hands-on learning of this type should continue all the way through elementary school and on into junior and senior high.

One of my first days at kindergarten the teacher brought us some toothpicks and semidried peas and told us to make structures. The other children, who had good eyes, were familiar with houses and barns; with my bad sight, I was used to seeing only bulks—I had no feeling at all about structural lines. Because I couldn't see, I naturally had recourse to my other senses which were very sensitive. When the teacher told me to make structures, I tried to make something that would work. Pushing and pulling, I found that a triangle held its shape when nothing else did. The other children made rectangular structures that seemed to stand up because the peas held them in shape. Meanwhile after pushing and pulling, the triangle I made felt good. The teacher called all the other teachers in the primary school as well as the kindergarten to look at this triangular structure. I remember being surprised that they were surprised. I began to feel then that all nature's structuring and patterning must be based on triangles.

R. BUCKMINSTER FULLER

I remember looking at the bathroom floor [as a child], and observing the different patterns that I could see by combining larger and smaller tiles. I also did arithmetic in my mind, rather obsessively, adding things endlessly, and also looking for patterns in numbers.

MATHEMATICIAN
RUEBEN HERSH

REDUCING MATH ANXIETY AT HOME

While the schools can do a lot to help turn around a child's attitude toward math, parents should also work hard to free themselves of negative feelings and stereotypes about mathematics that they may have developed from their own school and home experiences so that they can nurture a positive attitude in their children. One program that helps parents do this is the Family Math Project at the Lawrence Hall of Science in Berkeley, California. In this program, children and parents study math concepts together in a nonthreatening environment using games, puzzles, manipulatives, and challenging problems.

According to Nancy Krienberg, director of the project, "It doesn't take more than a half hour for parents to see that they're not going to be in a situation where they will have anxieties." What seems to help most of all, says Krienberg, is the recognition that "there are many ways to solve problems. It's not just that you get it or you don't. People 'get it' in lots of different ways. We provide an approach to math that's different from worksheets, timed tests, and competition—that has more to do with thinking, talking, and enjoying." Family math programs have been started in libraries, community centers, schools, and agencies across the country (see Resources at the end of this chapter for information about starting your own group).

In order to make this kind of math program work, it is important for parents to engage in math activities that focus on the *process* of thinking and that involve problems that may not necessarily have a right or wrong answer. By showing a genuine curiosity and interest in everyday math—from baseball averages in the living room and cooking recipes in the kitchen to carpentry measurements in the workshop and money management in the study—parents can model logical thinking and prepare their kids for what is shaping up to be an increasingly mathematical world. As Marilyn Burns puts it, "Whatever challenges kids are going to have to face in mathematics in the future, they're not the ones we have now." By providing a home and school environment where math counts for everybody—not just the wizards and the nerds—we can help kids realize their natural genius and natural joy for mathematics and logic.

★ WHAT PARENTS CAN DO ★

The single most important thing parents can do to help children with math is to learn to be comfortable with it themselves. That's why the suggestions and activities below are designed to be used by the whole family. Do these activities with your child, and notice if your own math phobia surfaces during a game or exercise. If it does, don't be afraid to show it—remember that success in mathematics depends upon your being able to make mistakes in front of others. After all, it's the process that's important in this new way of doing math, not the right answer.

If you happen to feel confident of your math abilities, watch out for the pitfall on the other side as well: the danger of making your child feel inadequate compared to your own high level of expertise. Allow yourself to participate in these activities and games with a noncompetitive and playful spirit. In this way, you can transmit your love of numbers and logic to your child in a spontaneous manner. Here are some general guidelines.

Stimulate your child's mind with interesting mathematical questions. John Allan Paulos suggests that parents ask imaginative questions to cultivate mathematical thinking: How many trees are there in the city park? How many nickels would it take to reach the top of the Empire State Building? How many hairs are there on the average human head? Using tools of measurement, estimation, and logic, parents and kids can together work out solutions to these seemingly whimsical problems.

Everyday situations also offer excellent opportunities for mathematical exploration. If you have three children in your kitchen and only one apple, you can ask, "How would you share this apple fairly among all three kids?" This sets the stage for an impromptu lesson in fractions. Or, if your child wants a dog for a pet, you can ask questions that help her figure out what the long-range cost of such an endeavor would be, making sure to include amounts for dog food, kennel and veterinarian fees, adjustments for inflation, and even the money you'd have to pay the neighbors to compensate them for the lawn chair your pet may conceivably chew up!

"The rule is, jam to-morrow and jam yesterday—but never jam today."

"It must come sometimes to 'jam to-day,'" Alice objected.

"No, it can't," said the Queen. "It's jam every other day; to-day isn't any other day, you know."

"I don't understand you," said Alice. "It's dreadfully confusing!"

"That's the effect of living backwards," the Queen said kindly. "It always makes one a little giddy at first—"

LEWIS CARROLL'S
*THROUGH THE
LOOKING GLASS*

Play math games with your kids. Simple board games like Candy-land and Chutes and Ladders give your child a chance to add dice amounts and calculate square moves. Dominoes are a great way for kids to learn about numbers, patterns, and addition. Chess and checkers help develop visual thinking and strategy skills. The game Clue requires making logical deductions, while Battleship helps develop a familiarity with the Cartesian coordinate system, where points are plotted on a grid defined by an x and a y axis.

"It's possible to talk about applications of mathematics—for example, probability—through games such as Monopoly," suggests John Allan Paulos. "If you land on the square Community Chest, are you more likely with the next roll of the dice to land on Boardwalk or Luxury Tax?" (Answer: on Boardwalk because there are more ways to roll a six than a five with two dice.)

Remember, though, that game time is fun time and not skill time. Your child could easily become game-phobic if he feels he's *supposed* to be learning something as he plays.

Buy your school-aged child a hand calculator. Contrary to many parents' beliefs, calculators will not make kids dependent and keep them from progressing in math. In fact, the National Council of Teachers of Mathematics endorsed the use of calculators several years ago and recommends that every student have access to one. In a position statement on calculators issued in 1986, the Council reported:

> Although extensively used in society, calculators are used far less in schools, where they could free large amounts of the time that students currently spend practicing computation. The time gained should be spent helping students to understand mathematics, to develop reasoning and problem-solving strategies, and in general, to use and apply mathematics.

"A calculator is a birthright," according to Marilyn Burns. "It gives children access to a world of numbers they wouldn't otherwise know about." Let your child see you using a calculator in your own work and have "calculator conversations" to help solve some of the mathematical questions that you raise with her.

Make sure your child's school has a practical, hands-on approach to mathematics education. First, see to it that your child's elementary school math program does not spend most of its time on a drill-and-skill approach to learning but instead includes a broad range of mathematical topics, such as logic, geometry, problem solving, graphing, probability, and measurement. Next find out whether your child's program involves hands-on learning materials. Any good elementary school math program should make use of manipulatives. These are concrete materials—such as blocks, rods, dice, and plastic chips—that kids actively touch, move, stack, and maneuver to explore mathematical relationships. Finally, check to see that the school helps kids learn math in practical ways; for example, setting up banks and stores to learn about money, measuring the schoolyard to study the metric system, or designing art projects to illustrate geometric concepts.

The national spotlight is turning on mathematics as we appreciate its central role in the economic growth of this country. . . . It must become a pump instead of a filter in the pipeline.

ROBERT M. WHITE
PRESIDENT OF THE
NATIONAL ACADEMY
OF ENGINEERING

 STARTING POINTS

Sorting systems. Find household items that can be classified.

- While doing the laundry, ask your child to sort the socks in different ways (by color, size, texture, etc.).
- Provide your child with a can of old buttons, coins, stones, or other small objects, and ask her to sort them (according to her own system of classification) into various compartments of an egg carton or ice-cube tray.

Food facts. Employ food in different ways to cultivate mathematical interest.

- Cut sandwiches in different geometric shapes (circles, triangles, squares, pentagons, octagons, parallelograms). Talk about the shapes (their names and features) as you eat them with your child.
- Use cereal bits as simple math manipulatives, for simple counting as well as for more complex math concepts such as estimating the number of bits in a handful of cereal or arranging clusters of 10 nuggets in groups of

Equations are just the boring part of mathematics. I attempt to see things in terms of geometry.

STEPHEN HAWKING

5 and 5, 4 and 6, 3 and 7, and so on, to illustrate basic addition properties.

♦ Let your child measure different quantities of liquid or solid food using measuring cups and spoons. For example, estimate how many cups of liquid there are in a gallon jug full of water.

♦ For older kids, explore the value of fractions (or the metric system) while following specific recipes.

Shape search. Concepts of geometry can be learned first within the context of everyday life.

♦ Suggest to your child that she pay attention to the shapes around her. What things in the house are made up of circles? Why do so many roofs consist of triangles? How many different shapes can she see in road signs?

♦ Find small objects around the house (blocks, cups, coins) and trace their shapes onto construction paper to cut out. Take one of these shapes and use it as a template or pattern. Trace around the template on a clean sheet of paper. Show your child how she can make repeated tracings of the shape on the paper to create interesting designs called *tessellations*.

Time tracking. Use a stopwatch to measure the passage of time in different ways (many multiple-function wristwatches include a stopwatch component).

♦ Ask your child to tell you when he thinks a minute has passed (or ten seconds, or three minutes).

♦ Time how long it takes to walk from the front of the house to the back (or how long it takes to skip or run the same distance).

♦ Think of other things you can time (examples: how long you can stand on one foot, how far you can run in a minute, how fast you can thread a needle).

Measuring up. Whether you use metric or English standard, there are plenty of things you can do around the house to sensitize your child to the important role of measurement in mathematics. Some examples:

◆ Measure different things around the house using a ruler or tape measure. Things to measure: the perimeter of the living room, the length from your child's waist to her shoulders, the width of your dog.

◆ Use other units of measurement (how many "hands" does it take to span the front yard?). Make up ridiculous-sounding terms to represent specific measurements; for example, how many *gleebs* long is the average pencil, where one *gleeb* equals the diameter of a quarter?

Toothpick tricks. Use toothpicks to make different geometric shapes.

◆ How many different shapes can you make with five toothpicks?

◆ How many toothpicks does it take to reach from one end of the table (or room) to the other (estimate first, then try it).

◆ For older kids, try making five triangles using only nine toothpicks.

Graph it. Make graphs with your child that present information about things that are important to him.

◆ Create a pie graph together showing what portion of each day is allocated to different activities in your child's life (sleeping, eating, watching television, playing, going to school).

◆ Draw a line graph with him indicating the amount of money in his piggy bank or savings account on a weekly or monthly basis.

◆ Construct a bar graph showing how many bowls of cereal each family member consumes during a thirty-day period.

Travel time. Bring math into family travel times.

◆ Estimate distances between towns, checking speedometer and odometer readings and road maps for accurate measurements.

◆ Count selected objects passed during the trip (number of Ford pickups, overpasses, barns, billboards).

When I was about thirteen, the library was going to get Calculus for the Practical Man. *By this time I knew, from reading the encyclopedia, that calculus was an important and interesting subject, and I ought to learn it. When I finally saw the calculus book at the library, I was very excited. I went to the librarian to check it out, but she looked at me and said, "You're just a child. What are you taking this book out for?" It was one of the few times in my life I was uncomfortable and I lied. I said it was for my father.*

RICHARD FEYNMAN

Weight watching. In addition to the health benefits, you'll also stimulate mathematical thinking in your child by doing the following activities together.

- Have a family "weigh-in" where members weigh themselves and compare their weights to household objects that can be placed on the scale (television set, lamp, teddy bear).
- At the grocery store, estimate weights of different meats, fruits, and vegetables, and then check your answers on a scale.

Family finance. Let your child open up a small bank account complete with checking account.

- Show her how to balance her checkbook.
- Go over bank statements with her, explaining concepts such as dividends or interest.
- Help her create a savings plan for a future purchase.

Number magic. Show your child how to perform magic using numbers. For example: "Think of a number. Double it. Add 8. Divide by 2. Subtract the original number. The answer is 4." The answer will *always* be 4, regardless of the original number. Talk with your child about why this might be so. Marilyn Burns's books (see Resources) contain other examples.

Newspaper math. Newspapers can be very useful in generating interest in math in a number of areas.

- The sports section contains baseball averages that help teach about decimals. (Ask your child: "What does a .333 batting average tell you about how often a player hits the ball safely?")
- Recipes in the food section allow you to have fun with fractions. ("Would ½ cup of flour added to ½ cup of water equal 1 cup of dough?")
- The television schedule provides a means of working with time values. ("How long is it from the present moment until your favorite TV program tonight?")

◆ Read the weather column to learn about temperatures. ("How many degrees Fahrenheit difference is there between the highest and lowest temperatures in the nation?")

Probability games. Some of these games can lead your child to think more critically about concepts such as *luck* or *chance*.

◆ Flip a coin and keep track of the number of heads and tails on a sheet of paper. Are there external factors that affect the results?
◆ Toss a pair of dice and record the results of each roll. What patterns emerge from the data?
◆ Look up the probability of winning the grand prize of your state lottery or a national direct-mail contest. Does this affect your belief that you can win?

Mathematics possess not only truth but supreme beauty.

BERTRAND RUSSELL

RESOURCES

Baratta-Lorton, Mary. *Mathematics Their Way*. Menlo Park, CA: Addison-Wesley, 1976. A kindergarten through second grade hands-on mathematics curriculum using common household materials. Parents can use ideas from this classroom program to help their children at home. See also her program for preschoolers, *Workjobs . . . For Parents* (Addison-Wesley, 1972). Available at teacher supply stores or by ordering through a bookstore.

Burns, Marilyn. *The I Hate Mathematics! Book*. Boston: Little, Brown, 1975. A classic book for kids (grades four through eight) loaded with practical math tricks, games, and experiences. Other books by Burns include *The Book of Think* (Little, Brown, 1976) and *Math for Smarty Pants* (Little, Brown, 1982).

National PTA and Mathematical Sciences Education Board. *Math Matters: Kids Are Counting on You*. Chicago: 1989. This kit of parent education materials is available only through local PTAs and elementary schools. It includes a seven-minute video on the importance of math in the home, a hand calculator, and specific math activities parents can do at home with their kids using inexpensive materials.

Paulos, John Allan. *Innumeracy: Mathematical Illiteracy and Its Consequences.* New York: Vintage, 1988. Best-selling indictment of mathematical ignorance among adults. Suggests that knowledge of logic and numbers is critically important in everyday life and that virtually everyone is capable of becoming mathematically literate. Includes easy-to-comprehend examples drawn from the stock market, astrology, medical statistics, and many other popular topics.

Organizations

Creative Publications, 5005 West 110th St., Oak Lawn, IL 60453; (800) 624-0822; (800) 435-5843 in Illinois. Mail-order service for innovative materials in mathematics, including manipulatives, games, puzzles, computer software, and books. Free catalog.

Family Math Program, Lawrence Hall of Science, University of California, Berkeley, CA 94710; (415) 642-1823. Trains parents and teachers to provide family math courses (parents and children learning together) at schools, community centers, libraries, and social service agencies. Also publishes a book of activities entitled *Family Math*, available for $15 from the program, and rents a seventeen-minute video showing parents and children working on cooperative math activities.

National Council of Teachers of Mathematics, 1906 Association Drive, Reston, VA 22091; (703) 620-9840. Professional organization for mathematics teachers focused on elementary and secondary education. Publishes a journal and other resources in math education that parents may find helpful in assisting their children with math at home or in pushing for better math programs at school.

6. *Hands-On/Minds-On Science for Your Child*

A two-year-old boy picks up a piece of paper, examines it, and crumples it in his hands. A three-year-old girl drops her rubber duck into the bath water and marvels at the ripples that she's made. A four-year-old pours his milk into a glass of water at the dinner table, then dumps the mixture into a bowl of soup.

These are all relatively mundane activities in the lives of young children. But it may surprise you to realize that when kids do these kinds of things they're engaged in scientific research. As kids explore, test, and modify the properties of the natural world, they use the same thinking processes fundamental to biology, physics, chemistry, and every other field of science. "Kids are natural scientists," says Vicki Cobb, author of *Science Experiments You Can Eat* and other science activity books for children. "They're naturally inquisitive. And they're always asking questions that are testable."

These fanciful investigations are the foundation for the kind of inquiry that later develops into mature scientific thinking. A look at some of the greatest scientists of Western culture

There are children playing in the streets who could solve some of my top problems in physics, because they have modes of sensory perception that I lost long ago.

J. ROBERT OPPENHEIMER

Science can be introduced to children well or poorly. If poorly, children can be turned away from science; they can develop a lifelong antipathy; they will be in a far worse condition than if they had never been introduced to science at all.

ISAAC ASIMOV

Seen only as a laundry list of theorems in a workbook, science can be a bore. But as a "hands-on" adventure guided by a knowledgeable teacher, it can sweep children up in the excitement of discovery.

WILLIAM J. BENNETT

reveals that they possessed a playful and childlike attitude toward their work. Sir Alexander Fleming, the Scottish bacteriologist who discovered penicillin, used to create little pictures of ballerinas and houses in petri dishes using microorganisms as his medium. Being intimately acquainted with microbes—their colors, textures, growth rates, and other features—he would arrange different colored germs in the dishes in such a way that they would grow into recognizable images. "I play with microbes," said Fleming. "It is very pleasant to break the rules."

Similarly, Nobel Prize winners James Watson and Francis Crick discovered the structure of DNA essentially by playing in unconventional ways with a three-dimensional Tinkertoy-like model. Like great scientists, children are constantly playing around with great ideas, experimenting with things, trying to ferret out their mysteries, and always asking questions that probe to the very heart of matter.

This curiosity appears to be at risk for early extinction when children enter public school. In the classroom, science no longer has to do with the mysteries of life but is confined to a *subject* that is *covered* by a textbook. The playfulness children exhibit in exploring, testing, and questioning the laws of nature gives way to memorizing, classifying, and quantifying a body of knowledge in preparation for a test. A recent report published by the American Association for the Advancement of Science suggested:

> The present science textbooks and methods of instruction, far from helping, often actually impede progress toward scientific literacy. They often emphasize the learning of answers more than the exploration of questions, memory at the expense of critical thought, bits and pieces of information instead of understanding in context, recitation over argument, reading in lieu of doing.

Douglas Lapp, director of the Smithsonian Institution's Science Resource Center in Washington, D.C., estimates that only 1 to 2 percent of American elementary school students are taught science correctly. The rest—if they receive science instruction at all—wallow in meaningless facts and numbers.

This educational mismanagement of children's natural scientific genius causes most children to view science as drudgery. According to Edward Pizzini, associate professor of science education at the University of Iowa, by the third grade half of all students don't want to take science in school anymore. By the middle of junior high school, 80 percent of all students dislike the subject. This massive rejection of science in American classrooms creates problems at the college and university level, where engineering and natural-science graduate programs are increasingly being filled by foreign nationals who presumably have been exposed to a more stimulating science curriculum during their youth. Many analysts predict a shortage of Ph.D. scientists by the mid-1990s unless more students are attracted to the field.

The impact of poorly taught science courses finds its way into the life of the average American adult as well. In one survey, only 45 percent of Americans knew that the earth orbits around the sun in one year, barely 43 percent reported that electrons were smaller than atoms, and a mere 37 percent understood that dinosaurs lived before the earliest human beings. This level of scientific illiteracy may create a nation of workers unequipped for twenty-first century jobs requiring increasingly technological skills. It also threatens to produce a generation of voters ill informed on scientific issues of increasing importance to our culture, such as waste management, nuclear proliferation, and genetic engineering.

Children are born true scientists. They spontaneously experiment and experience and reexperience again. They select, combine, and test, seeking to find order in their experiences—"which is the mostest? which is the leastest?" They smell, taste, bite, and touch-test for hardness, softness, springiness, roughness, smoothness, coldness, warmness; they heft, shake, punch, squeeze, push, crush, rub, and try to pull things apart.

R. BUCKMINSTER FULLER

PROMOTING SCIENTIFIC LITERACY

To help combat this wholesale apathy and ignorance, educators need to provide science education programs right from the start of school that embrace the child's natural tendency to wonder about the world. Rather than studying science from a distance, children need to be exposed to a hands-on approach to science education. *Hands-on* means that students *do* things to learn about scientific principles. Instead of reading about the wind, a first-grader in a hands-on classroom might go outdoors with a weather vane and determine the wind's direction.

*By the time I was eight
I began to be interested
in birds. One day down
Charterhouse Hill, I saw a
queer little bird, blue-grey
above and russet below:
It was just a common
nuthatch, but to me it was a
revelation. . . . All through
my Eton and Oxford days, I
kept an elaborate bird diary,
noting which species of
birds I saw each day, their
approximate number,
whether they were singing,
the nests I found (with the
number of eggs or young)
and notes on their peculiar
behavior.*

JULIAN HUXLEY

Rather than memorizing the definition of the term *evaporation* for a multiple-choice quiz, a second-grader in a hands-on classroom might keep a glass of water on the windowsill for a week, recording changes in water level on a daily basis.

Activities in a hands-on science program engage children in a whole range of important processes: observing, describing, comparing, classifying, measuring, predicting, graphing, and researching in many other ways. These experiences more nearly imitate the actual work of a scientist in the laboratory than do textbooks and lectures.

Children are also more naturally inclined to want to learn in such environments. In Mesa, Arizona, educators inadvertently had the opportunity to compare the effects of hands-on classes with more traditional programs when they offered seventh-graders the option of continuing science education in junior high or abandoning it for other electives. Ninety-six percent of the kids who had spent their elementary school years in hands-on programs chose to continue taking science. In these elementary school classes, they had measured their heartbeats, watched tadpole eggs hatch, reassembled chickens from after-dinner bones, played games demonstrating the roles of predator and prey in nature, grew plants from seedlings, and engaged in hundreds of other practical demonstrations of scientific principles.

In contrast, only 4 percent of kids in the traditional programs, where students spent most of their time reading textbooks and answering questions at the end of each chapter, opted for a science future. This experience led the district to develop hands-on programs for all of its elementary schools. Since then, the Mesa Public Schools have been cited as exemplary by the National Science Teachers Association.

Well-designed hands-on science programs break down traditional barriers between science and the rest of the curriculum. Indeed, they seek to bridge the gap between the traditional school world and real life by making science instruction relevant to significant social issues. In one New York City program, elementary school students try to understand the effects of oil spills by creating their own mini-disasters—pouring vegetable oil into pans of river water and attempting to clean them up using a number of different approaches, including cotton balls, Popsicle sticks, and detergent.

In another multischool project funded by the National Science Foundation, students learned about the acid rain problem by collecting pond water, tap water, and rainwater, measuring their acidity, running the results through a computer, and comparing figures with what kids in other parts of the country had found. By equipping children with the ability to personally investigate real-world problems, teachers are preparing them for adult roles as voters, consumers, and policymakers.

PARENTS ARE EXPLORERS TOO

Schools can only do part of the job in tapping the child's innate scientific spirit. Parents need to recognize their own important role in encouraging their child's interest in science. Kids look most often to parents for signs that the world is an interesting place worth studying. The problem for many parents is that the word *science* conjures up joyless memories of endless hours spent in high school chemistry or physics classes. As with mathematics, some parents also associate success in science with being a "nerd." Reflecting upon his own science education in the 1940s, Harvard biologist Stephen Jay Gould recalled, "Any kid with a passionate interest in science was a wonk, a square, a dweeb, a doofus, or a geek. . . . I was called 'fossil face' on the playground. It hurt."

Science does not have to be boring or painful. Parents and children alike can discover the excitement that comes from exploring the world with a scientific attitude. As George Hein, one of the developers of the highly innovative Education Science Study materials, puts it, "The more parents appreciate, enjoy, and are interested in nature and the objects of the world, the more likely their kids will be curious." Parents should start to nurture their own interest in the natural world by asking themselves the kinds of questions they used to ask when they were kids: How big is the universe? Why is the sky blue? What makes a seed grow? By awakening their own inner sense of wonder, they can help to stimulate it in their children.

Joseph Lister, aged ten, was waiting for his father to inspect his lessons, when he happened to look out of the window. He was startled by a remarkable sight; owing to a defect in the glass, a kind of bubble had formed, and when he looked through the bubble he could see everything outside much more clearly than he could when he looked through the rest of the glass. He asked his father for the explanation. His father told him that the bubble was acting as a magnifying glass, and could not explain it, but promised to look it up in a book of optics. This aroused Joseph's interest in optics. He was to invent the achromatic lens and to become a Fellow of the Royal Society.

R.S. AND C.M. ILLINGWORTH

True science, teaches, above all, to doubt and be ignorant.

MIGUEL DE UNAMUNO

★ WHAT PARENTS CAN DO ★

The best way to encourage your child to study science is by providing an environment at home that promotes curiosity and exploration of the world. Many parents think they can simply buy their kids a microscope, a computer, or a chemistry set and leave it at that. These resources are helpful, but the best science education comes from everyday activities that you engage in with your child using household supplies and your combined sense of enthusiasm for the object of your exploration. Here are some general suggestions.

Ask your child questions that awaken a scientific spirit of inquiry. As Vicki Cobb points out, "The business of science is raising questions. Even if you find answers, the best experiments raise more questions." Good questions are generally open-ended and allow for a variety of responses. Some effective ways to begin the questioning process include: "What would happen if . . ." "What do you think is going on here?" "How do you explain that?" Stay away from questions that begin, "Don't you think that . . ." or "Isn't it true that . . ." Leading questions place subtle pressures on children to comply with parental beliefs.

While parental inquiry can stimulate a child's scientific mind, avoid peppering your child machine-gun style with rapid-fire questions that scarcely give him time to respond. Research suggests that kids need time after being asked a question in order to properly think about their reply. Wait at least three full seconds after asking a question before saying anything else. Listen in a nonjudgmental way to the answers your child provides. Even wrong answers can lead to highly productive avenues of inquiry. And encourage your child to formulate his own questions as he explores scientific concepts.

Use the news to spark scientific interest. Pick up any daily newspaper or weekly news magazine and you will find it packed with information on scientific subjects from space exploration and genetic engineering to earthquake prediction and ecological accidents. Use these subjects as opportunities to begin researching and talking about scientific principles in everyday

I do not know what I may appear to the world; but to myself I seem to have been only like a boy playing on the sea shore and diverting himself and then finding a smoother pebble or a prettier shell than ordinary while the greater ocean of truth lay all undiscovered before me.

ISAAC NEWTON

All things are filled full of signs, and it is a wise man who can learn about one thing from another.

PLOTINUS

life. How does a space telescope work? What kinds of problems might arise from gene-splicing? Why can't scientists do a better job of forecasting earthquakes in populated areas? A trip to the library or a simple dinner-table conversation can open up these topics to closer scrutiny and make scientific investigation a controversial and exciting avenue of inquiry for your child.

Visit people and places that activate scientific curiosity. Nature offers practically an unlimited number of opportunities for engaging in the business of science with your child, including explorations in astronomy, geology, botany, biology, and meteorology. In addition, day trips to more specialized centers of scientific investigation, including science museums, zoos, aquariums, planetariums, and arboretums help stimulate scientific interest. Take your child to the library and check out books on science (listed under the 500s and 600s in the Dewey decimal system used in most public libraries). Seek out experts in your child's particular areas of interest. "There are wonderful people in the world who know everything there is to know about beetles, for example," notes George Hein, "or people who are terrific guides through nature." Introduce your child to friends and colleagues who use scientific methods in their work, such as engineers, chemists, physicists, horticulturists, and ecologists. The more your child can witness people using the skills and principles of science, the more relevant science will become in her own life.

Focus on the process of science rather than specific skills, facts, and fixed outcomes. Many parents are tempted to teach their children specific facts and skills in science, or to structure their scientific explorations so that the kids learn specific concepts the parents want them to learn. This defeats the very purpose of the scientific method, which requires asking good questions, creating hypotheses, keeping careful observations, setting up situations that test hypotheses, and changing hypotheses as new facts emerge. In the scientific method, the process of inquiry is more important than individual facts or principles.

The history of science has repeatedly shown that tangents, mistakes, accidents, and errors often prove to be particularly

And hark! how blithe the throstle sings!
He, too, is no mean preacher:
Come forth into the light of things,
Let Nature be your Teacher.

WILLIAM WORDSWORTH

Science invites us to let the facts in, even when they don't conform to our preconceptions. It counsels us to carry alternative hypotheses in our heads and see which [ones] best match the facts.

CARL SAGAN

helpful in generating new questions leading to revolutionary discoveries. So, resist the tendency to expect your child's investigations to lead to any fixed outcome. It's not particularly important that your child *get* the idea, for example, that blue plus red equals violet on the color wheel when mixing food dyes together, or that a paper airplane's flight is determined in part by wind resistance. What is important is that he develop the ability to form hypotheses, ask questions to test them out ("what would happen if . . ."), and begin to observe patterns and regularities for which he can then offer explanations.

✎ STARTING POINTS ✎

Sink or float. **Fill the bathtub up halfway. Provide your child with different objects to place in the tub, including sponges, soap, wood blocks, paper, stones, and styrofoam plates. Which ones sink? Which ones float? Can your child predict which objects will sink or float? Can heavier objects be supported by lighter ones?**

Bubble blowing. **Place some dishwashing liquid in a kitchen or bathroom sink filled with a couple of inches of water. Provide bubble-blowing equipment, including straws, hollow cans, plastic tubing, or wire shapes made from paper clips or coat hangers. Questions to ask: How large can you make your bubbles? Can you make them even larger? How long do they last? Can you make them last even longer? What can you do to change their shape? Can you make bubbles in things other than water? (Try egg whites, vegetable oil, or root beer.)**

Treasure hunt. **Select a descriptive quality like *soft* or *shiny* and ask your child to find things around the house that match that attribute. For example, find all the *fuzzy* things in the house. Find all the *gooey* things. Find all the things that bounce. Questions to ask for each group: How are they similar to each other? How are they different? Which ones are most useful? Which ones are the most fun to play with?**

In science the stories of making fundamental discoveries while poking around in places we don't belong are legendary: Johannes Kepler . . . discovered the true elliptical shape of the planetary orbits after devoting a lifetime to trying to prove they had to be circles. Kepler's method was nothing more than an elaborate game of blocks . . . trying to fit spherical orbits into cubic (and tetrahedronal) holes.

K.C. COLE

Sprout a seed. Gather seeds from different sources, including household fruit, organic grocery bins, gardening packets, and the outdoors. Place them on paper plates covered with wet cheesecloth. Keep the cloth damp for a period of several days. Which seeds sprout first? Which seeds don't sprout at all? What might be some reasons they did not sprout? How do the sprouts differ in appearance? Plant the sprouts and unsprouted seeds in tiny flower pots, one to a pot. Keep track of observations as the seeds grow into plant form. Older kids can draw the plants at different stages of growth and or write about what they see.

Color mixing. Get out several colors of food dye and a styrofoam egg carton with each compartment half-filled with clear water. Using an eyedropper, have your child mix colors together. What happens when blue and red are mixed? How about red and green? Can you make your favorite color? Older kids may want to create a color spectrum or choose one color and make a graduated series of shades from light to dark.

Magnet magic. Purchase two simple magnets at a variety or toy store. Place several different kinds of objects on a tray (examples: stones, jewelry, office supplies, kitchen utensils). Which objects attract the magnet? How are those objects similar? What happens when the two magnets come near each other? What makes a magnet work? Older kids may want to magnetize objects or create an electromagnetic force with two C or D flashlight batteries, some copper wire, and a nail.

Mystery powders. Place a few glasses of water on a table and get out several dry substances from the kitchen pantry, including salt, baking soda, flour, sugar, and cornstarch. Put each dry ingredient into an unmarked container so that its identity is unknown to the child. Then invite your child to mix each substance into a glass of water, observing what happens. Questions to ask: Can you guess what the substances are? How did you know? What happens when you mix dry ingredients together? Does the amount of substance mixed into the glass affect the appearance of the water?

always the beautiful answer who asks a more beautiful question

E.E. CUMMINGS

It's better to know some of the questions than all of the answers.

JAMES THURBER

I spy. Buy a simple magnifying lens at a dime store. Look at different things under the magnifying lens: a piece of paper, an ant, your skin, a leaf, the carpet, a food item. What changes as you look at the object under the lens? Which objects look most changed? How can you explain the new things you see? What do you think you'd see if you had an even stronger lens? You may want to obtain a good quality microscope for older kids to use in their explorations.

Flying machines. Provide your child with several sheets of paper and ask her to design a paper airplane that flies as smoothly as possible, or as far as possible, or as high as possible, or does a loop-the-loop or accomplishes some other specific acrobatic feat. Is there one design that will achieve all of these aims, or does your child have to create different designs to accomplish each objective? Do size, shape, and thickness of the paper make a difference?

Skyscrapers. Give your child a deck of cards and ask him to create the highest structure possible. Which card arrangements seem to work best? Suggest he create a stable structure and try putting objects on top. How heavy can an object be before the structure collapses? Which card arrangements seem to support the most weight? Try this activity with other materials as well, including clay, wet sand, blocks, or tin cans.

Ice cube melt down. Put an ice cube on a plate and measure the time it takes to melt. Try different ways of speeding up and slowing down the melting process. Which methods work best? Does the shape of the ice cube determine how fast or how slowly it melts? Try creating ice cubes in different shapes for this purpose by pouring water into molds made from cardboard, styrofoam, or plastic.

Weather watch. Go outdoors with your child periodically to observe the weather.

- Keep track of specific cloud formations, forms of precipitation, humidity, and other meteorological factors.

- Ask your child to figure out simple homemade ways to measure precipitation or the direction and strength of the wind.
- Listen to weather reports on the news and compare them with your direct observations.
- Purchase a barometer or another piece of commercially made weather equipment and explore with your child how it works.

Star search. The nighttime sky provides endless opportunities for scientific investigation.

- Go out at night and look at the stars. Tell your child a little about the ancient belief that groups of stars represented specific animals and humans. Ask your child if she can see her own pictures among different groups of stars.
- Buy a star chart (available from The Nature Company or Edmund Scientific—see Resources) and use it to locate specific constellations in the sky. Keep track of changes that occur over time, including the phases of the moon.
- Create your own homemade planetarium by purchasing a black umbrella, marking in chalk some key stars and constellations, pricking a small hole with a pin in each mark, and then shining a flashlight through the umbrella in a dark room. (You can create a simpler version by placing a piece of construction paper over one end of a cardboard tube.)

Rock hounds. Take a nature walk and collect some interesting stones (have a knapsack pouch or other container available for storage). Do particular geographical areas have a preponderance of certain kinds of stones or rock formations? Back at home, investigate the properties of the rocks. Examine color, shape, and other distinguishing characteristics. With a hammer, crack selected rocks in half. Can you predict what the insides will look like based on their outer appearance? Try scratching the surface of selected rocks with a jackknife. Arrange the rocks in order based on the ease with which they are scratched.

Purchase a field guide and use it to formally identify the rocks in your collection.

Circuit search. Provide your child with two or more standard flashlight D or C cells, some assorted strands of bare and insulated copper wire, some strips of aluminum cut from pans or cans, masking tape or thumbtacks, and one or two flashlight bulbs. Ask him if he can get the bulb to light using these materials. Are there different ways to make the bulb shine? Can he cause the bulb to shine more brightly? What kind of switch could be made to turn the light on and off? Try substituting an electric buzzer (available at a hardware store).

RESOURCES

While a hands-on approach to science generally does not require books (especially textbooks), there are some excellent guides for parents, teachers, and children that can help structure your explorations together. Here are some of the best.

Allison, Linda. *Blood and Guts: A Working Guide to Your Own Insides* (grades 5–12). Boston: Little, Brown, 1976. Motivating activities for exploring physiology, such as measuring lung capacity, dissecting soupbones, taking skin prints, and creating your own stethoscope. Part of the *Brown Paper School Book Series,* which includes *Good for Me: All About Food in 32 Bites; Beastly Neighbors: All About Wild Things in the City or Why Earwigs Make Good Mothers;* and several other titles.

Cobb, Vicki. *Science Experiments You Can Eat* (grades 5–8). New York: Harper and Row, 1972. Helps kids learn chemistry while making mayonnaise, fruit coolers, and a host of other eatables and drinkables. See also *More Science Experiments You Can Eat* and some of Cobb's books for younger readers (grades 1–3), including *Gobbs of Goo, Fuzz Does It,* and *Lots of Rot.*

Education Science Study (ESS). Delta Education, Box M, Nashua, NH 03061-6012; (800) 258-1302. Developed in the early 1970s for teachers, these guides still represent some of the finest examples of experiential science available. Titles include "Waterflow," "Growing Seeds," "Colored Solutions," and "Balloons and Gases."

Ontario Science Centre. *Scienceworks.* Reading, MA: Addison-Wesley, 1986. Includes sixty-five simple experiments for kids, (grades 2–7), including making butter, reinventing the camera, and having fun with magnets.

Saul, Wendy, with Alan Newman. *Science Fare: An Illustrated Guide and Catalog of Toys, Books, and Activities for Kids*, New York: Harper and Row, 1986. Excellent guide for parents, providing tips on buying science equipment, safety recommendations, and lists of children's science books and magazines.

Stein, Sara. *The Science Book* (grades 4–7). New York: Workman, 1980. Provides children with practical answers to everyday science questions, such as why the honeybee dances, whether space has shape, and why your hair stands on end.

Zubrowsky, Bernie. *Messing Around with Water Pumps and Siphons* (grades 3–7). Boston: Little, Brown, 1981. Descriptions of how to make simple fire extinguishers, thermometers, suction pumps, and other devices using bottles, rubber stoppers, plastic tubing, basters, and balloons. Part of the award-winning Children's Museum Activity Books series with titles such as: *Bubbles, Ball-Point Pens, Milk Carton Blocks,* and *Messing Around with Baking Chemistry.*

Organizations

American Association for the Advancement of Science, 1515 Massachusetts Ave. NW, Washington, DC 20005; (202) 326-6400. The largest science organization in the country. Publishes *Science Books and Films* five times a year, a review of recent children's books, films, and videos on science, *Science Education News* (quarterly), and an annual entitled *This Year in School Science.* Check with your child's school or public library to see if they have these publications.

Edmund Scientific Co., 101 E. Gloucester Pike, Barrington, NJ 07410; (800) 222-0224; (609) 547-3488 in New Jersey. Excellent mail-order supplier of microscopes, telescopes, science kits, and other science resources.

National Science Resources Center, National Academy of Sciences, Smithsonian Institution, Arts and Industry Building, Room 110, Washington, DC 20560. Provides resources and assistance to schools in creating hands-on science programs in classrooms around the country.

National Science Teachers Association, 1742 Connecticut Ave. NW, Washington, DC 20009; (202) 328-5800. Professional association of teachers seeking to encourage quality science teaching in the schools.

Publishes periodical *Science and Children* reporting on innovative science teaching methods.

The Nature Company, P.O. Box 2310, Berkeley, CA 94702; (800) 227-1144. High-quality toys and resources in science and nature study. Free catalog.

Things of Science, 1950 Landings Blvd., Suite 202, Sarasota, FL 34231. A service for children ages nine through fourteen. Every month members receive a different science kit that includes instructions and materials for carrying out experiments in specific fields.

7. *Forward into the Past—Making History Come Alive*

Not long ago, I happened to watch an old Alfred Hitchcock thriller, *Shadow of a Doubt*. The movie was filmed in 1942 in Santa Rosa, California, where I currently live. I was filled with a sense of amazement in looking at the Santa Rosa of almost fifty years ago. A few landmarks were easily recognizable, but many other intriguing features of the town shown in the film had vanished during the intervening years.

I rushed to the public library to find out where all the neat old buildings had gone, and discovered a special historical room where I began to look into Santa Rosa's past. As I pored over the old photos and newspaper clippings, I was reminded of the thrill I'd once had as a fourth-grader studying the history of my birthplace—Fargo, North Dakota—and remembered the moment when I realized for the first time that I was part of a bigger picture in the historical scheme of things. As nearly as I can describe it, I had the sense that just as I stood upon the surface of the earth yet was supported by layer upon layer of subterranean soil, so too did I exist *on top of history*, as it were, the product of everything that had gone on before me.

The subject of history is always and finally what it means to be a human being.

JOHN WILLIAM WARD

Children have an almost universal attraction to things of the past. They're fascinated with antique cars and trains, mummies, arrowheads, old buildings, and ancient coins. In their natural play experiences, they replicate—although unconsciously—many of the rituals, battles, customs, and ceremonies of past cultures. They may not understand the precise chronology of history, but they know all about "once upon a time" and "long, long ago." Specific events and dates may not have much of an influence on their young minds, but the powerful emotional struggles of villains and heroes, gangsters and generals, and kings and saints reach deeply into their souls, connecting them on a very deep level with all that has preceded them.

Businessmen agree with the elder Henry Ford that history is bunk. The young no longer study history. Academics turn their backs on history in the enthusiasm for the ahistorical behavioral "sciences."

ARTHUR SCHLESINGER

SCHOOLHOUSE AMNESIA

Children seem to have limited opportunities in school to explore this sense of history. Few elementary schools even teach history as a discipline anymore. According to Diane Ravitch, adjunct professor of history and education at Teachers College, Columbia University, history was largely dropped from the elementary school curriculum in the 1930s when educators urged school officials to make coursework more relevant to the needs of their students. The result was a devaluing of traditional historical studies and an emphasis upon *social studies* where children learned about themselves, their families, and their communities. Out went the Gettysburg Address, Greek heroes, and William Tell. In came personal hygiene, the duties of postal workers, and learning to be a good neighbor.

While social studies is an important part of young children's growth, the study of the distant past may also be an essential ingredient in their learning. According to Jerome Bruner, whose *Man: A Course of Study* represented one of the most innovative social studies courses ever developed for American elementary school classrooms, "It is inconceivable that one could grow up and feel fully in the world without a sense of history . . . without the imagery of the great turning points that created the present."

Children exposed to a nonhistorical social studies curriculum in the elementary grades have little to look forward to in the way of a substantial history curriculum as they progress in school. According to a survey conducted by the National Endowment for the Humanities, fewer than twenty states require more than one American history course in high school, and thirty-four states require no world history. Even in those schools that require history, instructors are often poorly equipped to teach it. Since teachers spend an average of 41 percent of their time in college studying general principles in education and teaching, they have few opportunities to take substantial coursework in history. Instructors often end up teaching history on the side as they fill a position considered more important by the school, such as coaching a sport. In one midwestern state, for example, one out of every five history teachers majored in physical education in college.

The best of prophets of the future is the past.

LORD BYRON

Those who cannot remember the past are condemned to repeat it.

GEORGE SANTAYANA

HISTORICAL ILLITERATES

Such neglect of history in the schools seems to have taken its toll on our youngsters' "HQ" (historical quotient), if recent studies are any indication. One investigation administered by the National Assessment of Educational Progress found that over a third of participating high school students thought that the Magna Carta was signed by the Pilgrims, and two-thirds of the sample were unable to place the Civil War within the correct half-century. Another survey conducted recently by the National Coalition on Television Violence discovered that ten- to thirteen-year-old children appeared to know much more about movie monsters than about historical figures such as Abraham Lincoln and George Washington. This poverty of knowledge about the past raises concerns among educators that our culture may be in jeopardy, since the nation's youth appear incapable of transmitting its heritage to future generations.

Part of the problem seems to be that when history is taught at the later elementary and junior and senior high school levels,

People will not look forward to posterity who never look backward to their ancestors.

EDMUND BURKE

A page of history is worth a volume of logic.

OLIVER WENDELL
HOLMES, JR.

it's presented as a collection of boring facts and figures. Historical textbooks in particular have come under attack for portraying history in a bland and mechanical way. Seeking to avoid controversy that might stir up special-interest groups and prevent adoption of their books by state departments of education, textbook publishers and educational committees have steered a middle-of-the-road course in presenting historical events, and the result has been a mediocre product. As Lynne V. Cheney, chairman of the National Endowment for the Humanities, puts it, "The 'great textbook machine' grinds away, trying to satisfy almost every interest group imaginable—except our children." These books contrast sharply with school texts of the nineteenth century such as *McGuffey's Eclectic Reader*, which offered a rich selection of historical literature, including material from political speeches, Shakespeare, and ancient myths and legends.

Another dilemma faced by many educators is the requirement that teachers cover a fixed body of historical knowledge over a given period of time. This limits the amount of time that can be taken for an in-depth exploration of specific historical periods or themes. "History should not be just a mad dash through the centuries with teachers trying desperately to get to the 1990's before school lets out in June," says Kenneth T. Jackson, chairman of the Bradley Commission on History in the Schools, in a privately funded study. Instead, history needs to be seen as lived experience.

To this end, the commission recommends that students be taught history from the perspective of the individuals who lived at that time, with all their varying points of view fairly represented. The common folk have as much to say about history, in this approach, as the leaders. The simple events of home life reflect the past as well as the battles and treaties. The commission also called for history to be better integrated with other fields of study, including geography, politics, economics, sociology, and literature, so that students can experience the complex forces that served to shape the past and use this knowledge to help interpret current and future issues and events.

On a more pragmatic level, the commission urged a substantial increase in the time allotted to the study of history beginning in the early elementary years. One state—California—has already redesigned its social studies curriculum to reflect the increased importance of history. Students will now take American history for three years (in grades 5, 8, and 11) and world history for three years (in grades 6, 7, and 10). Children in the elementary grades will be exposed to the study of local, family, and state history and focus on biographies of great men and women in different cultures. In addition, high school seniors will be required to spend a full year studying economics and government. These changes do not ensure that students will become motivated to learn history, but they at least provide the framework and philosophy within which exciting programs can be designed.

PROGRAMS IN THE PAST

The critical component in any good history program is the creativity of its instructor and the enthusiasm he or she brings to the study of the past. Many excellent examples already exist around the country of teachers who have been inspiring kids to think historically. One Madera, California, teacher led his twelve-year-old students in an exploration of the lives of a local nineteenth-century family after a friend discovered their long-forgotten tombstones while spraying insecticide along a weed-choked river bank. The sixth-grade study culminated in the class collectively writing a biographical novel about the family, which was published with a foreword by the renowned historical novelist Irving Stone.

In West Hartford, Connecticut, teachers and staff of the Noah Webster Historical Society directed children through a simulated experience of being in an eighteenth-century classroom, complete with texts, drills, and discipline ("offending" students had to kneel with their noses in knotholes just as their counterparts did 200 years ago). At Grace Church School in Manhattan, fourth-graders learned about Greek history by putting on a production of *Antigone*. Still other teachers are using computer simulations where students can interview Christopher Columbus, participate in the Constitutional Convention, or experience life on the Oregon trail.

Faithfulness to the truth of history involves far more than a research, however patient and scrupulous, into special facts. Such facts may be detailed with the most minute exactness, and yet the narrative, taken as a whole, may be unmeaning or untrue. The narrator must seek to imbue himself with the life and spirit of the time. He must study events in their bearings near and remote; in the character, habits, and manners of those who took part in them. He must himself be, as it were, a sharer or a spectator of the action he describes.

FRANCIS PARKMAN

The present contains nothing more than the past, and what is found in the effect was already in the cause.

HENRI BERGSON

Historical documents are replacing textbooks as the preferred instructional materials in many of these classrooms. Working in conjunction with libraries, archival museums, or historical societies, teachers provide students with access to diaries, journals, photos, letters, artifacts, speeches, news articles, and other products of a particular historical period. In one Illinois program, children were presented with a picture of a grade-school classroom taken in 1888. Each child was given the name of one of the children in the photograph. Students were responsible for researching as much as they could about the child in question. Each student searched through attendance reports, grade reports, newspapers, and excerpts from the nineteenth-century teacher's diary (made available by the local museum), to fill in as many details about the child's life as possible. Then each student assumed the role of his or her assigned child in school, bringing a lunch that reflected what that child might have eaten, wrapping it in cloth napkins or rags according to the custom of the times, and even copying the clothes and hairstyle of the child.

"History comes to life when students imagine what it was like to be alive then," according to Diane Ravitch. The best way of fostering this imagination is through active learning where children can visit original historical scenes or re-create them at home or in the classroom. When kids begin to see that historical figures were flesh-and-blood human beings, not simply names in a textbook, they can begin to identify with their hopes and dreams, their conflicts and problems, and their unique perspectives on the world. Moreover, they can borrow from the experiences of these historical characters to shape their own lives.

But they can only do this when parents and teachers begin to nurture their own interest in the past and share with their kids what they have discovered. "History must be taught, really told, as a story," according to David W. Moore, associate professor in the department of history at Loyola University in New Orleans. "The teacher [or parent], with all the dramatic devices he or she can muster, is the storyteller. What could be more simple or appealing?"

★ WHAT PARENTS CAN DO ★

Rather than attempting to get your child to understand the entire chronology of the human race, you should focus on helping him cultivate a basic appreciation for history. Find out what things of the past really excite your child. Perhaps it's naval battles, or colonial customs, or knights in shining armor. Provide your child with resources—books, films, field trips, materials—that allow him to explore that period in his own way. Avoid teaching him facts about the period. Instead, connect him with the spirit of the time. In this way, you will be helping him establish an important emotional connection to history that he may never forget. Here are some other general suggestions for awakening your child's natural historical genius.

Create a family tree. By digging through old photos and archival records you can reconstruct a picture of your family's past that your child will be able to relate to personally. See how far back you can go in discovering your ancestors. Keep track of your discoveries on a large sheet of paper showing all known branching family lines (forms for this purpose are available by consulting genealogy books like the ones listed at the end of this chapter). Pay particular attention to occupations and significant life events of ancestors and how these factors relate to what was going on in the world at the time. Were there more career military people during times of war? Were there more unemployed relatives during hard economic times? History takes on an entirely new dimension when it involves real people living real lives.

Get to know your community and your country as a historical resource. Visit historical landmarks and museums in your area. The public library can provide information about locations of important historical structures and monuments. Go to the local cemetery and read the history of the town from the gravestone inscriptions. During summer vacations, plan on visiting historical sites such as Colonial Williamsburg in Virginia, the Spanish missions in California, Mystic Seaport in Connecticut,

The Mystic Chords of Memory, stretching from every battlefield and patriot grave to every living heart and hearthstone all over this broad land, will yet swell the chorus of the Union when again touched, as surely they will be, by the better angels of our nature.

ABRAHAM LINCOLN

Sturbridge Village or Plymouth Rock in Massachusetts, the Pueblo cave dwellings in Arizona, or the Smithsonian Institution in Washington, D.C. These places provide visitors with a feeling of total immersion in specific historical periods.

Use holidays as a time to focus on special historical periods and events. During holiday times, we often tend to focus on recreation and relaxation and forget that the time is celebrated precisely because it is rooted in a significant event or series of events in history. The Fourth of July offers an opportunity to go beyond roasting wieners and exploding firecrackers in finding out more about the founding of our country. Memorial Day or Veterans Day can be a time to look into one of the major wars that we have fought as a nation. Five or ten minutes taken during a break in the usual festivities of a holiday to read or talk about the origins of the day can help set it in a historical context and awaken curiosity in your child so that he may want to find out more about what went on during that time.

Share your own life history with your child. Anecdotes about what life was like when you were a child ("We only had *three* television channels!") can provide your child with a temporal framework within which to view her own experiences. You might talk about what you were doing during particularly significant moments in the history of the culture, including the bombing of Pearl Harbor, the Korean War, the assassination of Kennedy, and the first walk on the moon. Your child can similarly talk about her personal experiences during important events in her own lifetime, such as the Challenger accident, the fall of the Berlin Wall, and the war with Iraq. These discussions reinforce the idea that history is about people and that it has a tangible effect upon the lives of those it touches.

Talk with your child about special family antiques or heirlooms. A search of your attic or cellar (or those of relatives) will probably reveal one or more objects of historical interest that you can share with your child. My grandparents' basement was a virtual treasure trove of historical documents and artifacts. At one time it contained a sword reputedly used by Mexican gen-

To know nothing of what happened before you were born is to remain forever a child.

CICERO

There is a history in all men's lives.

SHAKESPEARE

eral Santa Anna and a letter written by President Ulysses S. Grant. You might have an old coin or stamp collection, a treadle sewing machine, a collection of nineteenth-century dolls or milk bottles, or a yellowing photo album that deserves to be dusted off and examined. Each item tells a story and can serve as a springboard for learning more about a particular period in history.

Encourage your school-aged children to read historical fiction and nonfiction. Excellent selections abound of children's literature at all levels from picture books to adolescent fiction that weave their plots against the backdrop of history. Some examples from the Newbery Medal Books include *Lincoln: A Photobiography, A Gathering of Days: A New England Girl's Journal, 1830–32*, and *The Whipping Boy* (medieval times). In addition, you can subscribe to magazines with a historical focus such as *Smithsonian*, or to a mail-order book service such as *American Heritage* or Time-Life's historical series.

Be on the lookout for movies and television programs that chronicle important historical events. Many of the important TV miniseries during the past twenty years have been placed in a historical setting, from *Roots* (history of slavery in Africa and America) to *War and Remembrance* (World War II). TV networks sometimes create study guides for classroom use based on a miniseries (check your local network affiliate for details). There's also a wide range of historically significant movies available on videotape, including *Ben Hur* (Roman times), *The Grapes of Wrath* (Depression era), *Gandhi* (the Indian independence movement), and *Reds* (the Russian Revolution). Use these films as opportunities to begin talking and reading about the historical forces that helped shape the lives of their main characters.

On no other stage are the scenes shifted with a swiftness so like magic as on the great stage of history when once the hour strikes.

EDWARD BELLAMY

 STARTING POINTS

Sensory simulations. To help your child understand what individuals in the past really experienced, create an environment that mimics the sensory world of a particular historical period. For example, to re-create the visual world of the nineteenth century, turn off the electric lights and distribute some kerosene lamps safely around the house. Provide two or three authentic foods of the period to re-create some of its smells and tastes. Find examples of the kind of cloth worn by the people of that time and experience what it must have felt like on the body. Get records of period music played on the original instruments. Through these simulations, your child can begin to sense the world as it was at that time.

Birthday newspaper. Go to the public library and look up the local newspaper issued on the date of your child's birth (or choose a major newspaper such as *The New York Times* or a magazine such as *Time*). These documents will usually be found on microfilm. You can make a copy of the front page of the newspaper or magazine (and additional pages as desired) using the special photocopying feature found on the microfilm machines in many libraries. A birthday is an excellent time to give a gift like this to your child. Talk with your child about the events that occurred on his birthdate. Discuss how life has changed since then.

Time capsule. Purchase a metal or plastic lunch bucket (or find a container of similar size and durability) and designate this as your family time capsule. Ask each family member to choose one or two items to include in the capsule that would help to provide future generations with a sense of this current period in history. This exercise challenges each participant to think about the present as the future's past and thus stimulates historical thinking. After you have decided upon the items, write a family letter (with contributions from all members) to future generations describing the importance of these things and adding anything further you wish to communicate about the present day. Then find a spot in your backyard or in a remote area of the countryside (check to make sure you are not violating any laws) and bury the time capsule in a family ceremony.

Plays of the past. Engage in improvisational dramas with your family to re-create historical events. Pick a specific time and place to reenact—for example, the discovery of gold in California in 1849. Go to the public library with your family and together become familiar with the time in question. Then work out who will take the various roles in the play and collectively establish a basic scenario. Gather any costumes or props you may need. Then start the action, letting it unfold naturally and spontaneously. Don't worry if the play strays from the facts. It's more important that your child see history as a process of real people engaging in real experiences than as a succession of specific events.

Tales on tape. Interview aging family members who are still able to reflect upon life in the distant past. Record the interview on audio or videotape. Let your child be an integral part of the recording process. Afterwards, review the tape with your child and discuss life as it was then compared with today. The process of recording oral histories will help your child understand how different the life experience of an older person can be from her own personal world (and also assist her in appreciating the similarities).

House history. Find out about the origins of your residence. Building records can often be found in your local courthouse. Information sometimes can also be found in remote corners of an attic or basement. If possible, determine who built the house and why it was built. A project like this can develop into a broader exploration of a specific period in history.

Time lines. Create a large mural-sized time line as a family project, using colored felt-tip markers, pencils, crayons, collage materials, and a length of butcher paper (available from an art supply store) unrolled on the floor. Select a segment of time, such as the past 100 years, 500 years, or 1,000 years, and then label significant events along the way, illustrating famous battles, treaties, and discoveries with appropriate pictures, diagrams, and doodles. Make sure to spend time beforehand talking about the events, especially if your child is encountering them for the first time. You can also make a special time line just for the family, including birthdates of all family members, or for a child's individual life history.

RESOURCES

Brown, Cynthia Stokes. *Like It Was: A Complete Guide to Writing Oral History*. New York: Teachers and Writers Collaborative, 1988. Provides specific advice on using a tape recorder, conducting and transcribing interviews, and presenting the results in compelling ways.

"Building a History Curriculum: Guidelines for Teaching History in Schools." Available for $3.00 from Education Excellence Network, 1112 16th St. NW, Suite 500, Washington, DC 20036. The final report of the Bradley Commission on History in the Schools.

Cheney, Lynne V. *American Memory: A Report on the Humanities in the Nation's Public Schools*. This booklet stresses the importance of revitalizing the subjects of history, literature, and foreign languages in the curriculum. Available by writing: Superintendent of Documents, U.S. Government Printing Office, Washington, DC 20402 ($2.00 per copy; when ordering, specify title and stock number: 036-000-00050-3).

Grun, Bernard. *The Timetables of History: A Horizontal Linkage of People and Events*. New York: Simon and Schuster, 1982. Chronicles the events of history in time-line fashion from 5000 B.C. to 1978, including separate columns for history and politics; literature and theater; religion, philosophy, and learning; the visual arts; music; science, technology, and growth; and daily life. Excellent reference work for locating specific events in history. A related resource is the World History Chart, a three-feet-high and eight-feet-long wall chart that lists important dates and events in fifteen cultures from 4,000 B.C. to the present. Available from International Timeline, Inc., 2565 Chain Bridge Road, Vienna, VA 22180; 800-621-5559, 800-972-5855 in Illinois.

Ravitch, Diane, and Chester Finn. *What Do Our 17 Year Olds Know?* New York: Harper and Row, 1987. Report of the first national assessment of seventeen-year-olds in history and literature. Includes recommendations for improving history teaching in the schools.

Weitzman, David. *My Backyard History Book*. Boston: Little, Brown, 1975. Offers guidelines for researching in old diaries and cemeteries, interviewing relatives and neighbors, making rubbings, taking photographs, and sharing the research with others. For children eight and older.

Westin, Jeane Eddy. *Finding Your Roots* New York: Ballantine, 1989. Concise handbook for reconstructing your family tree, determining if you have a coat of arms, and writing a family history. Includes charts and diagrams for genealogical record keeping.

Organizations

American Association for State and Local History, 708 Berry Rd., Nashville, TN 37204; (615) 255-2971. Organization of historical societies, museums, and other institutions that provide services to the public. Publishes "Directory of Historical Societies and Agencies in the U.S. and Canada." Their pamphlet "Training for Docents: How to Talk to Visitors" (technical leaflet #125) includes examples of questions that can elicit historical thinking.

American Historical Association, 400 A St. SE, Washington, DC 20003; (202) 544-2422. Professional association of historians, educators, and others interested in promoting historical studies and the preservation of historical documents.

Genealogical Institute, P.O. Box 22405, Salt Lake City, UT 84122; (801) 532-3327. Publishes and distributes "how-to-do-it" materials on researching ancestry.

National Archives, Washington, DC 20408. Will look up military service records of any family veteran who served in the armed forces at least seventy-five years ago. Also provides historical documents to schools for instructional purposes.

Part Three

◆ ◆ ◆ ◆

Growing Through Arts and Leisure

8. *Play and Toys—Creative Pathways to Learning*

Play is perhaps the most basic outcome of a child's natural genius. As we observed in the previous section, play lies at the heart of many of humanity's noblest pursuits. The capacity to create new ideas, revel in novelty, and engage in world-making for its own sake may be the single most important factor responsible for the development of civilization. Play is essentially nature's way of forging fresh evolutionary possibilities. A child's innocent creation and re-creation of new ways of seeing, acting, feeling, and believing provide a direct pathway along which those behaviors that are particularly useful or adaptive to culture can later be incorporated into the fabric of a more advanced society.

The tragedy is that this natural and spontaneous phenomenon could be on the decline in our culture as unstructured types of child-directed play give way to more regimented forms of leisure. As children lose touch with their instinctive tendency to be creative in using free time, their social, emotional, and intellectual lives, as well as the destiny of the human species as a whole, may suffer the consequences.

The spirit of playful competition is, as a social impulse, older than culture itself. . . . Ritual grew up in sacred play; poetry was born in play and nourished on play; music and dancing were pure play. . . . We have to conclude that civilization is, in its earliest phases, played.

JOHAN HUIZINGA

THE LOST ART OF FREE PLAY

Play takes many different forms, from games, sports, and art activities to interaction with toys, dramatic improvisation, and other imaginative explorations. But while children appear to be playing as much as they ever have, they seem to be doing it in ways that are more organized and more structured around formal games and technological recreation.

In one recent study of children's home play conducted at the University of Kansas, parents reported their children's primary recreations as involving television-based or computer-based games, as well as preparation for athletic-directed play. According to E. Peter Johnsen, professor of educational psychology and research at the University of Kansas:

> When play occurs, it tends to be motor-play that fits into activities organized by adults that have rules and that are fairly competitive. We're not talking about Red Rover and Hide and Seek, but rather getting ready for swimming, soccer, or Little League. And even here, we found children expressing themselves very little. We didn't find a lot of pretend play, where children use their imaginations in constructing play episodes.

Unstructured imaginative play may have a much greater value to a child's overall development than these more formal types of recreation. Pretend play allows children to test their own hypotheses about the world and modify their ideas as they go along. The toddler who revels in playing peekaboo appears to be working through in his mind whether an object that has disappeared from view can continue to exist. The five-year-old busily engaged in forming and reforming a juicy mud pie may be tentatively experimenting with what Swiss child researcher Jean Piaget described as the law of the conservation of mass: the cognitive understanding that a change in the shape of an object will not affect its quantity.

Imaginative play also allows kids to work through emotional conflicts in creative ways. Psychoanalyst Bruno Bettelheim, author of *The Uses of Enchantment*, suggests that "the most normal and competent child encounters what seem like insurmountable problems in living. But by playing them out, in the way he chooses, he may become able to cope with them in a step-by-

Whenever you trace the origin of a skill or practices which play a crucial role in the ascent of man, [you] usually reach the realm of play.

ERIC HOFFER

Everything during the first months of life, except feeding and emotions like fear and anger, is play.

JEAN PIAGET

step process." Playing monster, for example, allows children to experience a sense of power and control over what might be threatening forces in their lives. In one of my classes, I remember a student who was under a great deal of pressure from her parents to succeed in school. During the free playtime I provided each child during the day, I noticed that she had placed several dolls on chairs and was sternly lecturing them to be "good students." Play helped this girl release emotional tensions and channel her energies in a constructive direction.

Finally, play serves as a microcosm of society, allowing children to investigate social roles in preparation for their full-fledged participation in family and community activities. Children get to experience what it feels like to be a mommy, a daddy, a teacher, or a sibling, and thus they begin to develop the ability to see the world from another perspective. This role-taking component of play represents an important prerequisite to mature social behavior. Children discover in their pretend worlds new ways of relating to and negotiating with their peers. Research also suggests that free, unstructured, imaginative play contributes to language development and leads to a more focused attention span in children.

Fewer children, however, are getting the opportunity to engage in the kind of free play that leads to these benefits. Children of dysfunctional families often find their natural impulse to play thwarted by an atmosphere of depression and anxiety that hangs over the family. As Frank and Theresa Caplan observe in their book *The Power of Play*, "One of the most striking characteristics of an anxious child is a strong inhibition of play activity. Often such a child is not able to play at all." Many of these children grow up completely out of touch with their own spontaneous *inner child* and must essentially be shown how to play as adults in therapy and recovery programs.

Children of disadvantaged families, on the other hand, lack significant play experience in early development because of limited exposure to educational materials and activities around the home. This deprivation can cripple their ability to think flexibly later in life. Frank and Theresa Caplan comment:

> New research on the disadvantaged child indicates that his relating and patterning ability is limited because from between eight months and three years—a critical learning stage—he

Play is the highest level of child development. It is the spontaneous expression of thought and feeling. . . . It is the purest creation of the child's mind as it is also a pattern and copy of the natural life hidden in man and in all things.

FRIEDRICH FROEBEL

Because there can be no Recreation without Delight which depends not always on Reason, but oftener on Fancy, it must be permitted Children not only to divert themselves, but to do it after their own fashion.

JOHN LOCKE

When I was ten years old and I operated my first magic lantern—with its chimney, its petrol lamp, and its constantly repeating films—I found the above phenomenon exciting and mysterious. Even today, I feel in myself the nervous excitement of childhood.

INGMAR BERGMAN

has had too few personal manipulating experiences (fitting, sorting, matching, et cetera) with those play materials that foster relationship thinking. He lacks fitting toys that can give him a sense of accomplishment.

Finally, children of fast-track families have the opposite problem: too many materials and activities and not enough time simply to play in unstructured ways. These kids find their time filled up with lessons, competitive games, after-school classes, and other activities designed by concerned but overly busy parents. "The days of most middle-class children are filled with scheduled activities—Boy or Girl Scout meetings, music and dance lessons, organized sports—which leave them hardly any time simply to be themselves," says Bruno Bettelheim. What children really need, according to Bettelheim, is *spielraum*, a German word meaning "free scope, plenty of room."

It was this kind of freedom that allowed famous individuals of the past to incubate their own creativity in childhood. Charlotte and Emily Brontë, for example, created two imaginary worlds—Angria and Gondal—peopled with curious characters who later became the subjects of their world-famous novels. The Norwegian playwright Henrick Ibsen at the age of eight created his own doll theater from paintings he had cut out and pasted onto cardboard. In today's world, however, television, computers, the soccer field, French lessons, and Trivial Pursuit seem to be crowding out the precious free moments in which children can nurture their inner lives.

★ WHAT PARENTS CAN DO WITH PLAY ★

While a lot of the charm of childhood play stems from its being a refuge from the world of adults, parents do have an important role to play in the land of make-believe. As Joseph Chilton Pearce, author of *Magical Child*, points out: "The child can never learn to play without the parent playing with the child. Play . . . is a huge creative potential built within the child, which . . . never develops unless it is stimulated by the outer model, the parent." Here are some guidelines for awakening your child's natural genius to play.

Develop your own sense of playfulness. Because you represent the primary model for your child of what play is all about, you need to make sure you are a truly playful parent. Jerome Singer, professor of psychology at Yale University, suggests that parents picture themselves once again as a three- or four-year-old at play, or keep a dream log that may activate pleasant memories of play. Take time out to engage in free play activities just for yourself: finger painting, running in the woods, making up songs, dancing alone with the lights out, or engaging in dramatic improvisation or role-play with friends. These experiences and other lively activities can help to break the shackles of your adult conditioning and free up creative energies you can then use in playing with your child.

In the true man there is a child concealed—who wants to play.

FRIEDRICH NIETZSCHE

Observe children at play. Children incorporate a wide range of material into their unstructured play, including themes borrowed from children's literature, mass media, friends at school, and other sources. These themes cover a lot of ground: playing house, heroes and villains, space odysseys, animal fables, monster movies, war games, party time dress-up, and hundreds of other topics. Unless you understand children's current working vocabulary for play, you may be unable to establish a meaningful connection with them at these times. When you see your children playing, ask questions about what the ground rules are for their current play scenarios. If you understand the specific role (or roles) being played by each child, you may be able to join their play in a way that fits into the overall scheme they've created.

Do not be afraid to get messy or be noisy. Unless real harm is being done, relax your usual restrictions about aggression, messiness, noise, and other parental bugaboos. Play is a time for letting down your hair and giving your kids permission to get a little rowdy if need be. Don't be afraid to get down on your hands and knees and moo like a cow or scamper across the floor fire engine style. At the same time, if you see that the living room lamp might be destroyed by a thundering herd of cattle, or that there is a real need to keep the noise level down, make sure to clearly define the playtime parameters before starting the

127

Avoid compulsion and let early education be a manner of amusement. Young children learn by games; compulsory education cannot remain in the soul.

PLATO

action. Keep the rules simple, however, since play thrives under conditions of basic freedom and suffers under martial law.

Incorporate novelty into children's play. Once you have developed the ability to naturally join in your child's play activities, you can gradually introduce suggestions for modifying basic play themes. If you're playing a space monster in a futuristic scenario, for example, you might decide to transform yourself into a space marshmallow, or a space monster that can shrink itself to the size of a pinhead, or one that can be in two places at once. Transformations like these help challenge children to expand their own set of ground rules to incorporate new roles. If you suggest something that is developmentally inappropriate or overly intrusive, the child will ignore or resist your modifications. One child I recently played with, for example, got very upset when I introduced a magic carpet into his Ghostbuster fantasy. Start out with relatively minor modifications in the basic play motif and work your way into more significant possibilities.

Although free play tends to be associated with the preschool and early elementary school years, it is important to realize that you can play with your kids at any age. When your three-month-old baby gurgles and you gurgle back, you've initiated a play activity. When you find your eight-month-old child handing you her favorite toy, taking it back, and repeating this process over and over again, you've become party to her own version of free play. At the other end of the spectrum, when your twelve-year-old does an imitation of his favorite rock star and you join in to provide the backup vocals, you've engaged in a bit of improvisation. While older kids tend to prefer more structured games and activities, they still enjoy the chance to ham it up in a little family skit or game of charades.

THE TROUBLE WITH TODAY'S TOYS

"Welcome to our world," blares out a mechanical toy in the center of one of the nation's largest toystores. This refrain could well be the theme song for millions of children and parents in toy stores across America who are welcomed daily into fantastic worlds filled with computerized Lego robots, talking animals, toy guitars that play themselves, and electronic dolls, games, and action figures of every conceivable kind.

Children in the 1990s have never had it so good where play-things are concerned. With a market that has reached $13 billion a year in sales, there have never been so many choices available for so many children in the never-never land of toys. Yet this cornucopia of fun may be both a blessing and a curse for parents who are looking for just the right amusement to stimulate their children's active minds.

On the plus side, toy industry trends have recently moved toward a renewed interest in simple toys, including high-quality blocks, play sets, and dolls. This back-to-basics movement resulted in part from a glut of electronic toys during the mid- to late 1980s. According to toy designer Bill Seidel, "A lot of the toy companies started saying 'the heck with electronics, the heck with complicated, we want simple.' They started going to simple play elements, and that was a very big breakthrough for the toy industry. Now, all kinds of better quality toys are becoming available to everyone." In addition, there is an increased interest in learning toys, including games, puzzles, and educational computer software.

On the minus side, however, toy stores still stock aisle after aisle with trinkets and baubles that do little to activate children's potentials and may even be harmful to their growth and development. Of particular concern are toys that stifle the imagination. One line of dolls describes what each member of its family prefers to do ("loves to cook," "writes stories," "loves parties"), while some action figures now come complete with their own psychological profiles ("Monsterbot Repugnus has been kicked out of the Autobots many times for insubordination only to be asked back since he's always willing to undertake missions too low-down and dirty for anyone else to consider"). There are even toys capable of being activated through electronic signals emitted by selected children's television programs, and other toys that are self-programmed to essentially play with themselves.

From my earliest years, I had a great desire to enquire into the causes of all those little things and events which astonish the childish mind. My invisible question on receiving any new toy was: "Mamma, what is inside of it?"

CHARLES BABBAGE

These developments threaten to turn kids into passive observers of life instead of cultivating their drive to explore the world around them. As Brian Sutton-Smith, professor of education and folklore at the University of Pennsylvania and a noted play expert, observed, "The modern-day image of the child at play is now that of a youngster playing with his action figures in front of a television set."

★ WHAT PARENTS CAN DO WITH TOYS ★

These criticisms of contemporary toys should not lead parents to throw out the Barbie with the bathwater. Many contemporary toys, including certain high-tech gadgets, may be instrumental in preparing children for life. As Joanne Oppenheim, author of *Buy Me, Buy Me—The Bank Street Guide to Choosing Toys*, suggests:

> To just cancel out all high tech toys would not be realistic in a world where we're surrounded by high tech—even turning on a microwave or using a calculator or a computer are becoming so much a part of our everyday lives, that there's no reason to keep them away from children.

Moreover, kids will often insist on having these toys, since children are always tuned into the toys of their peers and of the broader culture.

Whether you are considering pick-up sticks and marbles or action figures and video games as Christmas or birthday gifts for your child, here are some things you may want to consider before making any purchases.

Provide a range of toys from all three toy groups. Stevanne Auerbach, author of the *Toy Chest* and director of the San Francisco International Toy Museum, notes that children should be exposed to a balance of toys that are *active* (jump ropes, roller skates, trains, yo-yos), *creative* (modeling clay and dough, percussion instruments, puppets), and *educational* (board games, puzzles, magnets, globes). Select toys that are well designed, durable, safe, and appropriate for the child's age and interests.

Give the child the so-called pretty doll, and the brain has nothing more to do. Instead of unfolding, it becomes stunted and dried up.

RUDOLF STEINER

A quality toy will last for years and provide countless hours of enjoyment and enrichment, compared with the short-lived flash-in-the-pan thrills of many current commercial offerings.

Choose open-ended toys over toys that have fixed outcomes. A simple doll with a minimum of features is preferable to one that speaks, crawls, and walks through the miracle of high-tech. When the doll does all the talking or controls the dialogue, kids don't have an opportunity to develop their expressive language skills by taking on the doll's voice. When dolls do all the walking, kids don't have to move them around the house, thus depriving children of important sensorimotor functions. In fact, Vicki Cobb, noted science writer for children, has observed that there may be some relationship between the poor physical fitness of our nation's youngsters and the increase in toys that essentially do everything for the child. Likewise, blocks or Legos from which kids can build their own castles are preferable to a prefabricated castle, and simple musical instruments that require real plucking, playing, or pounding are better than guitars or drums that play themselves.

Do not be discouraged if your child wants a toy that you dislike. As soon as kids are old enough to be aware of Saturday morning television, they are exposed to a whole range of toys that may not fit the desirable criteria outlined above. Larry Carlat, editor of *Toy and Hobby World*, notes, "At the preschool level, it's usually a parental decision, and they can go for whatever they'd like for their kids, and get open-ended imaginative types of toys. But once a child reaches the age of knowing what's going on around him, if he sees a toy advertised on television, then often that's what he'll want. So instead of 'get me Play-Doh,' it'll be 'get me Teenage Mutant Ninja Turtles,' or whatever the latest fad happens to be. The best thing you can do in this case is to talk with your child about why he likes the toy, share your own feelings honestly, and then use your intuition as to whether you are willing to buy the toy. Once you've made a decision to buy a questionable toy, however, make sure that you don't hold your negative feelings over your child as he plays with it.

Play is an essential function of the passage from immaturity to emotional maturity. Any individual without the opportunities for adequate play in early life will go on seeking them in the stuff of adult life.

MARGARET LOWENFELD

*Children's playings are not
sports and should be deemed
their most serious actions.*

MICHEL DE MONTAIGNE

In the final analysis, it may be impossible to say exactly what constitutes a truly good toy. As Professor Brian Sutton-Smith points out, toys mirror culture, and adults who provide advice about what toys are best (including myself) are simply reflecting current cultural values that could well change drastically over the next few years or decades. The ultimate criterion of a good toy, perhaps, is the extent to which it enables children to play. And play, according to Sutton-Smith, "is children's choice. Adults shouldn't try to interfere too much. Kids need to play to work out the world themselves, not the one adults want, but the one they're living in."

Johan Huizinga, in his landmark study of play, *Homo Ludens*, suggested that children's play shares certain commonalities with the religious rites of ancient peoples. We would do well to consider play as a sacred activity for kids and not meddle with it too much.

✎ STARTING POINTS ✎

Dress-up. Have a hinged box or special drawer that contains old coats, dresses, shirts, pants, shoes, hats, and other clothes. Let your child play dress-up with his or her friends and provide a space for them to act out different roles wearing their favorite costumes.

Big box. Obtain an empty refrigerator carton or similar large-sized box. With your kids, collectively decide what the box should become (for example, house, mountain, post office, automobile, boat, department store). Cut appropriate holes for windows and doors, and paint it if desired. Keep detail to a minimum so that the identity of the box can be changed from day to day.

Space shifting. Using string or masking tape, mark off a circle of space ten to fifteen feet in diameter in an appropriate room of the house or outdoors. Let this space become an office, the center of the earth, an asteroid, or any other location your child wishes. Once inside this space, your child's imagination (and the imaginations of playmates) should determine the action that will follow.

Sand Play. Provide an indoor or outdoor sandbox space and lots of small dolls, houses, vehicles, plants, animals, and other miniature figures. Suggest to your child that she create her own little world inside the sand box.

Adventure playground. (For kids aged ten and above.) Have some wood, nails, and carpentry tools available in an open space in your backyard. Show your child how to use the tools, suggest some possible structures he might make, and then let him create his own special playspace (fort, tree, dollhouse, rocket ship) under adult supervision.

RESOURCES

Auerbach, Stevanne. *The Toy Chest: A Sourcebook of Toys for Children.* Secaucus, NJ: Lyle Stuart, 1986. Resource guide to toys with practical information about selecting toys for different age groups and needs, a history of toys, and a listing of toy manufacturers, stores, catalogs, museums, and organizations.

Caney, Steven. *Steven Caney's Playbook.* New York: Workman, 1975. Nicely illustrated book of games, puzzles, 3-D constructions, and other fun projects that can be made by kids or adults. See also Caney's *Toy Book* and *Invention Book.*

Caplan, Frank and Theresa. *The Power of Play.* Garden City, NY: Anchor Press/Doubleday, 1973. Well-documented volume supporting the many benefits of play. Includes an excellent chapter on pioneering educators who contributed to our understanding of play, including Friedrich Froebel, Maria Montessori, and John Dewey. Out of print but available in many libraries.

Toy Suppliers

There are thousands of toy manufacturers and hundreds of catalogs available. Here are a few of the best distributors of quality toys and play equipment. Each will provide a mail-order catalog upon request (sometimes for a small fee).

The parent who gets down on the floor to play with a child on Christmas Day is usually doing a most remarkable thing—something seldom repeated during the rest of the year. These are, after all, busy parents committed to their work or their success in the larger society, and they do not have much left-over time in which to play with their children.

BRIAN SUTTON-SMITH

ChildLife, 55 Whitney St., P.O. Box 527, Holliston, MA 01746; (800) 462-4445 or (508) 429-4639. Makers of outdoor playground equipment. Free catalog.

Childcraft Education Corporation, 20 Kilmer Rd., Edison, NJ 08817; (800) 631-5657. Indoor and outdoor toys for home or school. Free catalog.

Community Playthings, Route 213, Rifton, NY 12471; (914) 658-3141. High-quality toys and playground equipment made by the Society of Brothers, a religious community. Free catalog.

Constructive Playthings, 1227 E. 119th St., Grandview, MO 64030; (816) 761-5900 or (800) 255-6124. Focus on toys for younger children. Catalog $3.00.

Growing Child, P.O. Box 620, Lafayette, IN 47902; (317) 423-2624. Provides toys and parent information on play from a developmental perspective as part of a subscription to their monthly newsletter, *Growing Child*.

Johnson Smith, 4514 19th St. Court E. P.O. Box 25500, Bradenton, FL; 34206-5500; (813) 947-2356. Inexpensive toys, gizmos, and novelty items that children aged eight to twelve will find especially interesting. Free catalog.

Lakeshore Learning Materials, 2695 E. Dominguez St., P.O. Box 6261, Carson, CA 90749; (800) 421-5354 or (213) 537-8600. Excellent source for play materials of all kinds, including blocks, puppets, arts and crafts, doll houses, and play figures.

PlayFair Inc., 1690 28th St., Boulder, CO 80302; (800) 824-7255 or (303) 440-7229. Nonsexist, nonviolent educational toys for all age levels. Catalog $2.00.

Uniquity, P.O. Box 6, Galt, CA 95632; (800) 521-7771 or (209) 745-2111. Specializes in books, toys, and games for personal growth. Especially useful for play therapists. Free catalog.

9. *Music for Minors—A Major Key to Learning*

In no other area of human ability can the flowering of natural genius in childhood be better seen than in musical expression. Our culture offers many brilliant examples of children displaying highly proficient musical skills, from an eight-year-old Mozart composing symphonies to a ten-year-old Midori entrancing the world with her violin concertos.

Yet musical genius in childhood is much broader than the occasional prodigy. In a sense, music itself has emerged from the collective genius of all children. It has been suggested by some authorities, including the late American composer and conductor Leonard Bernstein, that through their spontaneous musical activities, children have originated an archetypal melody—the so-called Ur-song—that is the ultimate source from which all the world's diverse music flows.

Very young children exude music from every pore. Their babbling and earliest speech is musical in character. Their motor activity has a rhythmic quality. They sing like little composers, actively experimenting with different tone combinations and seeking ways of melding the sounds they hear around them

We grown-up people think that we appreciate music, but if we realized the sense that an infant has brought with it of appreciating sound and rhythm, we would never boast of knowing music. The infant is music itself. In the cradle it is moving its little arms and legs in a certain rhythm. And when our music falls on the ears of an infant it is of the lowest character compared with the music it is accustomed to.

HAZRAT INAYAT KHAN

with the promptings of their innermost feeling life. Their perception of sound is astonishingly accurate. Some studies have suggested that infants as young as two months are able to match the pitch, loudness, and melodic contour of their mother's songs and by four months can match the rhythmic pattern as well.

This musical acuity appears to blossom during the preschool years. Joseph Chilton Pearce reports of a musicologist who discovered virtually all of the four-year-olds in her study had perfect pitch yet lost this ability by age seven. Similarly, young children seem to possess a highly developed *inner ear* or sense of eidetic auditory imagery: They are able to hear tones in their head as clearly as if they were being played externally. Paul Randolf Farnsworth, formerly professor emeritus of psychology at Stanford University, observed that these auditory eidetic images "are known to be far more common among children than among adults, many of the latter having lost their eidetic potentialities through lack of practice."

What happens to these inborn musical abilities as the child matures? Is it possible to preserve a child's innate musical genius into adulthood? What kind of musical training, if any, should you give your child? This chapter will attempt to answer these questions and will suggest ways in which parents can help youngsters preserve or recover their innate sense of music throughout their lives.

From infancy I was surrounded by music. . . . To hear my father play the piano was an ecstasy for me. When I was two or three, I would sit on the floor beside him as he played, and I would press my head against the piano in order to absorb the sound more completely.

PABLO CASALS

THE BIRTH OF MUSIC

Your child received a great deal of musical exposure before she was even born. After spending nine months on intimate terms with her mother's heartbeat, an infant has learned much about rhythm. And because the fetus hears other sounds in her mother's body from around six months on, and by eight months in utero perceives noises from outside, a baby comes into the world already knowing much about pitch, melody, and other rudiments of music.

One of the best things parents can do to enhance the role of music in their babies' lives is to sing to them. This doesn't necessarily mean dusting off the old songbooks and launching into a fifteen-minute medley twice a day. During the first year of life, the infant is making her own music. Parents and others need only respond by rhythmically tapping and patting the child and melodically responding to her gurglings.

As your child matures, these informal physical/musical interludes should give way to a rich collection of nursery rhymes, lullabies, patty-cake and knee-bouncing songs, and tickling games ("This little piggy went to market"), all of which form the core of your child's earliest musical education. Then, as your child becomes more independent, she will carry her musical training into the playground with her jump-rope rhymes, counting songs, and other forms of musical childlore.

Unfortunately, many musical experiences of today's children are provided by television and radio. Jean Sinor, assistant professor of music education at Indiana University and former president of the Organization of American Kodály Educators, reports that "instead of playing ring-around-the-rosy in their yard, children may be watching cartoons or listening to the radio while playing with their space monster action figures." Such commercially prefabricated musical events may be crowding out the spontaneous music-making activities that are so much a part of a young child's natural musical genius. They also convey a subtle message to the child that music comes out of a box instead of emerging spontaneously from the human spirit.

I frequently hear music in the heart of noise.

GEORGE GERSHWIN

We are full of rhythms . . . our pulse, our gestures, our digestive tracts, the lunar and seasonal cycles.

YEHUDI MENUHIN

THE TYRANNY OF LESSONS

By the time children are four or five, they are usually physically capable of playing a musical instrument. Some parents use this as a cue to buy an expensive instrument. Many flock to systems such as the Suzuki Talent Education Program, which trains youngsters to play the violin or piano beginning as early as age two or three. However, I'd like to caution parents to be very careful when considering music lessons for kids. Some parents force lessons on children and make them practice against their will. This amounts to nothing short of child abuse since it turns many kids off to a lifetime of potential musical enjoyment.

At the age of 3, the drawing room became my paradise. . . . Half in fun, half in earnest, I learned to know the keys by their names and with my back to the piano I would call the notes of any chord, even the most dissonant one. From then on it became mere "child's play" to master the intricacies of the keyboard, and I was soon to play any . . . tune that caught my ear.

ARTUR RUBENSTEIN

Of course, if a child really wants to study a musical instrument, parents should try to provide appropriate training (see A Parent's Guide to Music Education Programs below). You might notice your child having a musical peak experience similar to Yehudi Menuhin's experience when he listened to a violin concerto at age three and asked for lessons. However, even among musically inclined children, it's important to provide a gradual introduction to music instruction.

◆　◆　◆　◆

A Parent's Guide to Music Education Programs

There are many music education systems available to children both in and out of the classroom that can help awaken or continue to cultivate their natural musical genius. Some, such as Suzuki and Yamaha, are focused on helping children master a specific musical instrument; others, like Orff-Schulwerk and Kodály, are designed to stimulate a child's music-making capacity more generally through a variety of creative activities. Here are descriptions of several of the major approaches.

Suzuki Talent Education Program. This method focuses on becoming proficient in a musical instrument (usually violin or piano). It was developed by Japanese violinist Shinichi Suzuki just prior to World War II and depends heavily on the involvement of the parent—who for a time takes music lessons along with the child. Children begin lessons as early as age two or three and practice from a set curriculum of short songs taken from the Western classical music tradition. Emphasis is placed on learning by ear (there is no teaching of musical notation) and on producing a perfect replica of a musical recording through regular repetitive practice sessions. Suzuki is concerned with developing character in children as much as helping them learn a musical instrument.

Yamaha Method. This approach was developed by the makers of Yamaha pianos in Japan during the early 1950s. Children are taught in groups of six to twelve students. As in the Suzuki method, parents are closely involved in the program and attend all classes. Classes for four- to six-year-olds stress singing, ear training, and learning to identify simple melodic and rhythmic patterns. After age six, children focus on piano and simple rhythm instruments.

Orff-Schulwerk Approach. Created in the 1920s by German composer Carl Orff, this approach to music instruction emphasizes improvisation and informal music-making rather than proficiency in the performance of set musical pieces. Children take part in group sessions that integrate music, movement, speech, and drama activities. Students engage in finger snapping, foot stomping, thigh slapping, and voice echoing exercises using simple musical rhymes and games. They also use barred percussion instruments such as xylophones, glockenspiels, and metallophones to create their own compositions. Kids learn simple musical notation with this method.

Kodály Education. Similar in many ways to Orff-Schulwerk, this approach is based on the work of Hungarian composer Zoltán Kodály, who declared that musical literacy (the ability to read musical notation with ease) should be part of every individual's birthright rather than being confined to an elite group. Kodály instruction uses group a cappella singing as a foundation for learning. It employs relative solfège (do-re-mi-fa-sol-la-ti-do) as an initial alphabet for learning the musical scale and, like Orff-Schulwerk, engages children in musical rhymes and games based on simple folk melodies. Kodály instruction is provided daily in most Hungarian classrooms. In the United States it has been integrated into many public and private musical programs.

Dalcroze Method. This method of instruction, based on the work of Swiss educator Émile Jaques-Dalcroze, was quite popular during the 1920s in the United States but is less well-known today. It combines solfège and improvisation techniques with a body movement system called *eurhythmics*. In a Dalcroze classroom, children engage in ear-training games (for example, finding the rhythm in their names), movement exercises (for instance, creating a series of bodily actions corresponding to the rests in a musical score), and they sing and play instruments as well. Dalcroze techniques are found at every level of music education in some public and private schools, as well as in private teaching studios.

African children in particular enjoy the benefits of musical life; they are as involved with music as our children are with television.

JOHN MILLER CHERNOFF

Which method is best for your child? That depends upon your child's specific needs and interests. If your child wants to learn to play the piano or violin, Suzuki or Yamaha may be most appropriate. However, if your child enjoys singing and dancing or wants to express himself more creatively, then Orff-Schulwerk, Kodály, or Dalcroze may be the way to go. To ensure that your child's experience is a positive one, here are some steps to follow right from the start. (These suggestions also apply to any other private music lessons your child may take.)

◆ Make sure your child really wants to become involved in formal musical training before taking any steps to provide a program.
◆ Let your child sit in on an introductory lesson in two or more of these approaches (if available), or with two or more teachers, and then choose the program that he prefers.
◆ Agree to begin with a specific number of classes or lessons, say one hour per week for five weeks, and then at the end of this series talk with your child about the experience and decide whether he wants to continue.
◆ Observe at least one class or lesson early in the program and discuss any concerns you may have with the teacher or your child before continuing.

◆ ◆ ◆ ◆

The process of pushing children too quickly into musical training can have long-lasting effects. As a six-year-old I had shown some interest in playing an old upright piano at my grandparents' house. I enjoyed climbing up onto the long wooden bench and banging out tunes I'd heard or making up little melodies of my own. Soon, I found our house full of keyboard instruments, including a harpsichord, a clavichord, two organs, and a Steinway grand. My two sisters and I were sent to music lessons for years, and my dad crowed on and on about our accomplishments. However, the pressure put on me to succeed musically turned out to be too great. Now, as an adult, I have difficulty reading music and approach piano playing with a great deal of conflict.

I know there are many parents who want to turn their children into little concert virtuosos. Take my advice: Please don't try! If your child is destined to become a musical legend, nothing you can do will stop him. Handel's father supposedly said he'd do anything short of cutting his boy's hands off to keep him away from music. On the other hand, you can do a lot of damage to a child if you insist on making him carry out the musical life that you wish *you* had lived.

Probably many parents reading this are thinking just the opposite: *Their* kids are so tone-deaf that giving them music lessons would be about as worthwhile as teaching a water buffalo to fly. Again, wrong. According to Frank R. Wilson, a University of California neurologist and the author of *Tone Deaf and All Thumbs?*, there are no tone-deaf children or adults. "The truth," he reports, "is that the ability to identify a pitch, or to produce a required pitch with precision, can be learned." I'd go further than that and say that this ability is not so much learned as it is *remembered* from a person's "musical years" in early childhood.

What I am pleading for, then, is a middle way. Instead of harboring grandiose illusions concerning their children's musical future or giving up entirely, parents can do the most simply by helping them learn to enjoy making music. There need not be a single nonmusical child in the United States. Other cultures offer proof of this. In Hungary, thanks to the pioneering work of contemporary composer Zoltán Kodály, all children take music in school every day. In Nigeria, children of the Anang culture can already sing hundreds of songs and perform dozens of intricate dances by the time they turn five. The point is, music-making should be for everybody, not just for the select few who perform in recitals or concert halls.

Beethoven never has learned anything and never will learn anything. As a composer he is hopeless.

JOHANN GEORG ALBRECHTSBERGER (BEETHOVEN'S TUTOR)

I am convinced that all of us have a biologic guarantee of musicianship. This is true regardless of our age, formal experience with music, or the size and shape of our fingers, lips, or ears. . . . We all have music inside us, and can learn how to get it out, one way or another.

FRANK WILSON

MUSIC IN THE SCHOOLS

Schools can play a large part in supporting the musical education of all children. If kids are lucky, they will be exposed to a gifted teacher who has spent years inspiring children with music. In my own life, that person was Marie Wilds, a music specialist at Clara Barton Elementary School in Fargo, North Dakota, who nurtured my own love of singing from second until

Musical training is a more potent instrument than any other, because rhythm and harmony find their way into the inward places of the soul.

PLATO

sixth grade. I always remember Miss Wilds when summer comes around and I am seized with the urge to sing "June Is Bustin' Out All Over," and at Thanksgiving when I insist on getting out my guitar and leading the family in a chorus of "We Gather Together" before mealtime.

Regrettably, however, fewer and fewer schoolchildren these days are getting the kinds of musical opportunities that existed twenty or thirty years ago. In some cases, budget cutbacks have entirely eliminated music programs from public schools; in other cases, instruction has been restricted to high school. Professor Sinor says that relatively few schools in this country are making quality music education a high priority, "especially nowadays, when emphasis is being placed on reading and math scores." This is a tragedy, considering the universal appeal of music and its importance in fostering a sense of self-esteem and well-being.

Even when it is offered, it is usually presented ineffectively for most kids. Sadly, most schools still seem ruled by the philosophy that music instruction must be *taught* as a body of knowledge, that some children are better than others in this *skill*, and that one must *perform* acceptably on an instrument and pass tests on musical theory in order to be a successful music student.

INTEGRATING MUSIC INTO THE REGULAR CLASSROOM

Parents and educators sometimes justify the minor stature that music has in the schools by suggesting that it has no practical usefulness in today's society. This conclusion is unjustified since educators are showing that it is even possible to use music to teach academic subjects. Grace Nash, a Scottsdale, Arizona, music specialist and author of twenty-one books in the field of music education, points out that spelling and vocabulary words, science terms, and historical facts all can be put into rhythmic patterns and conveyed through song, dance, and percussion instruments. When I taught a group of third- through fifth-graders in public school, I routinely led my class in a twelve-bar blues rendition of the multiplication tables on the guitar (we called it "The Times Tables Blues"). While teaching junior high kids, I set simple mathematical formulas to music and used popular songs as the basis for some reading lessons. The problem, according to Nash, is that there is virtually no teacher training in this creative and practical use of music-making. "The methods courses are still teaching music as a subject. Music should be a basic part of the whole school day," she argues.

★ WHAT PARENTS CAN DO ★

Parents can help make music an integral component of a basic education by letting schools know that they value this important human ability and want to see it reflected in the curriculum. If you find your child's school unwilling or unable to offer the kinds of musical experiences you feel your child deserves, try to provide what your child may not be getting in school by taking time at home to sing, dance, and make musical merriment together. Here are some suggestions for increasing the odds that music will enrich your child's life at home and school.

Encourage your child's school to offer a quality music education program. Acquaint school administrators with some of the innovative music education philosophies described in this chapter. Don't let budget cutbacks sabotage your child's right to at least some music education in school. If necessary, create a parent committee to develop funds for one or more of these programs. Even if funds are tight, the school should still be able to bring music into the regular classroom to teach other subjects. Suggest to your child's teacher that next week's spelling list or times tables be chanted rhythmically instead of copied out ten times in a notebook. Bring in records or tapes that can supplement a reading or history lesson (songs of the Civil War, for example, can illustrate certain points about that period in U.S. history). Try to have quality music played in the halls before and after school and during recess periods. Volunteer to lead students in singing on a regular basis, or to teach a music appreciation course after school as part of the extracurricular program.

For many children, the start of formal musical instruction marks the beginning of the end of musical development. The atomistic focus in most musical instruction—the individual pitch, its name, its notation—and the measure-by-measure method of instruction and analysis run counter to the holistic way most children have come to think of, react to, and live with music.

HOWARD GARDNER

My nurse brought me home from the village where we had been perambulating one afternoon, and my parents, who were trying to coax me to talk, asked me what I had seen there. I said I had seen the peasants and I had heard them sing, and I sang what they had sung. . . . Everyone was astonished and impressed at this recital, and I heard my father remark that I had a wonderful ear.

IGOR STRAVINSKY

Make music together regularly as a family. Pick a time on a weekly or monthly basis to share favorite musical pieces. Each family member should have a turn to sing a special song or play a treasured piece of recorded music. Others in the family must listen attentively, sing along, or even dance to the music, according to the directives of the individual in charge. This turn-taking format exposes participants to a wide range of musical experiences and can lead to a new openness toward the musical tastes of family members. You can also have sing-alongs during car trips (bring along a cassette tape player and a variety of tapes) or during special occasions such as birthday parties and holidays.

Sing to your child before bedtime. Along with the stories that you tell or read to your child during the bedtime ritual, include a few songs as well. These might be songs from children's literature (nursery rhymes set to music or stories where kids can sing along with the text), songs that you recall from your own childhood, or even songs that you make up as you go along. For older kids who don't want to be sung to, play soothing background music (either live or recorded) as they drift off into dreamland.

Go on musical field trips as a family. Let each family member have a turn choosing where they would like to go. Possibilities include rock concerts, classical piano recitals, musicals, choral productions, rap music sessions, and other community musical events. After each event, spend time as a family talking about what you liked or did not like about the music. Compare the musical styles from one event to the next. Keep a family scrapbook documenting these outings, saving advertising, program notes, and even audio cassettes of the performances if available.

Use music to help your child learn school subjects. If your child has some material to memorize for school (spelling words, math facts, history dates, science formulas), try setting the information to music. For example, any seven-letter word can be sung to the tune of "Twinkle, Twinkle, Little Star" (try it with M-U-S-I-C-A-L). Or, have your child recite homework assignments in rhythm to his favorite musical selection. Then suggest to him that he imagine that same music playing in the background when he takes tests on the material. (For other suggestions on using music to facilitate learning, see Chapter 16.)

✎ STARTING POINTS ✐

Percussion time. Gather a number of inexpensive percussion instruments, such as a tambourine, triangle, drum, and maracas. Most can be purchased inexpensively at a toy or variety store, or constructed with simple materials. Maracas can be made with dried peas or beans sealed inside orange-juice cans. A simple drum can be created by banging a stick or pencil against the bottom of an oatmeal box. Two old spoons can be made to click together like castanets. Other household items can similarly be creatively adapted. Let each family member make or choose a favorite percussion instrument. Then start a session by letting the youngest child create a rhythm that others must match with their instruments. Take turns creating new rhythms and matching them in the whole group. Finally, let out all the stops and have a regular down-home jam session improvising as a group using some or all of the different rhythms created. You can also put on recorded music and accompany the selections with your family's own percussion rhythm band.

Tone blending. Start by having one family member create a sustained and unvarying musical sound with his or her voice. Another person should then join in with a sound that blends in some way with the existing note. Additional participants should then add their voices to this musical stew in turn until everyone is "sounding." Keep this a cappella creation going for a few minutes and notice how it tends to change in different ways like a musical kaleidoscope (words may even come up to accompany the sounds). Then, when it seems that the piece has lived its life, choose a new individual and start the process all over again in a different key. Allow these sessions to turn into sing-alongs or song improvisations as the spirit moves you.

Visible music. Obtain a roll of white or beige wrapping paper at least eighteen inches wide and several yards long. Give your child about four feet of this paper and a pencil or other marker. Suggest that she sing a simple song such as "Happy Birthday to You." Then ask her to draw the song on the paper using a single line. Suggest that the line might go up on the high parts of the song and move downward when the melody dips. However, let your child create her own unique notation for the song. Then ask her to sing the song as she moves her hand along the diagram showing the parts of the song that correspond to the different curves of the line. Finally, suggest that she act out the song as if her body were the line or drawing, rising and dipping to the contours of the melody. Then, let her come up with her own songs to diagram and dramatize. Do this as a family and let each individual illustrate his or her favorite songs.

Name that tune. Take turns as a family coming up with tunes that family members try to guess in as few notes as possible. Either singing or playing an instrument, each participant should start out with a minimum of three or four notes to begin the song, and add notes as others continue to guess. Use songs and musical bits that are liable to be recognized by all or most of the participants, including well-known commercials, themes from television programs and movies, popular folk songs, and top-40 hits.

RESOURCES

Halpern, Steven, and Louis Savary. *Sound Health: The Music and Sounds That Make Us Whole.* San Francisco: Harper and Row, 1985. Underlines the importance of music in promoting physical and emotional health. Good suggestions for using music as a background environmental enhancer.

Judy, Stephanie. *Making Music for the Joy of It.* Los Angeles: Jeremy P. Tarcher, 1990. A course in enhancing your own musical abilities and interests as an adult.

Suzuki, Shinichi. *Nurtured by Love: A New Approach to Education.* Pompano Beach, FL: Exposition Press of Florida, 1982. The founder of the Suzuki Talent Education Program describes his philosophy of learning.

Wilson, Frank R. *Tone Deaf and All Thumbs? An Invitation to Music-Making for Late Bloomers and Non-Prodigies.* New York: Viking, 1986. Provides a sophisticated but readable explanation of the neurological basis for musical literacy. Suggests that virtually everyone can benefit from some musical training.

Organizations

American Orff-Schulwerk Association, P.O. Box 391089, Cleveland, OH 44115 (216) 543-5366. Disseminates information, assists in development of teacher training programs, and encourages research in the Schulwerk (Music for Children) philosophy of Carl Orff.

Children's Book and Music Center, 2500 Santa Monica Blvd., Santa Monica, CA 90404 (213) 829-0215. One of the country's largest distributors of children's records, cassettes, and musical instruments. Free catalog.

Music Educators' National Conference, 1902 Association Drive, Reston, VA 22091 (703) 860-4000. Association of public school music teachers. Write for information about promoting music education in your child's school.

Organization of American Kodály Educators, Music Department, Box 2017, Nicholls State University, Thibodaux, LA 70310, (504) 448-4602. Supports the implementation of Kodály methods in schools across the country. Write for information about Kodály teachers or programs in your area.

Suzuki Association of the Americas, P.O. Box 354, Muscatine, IA 52761 (319) 263-3071. Provides information about Suzuki teachers around the country. Conducts workshops and camps that parents and children attend together.

10. *The Art of the Matter—Drawing with Your Child*

It has often been observed that the earliest artwork of pre-historic man (and the abstract designs of many contemporary artists) resemble the drawings of children. The artful scribbling of the toddler, the detailed pictorial narratives of the eight-year-old, and the cartoons of the sixth-grader all seem to tap into streams of consciousness that lie at the heart of civilization's striving for artistic creativity.

Parents should honor and nurture the child's natural impulse to paint, to draw, and to engage in other art forms. These activities serve to bring out the natural genius in kids by giving them an opportunity to express their innermost feelings and thoughts in a visible way. Art challenges children to fashion products that respond to both the inner stirrings of the soul and the outer demands of the sensory world.

While children often need to be left alone to pursue the artistic process in their own way, parents and other adults may be vitally important to their aesthetic development when they provide fresh ideas and new approaches children can use to improve their abilities. How can a parent help keep a child's artistic urge alive as he matures? How can a parent support a

I used to draw like Raphael, but it has taken me a whole lifetime to learn to draw like a child.

PABLO PICASSO

child's drawing and painting without interfering in that process? This chapter will address this controversy and provide several options for parents in helping to nourish their children's creative development.

I shall like to recapture that freshness of vision which is characteristic of extreme youth, when all the world is new to it.

HENRI MATISSE

By the time the child can draw more than a scribble, by age three or four years, an already well-formed body of conceptual knowledge formulated in language dominates his memory and controls his graphic work. . . . As an essentially verbal education gains control, the child abandons his graphic efforts and relies almost entirely on words. Language has first spoilt drawing and then swallowed it up completely.

KARL BUHLER

FROM SCRIBBLE TO SKETCH: THE DEVELOPMENTAL STAGES OF DRAWING

Children move through stages in artistic expression just as they do in reading and math, although along different developmental pathways. As early as one and a half or two years of age, the toddler scribbles on a page using a form of gestural representation that is more physical than visual. For example, he might use a marker to represent a rabbit and hop across the paper, making "rabbit's feet" as he goes. Between the ages of two and three, the child's drawings become explicitly pictorial with the first representational shapes emerging. Around this time, the first image of a human being develops, often in the form of a tadpole-like figure consisting of a circle with two lines for legs.

From three to five, the child works on her ability to create likenesses of things she sees around her. Then, beginning around age five and continuing for two or three years, there is a flowering in creative expression when the child seems particularly concerned with expressing her inner feelings and sensibilities. Grass may be flaming red ("fire grass"), seals and seagulls may kiss, and tree branches may crawl like lizards through the sky.

As children move into middle childhood and early adolescence, they tend to strive toward greater realism in their drawings and develop the ability to represent objects in space using perspective. During this quest for accuracy in drawing, children often abandon the freshness and spontaneity of their earlier creations. Some research suggests that a substantial percentage of individuals stop drawing at this stage in their development (somewhere between the ages of eight and twelve) because of their frustrations over making their drawings look *real*.

Part of their passion for realism is due to their own adaptation to the world. As kids get older, they look more carefully at the visual world, think about what they are doing, and often do a lot of planning before actually making a drawing. But culture, too, has a lot to do with their growing frustration. Art classes reward children who produce "nice-looking" pictures, and parents praise kids who create realistic images. Kids themselves look to adults for accurate models of how to draw. Should parents feed this desire or simply encourage their children to draw in their own way?

TO COPY OR NOT TO COPY?

In an attempt to answer this question, I attended a class for parents and children based on a structured drawing method. Ten people—four children and six adults, including myself— sat at two large tables with sheets of paper and boxes of felt-tipped pens in front of us. Our task was to copy a picture of two exotic parrots sitting on a tree stump.

"We *always* start with the eye," began the teacher, "because it tells us where the rest of the body goes." I thought to myself, "Hey, I'll start where I feel like starting," yet for lack of knowing what else to do, I proceeded to draw an eye on the page just as she'd suggested. Line by line, the teacher led us through a complete composition of the birds. As we drew, a growing discontent filled my artistic soul. What was this structured approach to drawing doing to the creativity of the children in the room?

Toward the end of the class we all held up our drawings. The child who sat next to me had created some "punk" birds, complete with Mohawk hairdos. I noticed that the other kids had drawn birds that were equally original in color, shape, and form. Clearly, nobody's creativity was being destroyed. But as I walked out of the room, I was still bothered by some lingering questions: Is it wrong for children to copy other people's work? Should kids be allowed to paint and draw spontaneously from their own inner worlds? How much formal instruction should we provide for children who are just learning to draw?

The source of my ambivalence was a new approach to drawing developed by Mona Brookes, author of *Drawing with Children*. Brookes teaches children to go beyond stick-figure art in

I was such an oddball that wherever I went, alone as usual, I would pick up stray newspapers, torn books, discarded notebooks, and most of all, picture magazines, and with great joy would take them home making sure no one observed me. There, expectant, tense with excitement I would forage through the worthless pile of papers. . . . Driven by some kind of instinct I began to copy in pencil those I found the most appealing on a clean sheet of paper.

HUNGARIAN GYPSY
PAINTER JANOS BALAZS

[Louisa May Alcott] was never so happy as when copying flowers, designing fairies, or illustrating stories with queer specimens of art. Her teacher complained that instead of doing her sums she covered her slate with animals; the blank pages of her atlas were used to copy maps on, and caricatures of the most ludicrous description came fluttering out of her books at unlucky moments.

CAROLINE TICKNOR

Adults interfere with a natural biologic development of the child's motor, visual, mental, and artistic abilities when they try to influence the child's work in the early years. The adult's brain has accumulated much more visual and artistic memory than the child's, so there can be no true meeting of adult and child mind unless the adult knows how the child's mind . . . functions in art.

RHODA KELLOG

creating drawings based on a very specific system of representation. Her method teaches children to draw five primary elements of shape: dot, circle, straight line, curved line, and angle line. These five families of form, according to Brookes, constitute a primary visual alphabet that lies at the heart of all other shapes. She encourages students to notice these primal shapes in everyday life and to use them to build their own artistic creations. Students in her Monart schools, as they are called, begin by copying simple illustrations based on these forms, eventually building up to more complex pictures and finally drawing from real life.

Brookes developed her method in 1979 when the director of a Southern California nursery school asked her to develop an arts program for 150 preschool children. She discovered that already at this young age, children were churning out cliché-ridden images such as happy faces, hearts, daisies, and video game figures and competitively copying each others' stick-figure drawings. This experience raised her own level of awareness about children's visual illiteracy and prompted her to develop her drawing method. In addition to the five elements of shape described above, her method includes relaxation exercises, tips on using art materials, and tricks that professional artists employ in dealing with special problems (for example, covering up a mistake, such as a poorly drawn dog, by transforming it into a flowering shrub).

This approach to drawing with its emphasis on structure and visual models has some pretty vocal critics. Brent Wilson, professor of art education at Pennsylvania State University and author of *Teaching Children to Draw*, suggests that the most important function of drawing among young children should not be realistic portrayal or accurate representation, but communication and expression.

> What we've observed is that the children who draw most, sometimes spending four or five hours a day drawing, are narrating, telling very complex visual stories. If you take kids who are avid graphic narrators and tell them "let me show you how to make it better," what you do is cut off their narrating, take what was delightful and exciting, and fulfilling of their deepest needs, and make it into a kind of lock-step drudgery.

Wilson points out, "You can get kids to do anything you want—I've taken four-year-olds and had them draw better than some adults by giving them a penny for every detail they provide—but in the process we lose the fun and what it's all about for kids."

Similarly, Seonaid Robertson, a British art educator and author of *Rosegarden and Labyrinth: A Study in Art Education*, says that because so little time is devoted to art in the schools and at home,

> I am jealous of that time—and feel that it should be spent helping children develop confidence in their own representations, not somebody else's. If you draw from an artist's depiction of a cat, what you end up with is not your cat—it's a drawing of a drawing of somebody else's cat—rather like painting from numbers.

Brookes defends her method from critics by suggesting that her approach is not a replacement for children's natural drawing but simply a structure within which a child's creativity can flourish.

> There were a lot of methods in the 1920s and 1930s where artists were trying to get kids to copy pictures. Critics think that's what I'm doing. That's not what I'm doing. I'm teaching kids to see through the five elements of shape and giving them an environment that allows them freedom of interpretation to be creative. You would never consider it would stifle a musician's creativity ability to teach him the scales.

THE SPECTRUM OF DRAWING METHODS

Brookes's method is one of several drawing techniques that have become popular in recent years. These systems range from pure copying to totally free expression. At the you-draw-what-I-draw end of the spectrum, there's the Ed Emberley Drawing Books series, consisting of simple, step-by-step instructions for creating imaginary creatures, faces, and buildings. Developed for children from kindergarten to third grade, Emberley's method, like Brookes's, uses an alphabet of shapes and takes the reader from first stroke to final product in a series of

As a . . . boy I bought a box of oil-colors with pennies slowly and painfully saved. To this very day I can still see these colors coming out of the tubes. One press of my fingers and jubilantly, festively, or grave and dreamy, or turned thoughtfully within themselves, the colors came forth. Or wild with sportiveness, with a deep sigh of liberation, with the deep tone of sorrow, with splendid strength and fortitude, with yielding softness and resignation, with stubborn self-mastery, with a delicate uncertainty of mood—out they came, these curious, lovely things that are called colors.

WASSILY KANDINSKY

The scribblings of any . . . child clearly indicate how thoroughly immersed he is in the sensation of moving his hand and crayon aimlessly over a surface. . . . There must be some quantity of magic in this alone.

EDWARD HILL

155

If it were possible for children to develop without any interference from the outside world, no special stimulation for their creative work would be necessary. Every child would use his deeply rooted creative impulses without inhibition, confident in his own means of expression.

VIKTOR LOWENFELD AND
W. LAMBERT BRITTAIN

Pictorial playfulness has always been an important helper of artistic exploration. . . . Pictorial playfulness manifests the delight in the variety of visual shape, the elementary affection that every artist has for his medium. . . . Herein lies the oft-noted but nonetheless deep affinity between the exploration of the young child and the experimentation of the artist's conscious and unconscious faculties.

RUDOLF ARNHEIM

increasingly complex drawings, pointing out exactly what to draw and where to draw it. This method reminds me of the Jon Nagy learn-to-draw kits that were advertised on television when I was a child.

At the other end of the spectrum, art educator Viktor Lowenfeld, in his book *Creative and Mental Growth*, exhorts parents and teachers not to interfere one bit with what he describes as the child's natural tendency to draw. Lowenfeld maintains that a child's drawing is a spontaneous reflection of his maturity level; if children are taught to draw something they are not developmentally ready for, it will not enhance their drawing ability and may cripple their creative impulse. He criticizes the emphasis adults place on getting kids to produce realistic products and insists that a child's own spontaneous creations are far more important than externally imposed methods and models.

Somewhere between Emberley and Lowenfeld lie the Monart schools as well as another structured approach to drawing based on Betty Edwards's best seller, *Drawing on the Right Side of the Brain*. Edwards believes that children need to be taught how to draw, but she disagrees with the premise that they need a visual symbol system or alphabet of shapes to help them draw more effectively. "People need to be taught to set aside the symbol systems and to see what is really in front of their eyes, what is actually there," Edwards says. The exercises she uses include copying upside-down pictures, drawing a common object such as a paper bag or a household utensil without taking one's eyes off it, and paying attention to negative space, the empty space between solid objects. Edwards feels that the best age for children to begin learning to draw in this way is around ten, when the desire for realistic drawing is at a peak for many kids.

★ WHAT PARENTS CAN DO ★

A parent confronted with such a variety of drawing approaches needs to decide which ones to use with a child. Most often, the child himself will indicate which method is best, by showing a preference for a more structured approach or by choosing instead to be left alone to express himself more freely. Regardless of the philosophy or method, there are certain fundamental guidelines that parents should follow in stimulating a child's drive to draw, paint, or engage in other art-related activities.

Develop your own artistic impulse as a parent. Buy yourself a sketch pad and take time out during the week to draw, doodle, or diagram, especially if you are one of the many who gave up drawing in childhood and feel embarrassed to draw your stick figures in public. If your child senses that you are ashamed of your drawing ability, she may well learn from your example to shun the artist's easel for good. If you feel you'd like to have a more structured approach, buy one of the how-to-draw books suggested at the end of this chapter, or take a drawing class (or explore another medium like paint or clay) at a local community center or adult education school.

Draw together as a family. Professor Brent Wilson suggests that parents—even those who don't draw well—carry on a graphic dialogue with their kids. "Draw stories together, and simply make your figures a little more elaborate and complex than the children's, just as you do in conversation when you use a syntax and vocabulary slightly more complex than that of the kids' without even knowing it. In this way, you move them to a higher level." Have family painting or drawing times when everyone can paint or sketch together, either from imagination or using a common model. It can be interesting to share and discuss the different renditions of the family cat or the backyard tree and then display the drawings on a bulletin board set aside for this purpose.

Don't criticize or judge your child's artwork. Criticism is the great killer of creativity. If your child feels that her work doesn't measure up to some external standard or is being compared unfavorably to the drawings of other family members or students at school, she's likely to consider her accomplishments of little value and give up.

Even praise can work to stifle your child's urge to draw or

Many adults draw childlike drawings and many children give up drawing at age nine or ten. These children grow up to become the adults who say that they never could draw and can't even draw a straight line. The same adults, however, if questioned, often say that they would have liked to learn to draw well, just for their own satisfaction at solving the drawing problems that plagued them as children. But they feel that they had to stop drawing because they simply couldn't learn how to draw.

BETTY EDWARDS

paint. Avoid evaluative comments on your child's work, such as "That's pretty" or "Aren't you the little artist!" Instead, respond to the work in an authentic way that reflects upon the actual contents of the picture: "Your airplane looks like it's going a thousand miles an hour," or "The red in the girl's dress makes me think of the red roses in our garden." Talk about how two drawings are *different* rather than one being better than the other.

Provide your child with rich sensory experiences. The best art flows from the child's direct experience of the external world, even when that experience is transformed by the imagination. Before a child draws a picture of a tree, for example, it helps if he's been exposed to trees: touching them, climbing them, smelling them, examining their leaves, and looking at them from varying perspectives. Start some drawing periods with a specific sensory activity, such as dancing, smelling spice bottles in the kitchen, feeling the textures of different fabrics, listening to music, or being out in nature. Since young children are able to perceive the world synaesthetically (hearing colors, seeing sounds, tasting textures), these activities can prepare the way for a very interesting art session that may reflect a creative mixing of the senses.

Supply your child with plenty of materials and opportunities to do art at home. Fine drawing tools for kids include sturdy pencils whose points won't easily break, crayons, felt-tipped pens, and colored chalk. Provide drawing surfaces of varying dimensions to accommodate a child's different needs, including sketch pads (available at art and stationery stores), reams of inexpensive photocopying paper, and rolls of white wrapping paper.

While this chapter has focused upon drawing ability, it is important to recognize the importance of all the visual arts in stimulating your child's creative instinct. Make sure your child has access to clay, collage materials, watercolor paints, finger paints, tempera paints, and other art supplies.

Also, see that your child has a special creative space for drawing or engaging in other art activities. This space should include a table with a large flat surface for drawing, an easel for painting, a large basket or other container for holding drawing

Merely to see . . . is not enough. It is necessary to have a fresh, vivid, physical contact with the object you draw through as many of the senses as possible—and especially through the sense of touch.

KIMON NICOLAIDES

implements, and close-at-hand shelf space for storage of other materials.

Collect and keep your child's art. Provide her with an artist's portfolio that can be fastened or tied shut. Let her use this to keep images from magazines, newspapers, catalogs, junk mail, and other sources that interest her. She can also use this (or another) folder to keep her own drawings, doodles, diagrams, paintings, sketches, and photographs. This folder can serve as a library of ideas that she can refer to in future art activities. Finally, provide resources that will allow her to display her work in a suitable manner, including a bulletin board, empty photo frames, and even a special corner of a room that can serve as an art gallery.

Take your child to art museums or to art galleries on a regular basis. Field trips give your child an opportunity to experience the value that culture places on the visual arts. Talk about the art you see displayed. Share your own favorite (and unfavorite) works. Together, find out about the lives of the artists whose works you're observing. If possible, introduce your child to some living artists who can describe how they make their living, explain why they create art, and answer any questions your child may have. Follow up these excursions with an art activity at home so that your child can feel his own sense of connection with the art he's just seen.

Support art programs at your child's school that focus on process and not product. Too many school art programs still emphasize trace-and-cut-out art projects that leave little room for the imagination and stifle artistic creativity. Encourage the art specialist at your child's school to involve kids in activities where the exploration of the medium is most important so that children have the opportunity to experiment with the properties of clay, the different shades of color in a painting, the varied ways to use a pencil to create special effects in a drawing, and other open-ended exercises. If your child's school has no art program, even in the regular classroom, find out why and take steps to encourage administrators to make funds available for

Pablo Picasso resisted school stubbornly and seemed completely unable to learn to read or write. The other students grew used to seeing him come late with his pet pigeon—and with the paintbrush he always carried as if it were an extension of his own body.

MILDRED AND
VICTOR GOERTZEL

For as long back as I can recall, I have lived in space, not in time. . . . My childhood memories are not co-ordinated chronologically . . . but visually.

VIENNESE PAINTER
OSKAR KOKOSCHKA

this purpose. Failing this, offer to come to the school and supervise open art periods before or after school or during recess periods.

Drawing is a skill that all children and adults should have at their command; it is not just for those who are "artistically inclined." Most people stop drawing early in their lives because they become frustrated with their graphic efforts. Yet with today's emphasis on technology and rational thinking, the ability to draw, and the arts in general, are more important than ever. They provide a much-needed balance to our culture's predominately verbal and numerical thinking styles, giving children another way of communicating ideas and serving as a kind of oasis in which kids can begin to nourish their inner selves.

✎ STARTING POINTS ✎

Group pictures. Spread out on the floor a sheet of white wrapping paper about ten feet long. Participants should space themselves evenly along the length of the paper and begin drawing whatever comes to mind. As the drawing process continues, a common theme may or may not emerge—let the picture have its own life. As the drawings begin to merge, participants may want to mutually determine ways of combining the images or decide to keep them separate. At the end, suggest that group members decide on a title for the mural, place this somewhere on the picture, and hang it up for all to see.

Visual dialogue. Roll out a long sheet of white wrapping paper across a table or on the floor. Sit or lie next to your child (or, alternatively, on opposite sides of the paper) and have a *pencil conversation.* You can also use markers, crayons, or other drawing implements as desired. Draw something simple on the paper and have your child respond to it with a sketch of his own. Continue this graphic conversation until both sides have nothing left to say visually. Try doing this activity in silence. You can talk about it afterwards if you'd like.

Drawing diaries. Go to an art supply or stationery store with your child and let her select an artist's sketch book that she feels comfortable with. Suggest that she use the sketch book as her own private picture diary, to record anything she pleases from her inner imagination or from her observations of the outside world. Let her know that she doesn't have to share any of her drawings with you or others unless she chooses to do so.

Droodles. Draw a circle on a sheet of paper and suggest to your child that he create his own picture using the circle as a starting point. He might choose to create a face out of the circle, or a ball, a sun, or many other possible objects by filling in relevant details. Avoid making suggestions—let his own imagination dictate the direction of the drawing. Try other droodles besides a circle, including a straight line, a circle with a line passing through it, a square, a wavy line, a zigzag line, or any other simple configurations of your own (or your child's) choosing.

Word pictures. Play a game with your child where she must draw a picture of a word that she selects sight unseen from a bag or box. To prepare this game, write on slips of paper words that are relatively easy to draw (chair, hat, tree) for preschool kids, words that are moderately hard to draw (school, mailman, baby) for beginning school-aged kids, and words that are very hard to draw (avalanche, astronaut, magic) for older kids. The child selects the slip and then draws the word while other players try to guess it. Commercial versions of this game are available in toy stores under the names Pictionary and Win, Lose, or Draw.

Dual doodle. Tape a large sheet of drawing paper to the wall or fix it in place on the floor. Draw a vertical line down the center of the sheet. Give your child a pencil or crayon for each hand and suggest that he draw a picture. Tell him that he must draw with both hands at the same time and that he must make the exact same drawing on both sides of the line, so that they are essentially mirror images of each other. Demonstrate what you mean on a sample sheet of paper. This might be especially difficult

I am among the few who continue to draw after childhood is ended, continuing and perfecting children's drawing.

NEW YORKER
CARTOONIST
SAUL STEINBERG

for some children, so don't expect your child to do it accurately. But show him the ground rules and let him play with it in his own way.

RESOURCES

Brookes, Mona. *Drawing with Children*. Los Angeles: Jeremy P. Tarcher, 1986. Step-by-step instructions for using Brookes's alphabet of five shapes to create colorful drawings. Includes suggestions for creating a supportive environment and guidelines for materials to purchase. Can also be used by adults.

Edwards, Betty. *Drawing on the Right Side of the Brain* (rev. ed.). Los Angeles: Jeremy P. Tarcher, 1989. A guide for learning how to see the world with artist's eyes. Provides numerous exercises for developing artistic perception based on right-left brain research. Intended primarily for adults, this book includes a section on adapting the material for children in and outside of school.

Gardner, Howard. *Artful Scribbles: The Significance of Children's Drawings*. New York: Basic Books, 1980. Excellent discussion of the development of drawing ability in children from infancy to adolescence. Explores possible links between children's artwork and the creative expression of mature artists. Includes a chapter on the controversy over whether children should copy drawings from visual models.

Johnson, Mia. *Teach Your Child to Draw: Bringing Out Your Child's Talents and Appreciation for Art*. Los Angeles: Lowell House, 1990. Well-illustrated collection of drawing exercises designed to help children learn visual concepts such as point of view, proportion, shading, texture, and movement.

Lowenfeld, Viktor, and W. Lambert Brittain. *Creative and Mental Growth* (8th ed.). New York: Macmillan, 1987. Written as a textbook for teachers, this book includes important developmental information about children's artistic abilities. Emphasizes leaving children alone to draw in their own way.

McKim, Robert H. *Experiences in Visual Thinking* (2d ed.). Boston: PSW Engineering, 1980. A wonderful resource for using drawing to think more effectively, solve problems, generate creative insights, and more. Written for adult learners, the many exercises in the book can be adapted for use by older children (grade 4 and up).

Warner, Sally. *Encouraging the Artist in Your Child.* New York: St. Martin's Press, 1989. One hundred and one projects for kids aged two to ten in drawing, painting, sculpture, collage, clay, and other visual media.

Organizations

Children's Art Foundation, P.O. Box 83, Santa Cruz, CA 95063; (408) 426-5557. Promotes children's artistic and literary expression. Maintains Museum of Children's Art, conducts research on art by children from around the world, publishes books and periodicals containing child art.

National Art Education Association, 1916 Association Dr., Reston, VA 22901; (703) 860-8000. Clearinghouse for information on art education programs and materials and methods used in teaching art from kindergarten through college.

11. *High-Tech Ed—The Role of Computers and Television in Learning*

Whenever I talk to parent or teacher groups about the use of television or computers in learning, I feel I have to choose my words carefully in order to avoid misunderstandings about their potential value as learning tools. Not long ago, I was speaking to a group of homeschooling parents and started sharing how excited I was to see a recent popular television show portraying children learning the times tables through rap rhythms. I caught myself in mid-sentence realizing that many of the parents attending the conference frowned upon television as an educational experience for their kids. I felt guilty for a moment (because I too feel that television is making mincemeat out of our children's minds), but then I had to admit to myself that when TV is at its best it can truly inspire and educate.

I have the opposite problem with computers. Frequently, parents and teachers approach the topic of computers with stars in their eyes, thinking that *this* is the solution to their kids' educational problems. I have to soften their zeal sometimes and point out that many computer software packages touted

The best current evidence is that media are mere vehicles that deliver instruction but do not influence student achievement any more than the truck that delivers our groceries causes changes in our nutrition.

RICHARD CLARK

as learning programs are in reality nothing but electronic work-sheets—in other words, more of the same drivel that schools have been serving up to kids for years.

In the long run, however, I do not want to be pinned down to any one stand with respect to these technological tools. They are, after all, just that—*tools*—capable of being either used or abused depending upon how they are handled in a learning context. I offer this chapter as my own attempt to balance out what I feel have become some lopsided attitudes toward these two often misunderstood media, and to show how each can either help or hinder the unfolding of your child's natural genius.

COMPUTERS: LEGO OR LOGO?

Recently, I attended a home computer fair featuring the latest in fancy software for children. While wandering the aisles, I happened to stop at a booth where a child who couldn't have been more than three stood at a computer trying to follow her parents' instructions. By pressing a button, the girl could place a square around any one of three different animals on the right side of the screen (bear, elephant, lion). The object was to select the animal that matched the one on the left side of the screen (in this case, a lion). Just as she had selected the lion and her parents were about to praise her, she continued joyfully pressing the button to highlight the other animals. Her parents' attempts to explain that this was not the objective of the program seemed not to faze her as she continued to press the button, contentedly watching the golden square hop from one animal to the next.

I would be willing to bet that this kind of scenario takes place daily in thousands of homes across the country as parents push their kids headlong into mastering computer learning software. Worried that their children may not be getting the training they need in order to make them fully computer literate for the twenty-first century, parents are jumping onto the high-tech bandwagon and exposing their children to computers at earlier ages and higher levels of sophistication than

Children who can talk about their hard-disk systems and their laser printers might as well be talking about their Ralph Lauren shirts and Bally shoes. For many families, computers have become yet another symbol of leisure-class status.

DAVID ELKIND

ever before. Yet, many children may be pushing buttons when they should be pushing scooters and doll carriages instead.

COMPUTER CAUTIONS

During the years of early childhood, when the child's developmental needs require perceptually rich experiences such as water play, painting on large easels, and plenty of time outdoors, the computer appears to provide a relatively sensory-poor environment. "If the choice is between a preschooler playing in a mud puddle with his neighbors or sitting in the house with a computer program," says David Thornburg, educator and computer hardware and software designer, "I'd far rather see him out with his friends, making discoveries with natural objects than horsing around with a computer."

According to Harriet K. Cuffaro, a graduate faculty member at the Bank Street College of Education in New York City, even brightly colored computer graphics programs distort reality for the child. "In 'painting' via the computer [selecting a color from a 'palate' of hues and applying it by pushing a button or manipulating an electronic mouse] the experience is reduced and limited by eliminating the fluid, liquid nature of paint," notes Cuffaro. "In this painting there are no drips to control or spills to mop up." In addition, Cuffaro points out that computer use restricts a young child to fine motor movements (pressing buttons or manipulating joysticks or an electronic mouse) at a time when large motor movements (running, jumping, building, painting with large brushstrokes) are the order of the day for the growing child.

Other experts, however, disagree with the notion that computers and preschoolers should not mix. They point to research showing improvements in social and cognitive growth in four-, five-, and six-year-olds after they have engaged in motivating computer activities. "I'm really doubtful of the power of computers to benefit a normal two- or three-year-old," says Douglas Clements, associate professor of early childhood education at the State University of New York at Buffalo, "but from age four on for most kids, there is nothing to lose and potentially rich benefits to gain through informed use of computers."

There is not a flower or bird in sight, only a small screen on which lines are moving, while the child sits almost motionless, pushing at the keyboard with one finger. As a learning environment, it may be mentally rich . . . but it is perceptually extremely impoverished. No smells or tastes, no wind or birdsong (unless the computer is programmed to produce electronic tweets), no connection with soil, water, sunlight, warmth, . . . the actual learning environment is almost autistic in quality, impoverished sensually, emotionally, and socially.

JOHN DAVY

The computer is the Proteus of machines. Its essence is its universality, its power to simulate. Because it can take on a thousand forms and can serve a thousand functions, it can appeal to a thousand tastes.

SEYMOUR PAPERT

The value of computers in learning becomes less problematic when we consider the needs of children aged six to twelve. School-aged kids can comfortably sit for longer periods of time at a computer terminal, can more easily manipulate the traditional computer keyboard, and can productively explore a wider range of more highly abstract software programs than preschoolers.

In fact, the computer has the potential to serve as a tremendous tool of empowerment for many elementary-school-aged children. Children who learn best independently have the opportunity to teach themselves a wide range of school subjects through self-paced and self-correcting software programs. Problem-solving software provides kids who possess special logical-mathematical abilities with a chance to challenge themselves in ways not possible fifteen or twenty years ago. Word processors free up many youngsters from the constraints of penmanship in expressing their ideas. Spell checkers provide relief for the poor speller. Simulation software gives children the opportunity to practice fast-paced decision making in preparation for the demands of real life. Recent computer applications such as hypertext (where words, images, and music can all be stored and retrieved from a computer disk) and interactive video allow children to create polished multimedia presentations. The computer, in short, offers school-aged children many new avenues for the expression of their abilities.

At the same time, it is important to realize that many schools are still a long way from helping students explore these creative applications of computer technology. A recent article in the journal *Science* suggested that "although there are now an estimated 1.5 million computers in the public schools—one for every 30 kids—nowhere can they be said to have transformed education." According to the report, teachers still have little training in computer use, administrators have made few attempts to integrate computers into the heart of the curriculum, and school software remains for the most part dull and uninspiring.

Furthermore, even when computers are used creatively in the schools or at home, they still may serve to quietly distance children from real life—especially when kids log too much time on the terminals. Psychotherapist Craig Brod, author of *Technostress: The Human Cost of the Computer Revolution*, suggests that computers can promote in children a distorted sense of time, mental fatigue, social isolation, and an unhealthy attachment to machines at the expense of human contact. "Some kids become much more fluent with computers than with people," says Brod. As a result, they grow accustomed to the instant feedback and yes/no answers that computers provide, instead of learning about the subtleties and nuances of human interaction at a time when social understanding is still in the formative stages.

★ WHAT PARENTS CAN DO ★ WITH COMPUTERS

You may already have a computer and be thinking about how to get the most out of it to help your child learn more effectively. Or you may be considering buying a computer for the family and are questioning whether it will truly make a difference in helping your child learn. The following guidelines can assist you in thinking about computer use and your youngster.

Select stimulating computer software programs. Parents need to steer their way safely through the many pitfalls of the computer software market. On the one extreme, there are the electronic worksheets that occupy children with mindless rote tasks such as answering multiple-choice questions in math or reading. At the other extreme are the slam-bang supercolossal video games that provide lots of action but little real learning. It's true that certain creatively designed skill-and-drill software programs may be useful for kids who are having trouble learning through traditional means, and some imaginative arcade-type games have good entertainment value. However, studies suggest that open-ended software (programs that don't have fixed outcomes but allow for a variety of creative responses) provides children with more opportunities to experiment, hypothesize,

At a time when the nation's schools are widely perceived to be in serious trouble, the computer seems for many people to have come on the scene as a veritable deus ex machina *to put all things right, and to relieve parents, teachers, and all our sundry officials of any necessity for fundamental reexamination of self and society.*

DOUGLAS SLOAN

Standard computer-aided instruction treats knowledge as a fluid that can be transferred from the teacher vessel into the empty student vessel. A better system is one that gives the child an environment to explore.

ALAN KAY

and wonder about things than the more structured worksheet/video game software.

Recommendations for children's software include: a word-processing program where your child can create his own stories; a graphics program where he can draw his own pictures; a music program where he can create simple compositions and hear them played back; a program where he can use Logo (a simplified computer language) to control an animal or object on screen; and programs that include open-ended games such as concentration, tic-tac-toe, and anagrams. For the preschooler, add-on devices such as the Muppet Learning Keys, the Koala Pad, or a touch screen can enhance his ability to interact with appropriate software without being hampered by the traditional keyboard.

◆ ◆ ◆ ◆

A Parent's Guide to Kid-Compatible Software and Peripherals

There are thousands of educational software programs as well as numerous peripheral hardware devices seeking to gain a share of the lucrative home and school market. Here are only a few of the very best (prices indicated may change):

PRESCHOOL CHILDREN

Peripheral Hardware

TouchWindow. A screen that can be placed over a computer monitor to allow a child to control software by simply touching different points on the window. Available for Apple II ($249.95). Works with compatible software only (comes with several programs). Edmark, (800) 426-0856; in Washington, (800) 426-3118.

Koala Pad+. An add-on device that allows the child to draw directly on a special pad with a plastic stylus and have the drawing show up on the screen. Available for Apple II ($139.50) or IBM PC ($163.95). Modern School Supplies, (800) 243-2329.

Muppet Learning Keys. A special keyboard containing large-sized letter keys arranged alphabetically for easy access. Also includes special picture keys for printing, spacing, undoing commands, and making corrections; $99.00. Sunburst Communications, (800) 628-8897.

Software

Muppet Slate. A word-processing software program that works with Muppet Learning Keys. Children can type letters to create stories or write with pictures from a built-in picture library. Available for Apple family computers; $75.00. For older children, see Magic Slate II, which use a standard keyboard (20-, 40-, and 80-column versions available); $65.00. Sunburst Communications, (800) 628-8897.

EZ Logo. A software program that prepares children for Logo by letting them make one-letter commands on the keyboard to control a graphic Turtle on the screen. For Apple II; $59.00. MECC, (800) 228-3504; in Minnesota (800) 782-0032.

SCHOOL AGE CHILDREN

Software

The New Print Shop (age 6 and up). Allows users to create personalized greeting cards, signs, calendars, posters, banners, letterheads, and other printed materials. Contains a library of nearly 100 graphic elements, including borders, images, and typefaces. Available for Apple models ($49.95) and IBM PC and Tandy ($59.95). Broderbund Software, (800) 521-6263.

Safari Search (age 8 and up). Participants decipher clues to locate safari animals hidden in a 5" x 5" square grid. This program helps kids learn to think systematically by stimulating them to collect, organize, and analyze data, and then to make logical judgments. Available for most models; $65.00. Sunburst Communications, (800) 628-8897.

Science Toolkit (age 9 and up). Turns the computer into a scientific instrument by including external temperature and light probes that can be plugged into the terminal and used to conduct a number of experiments. Available for Apple II, IBM PC, and Tandy machines; $79.95. Additional modules exploring the human body, earthquakes, and speed and motion can be purchased for $39.95 each. Broderbund Software, (800) 521-6263.

Where in the World Is Carmen Sandiego? (age 10 and up). A detective game where players track down the criminal Carmen Sandiego or one of the members of her infamous gang through a series of clues provided by the program. The twist is that these individuals could be hiding anywere in the world. Numerous references and an accompanying almanac provide children with frequent opportunities to learn about geography, history, and culture. Other versions of this program include *Where in the USA Is Carmen Sandiego?* and *Where in Time Is Carmen Sandiego?* Broderbund Software, (800) 521-6263.

◆ ◆ ◆ ◆

> *It is infinitely more useful for a child to hear a story told by a person than by a computer . . . because the greatest part of the learning experience lies not in the particular words of the story but in the involvement with the individual reading it.*
>
> FRANK SMITH

Plan on being with your child when she is using the computer. According to psychotherapist Craig Brod, many parents have simply switched from TV to the computer in providing their kids with just a high-tech baby-sitter. Unlike television, "a computer interacts," says Brod, "and it's supposed to prepare children for the future, so many performance-oriented parents now pass the computer off without feeling guilty about the time they're not spending with their kids." Yet, recent research shows that when an adult is present during computer use, kids are more attentive, more interested, and less frustrated.

"Prior to school age," says David Thornburg, "I would almost insist that the child be sitting on a parent's lap just as he does when reading a book." Older kids and parents can sit next to each other in front of the terminal and take turns operating the computer or have access to their own individual joystick, keyboard, or computer mouse. Possibilities for adult-child computer play include drawing pictures on the computer together; having your child dictate stories that you input into the computer; creating a family newsletter with a desktop publishing program; and playing interactive learning games. Make sure to spend some time answering your child's questions about each software program that you use together.

Limit your youngster's computer time and encourage other forms of play. Professor Douglas Clements suggests fifteen to thirty minutes a day as a rough guideline for motivated preschoolers, up to one hour a day for grades one to three, and from one to two hours for older elementary school kids. These are general guidelines related to at-home computer use; some kids won't want to spend *any* time at the computer, while others may get absorbed for longer periods of time without harm. Remember, however, that the computer is a two-dimensional device, and young kids need lots of three-dimensional play. See that your preschooler still has the majority of her free time available for art, water and block play, outdoor games, make-believe activities, music, and other forms of unstructured learning. Monitor your older child's computer use, as well, so that he balances what he does at the terminal with activities that engage his social, emotional, and physical energies elsewhere in his life.

Above all, make sure not to force your child to become involved with computers in the hope that it will raise his IQ or make him a successful student. The computer is, in the final analysis, neither panacea nor poison to the child, but simply another medium through which he can express himself and explore the world of ideas. By treating it in this spirit, parents can ensure that their children will find their way safely through the silicon forest of the 1990s.

Between ages 6 and 18, an American child averages about 16,000 hours in front of a TV set; that same child will spend only about 13,000 hours in school. By my reckoning, in the first 20 years of his or her life, an American child will see approximately 700,000 TV commercials, at a rate of close to 700 per week.

NEIL POSTMAN

TELEVISION: THE SILVER LINING

It is popular these days to reject television as a learning tool for children—even among those of us who unashamedly enjoy watching it ourselves. And for good reason. TV is riddled with violence, sexism, and commercialism; it dulls the imagination; and it turns people into passive spectators instead of lively participants. But like it or not, the medium is here to stay. Ninety-nine percent of all families in the United States own a TV. To ignore television is to be essentially out of step with American culture.

I am of two minds on the subject. On the one hand it's clear that current TV offerings threaten to turn our children into a generation of couch-potato kids. Mind-numbing programs flood the airwaves providing children with inappropriate and

Just like the operating room light, television creates an environment that assaults and overwhelms the child; he can respond to it only by bringing into play his shutdown mechanism, and thus becomes more passive. I have observed this in my own children and I have seen it in other people's children. As they sat in front of a television set that was blasting away, watching a film of horrors of varying kinds, the children were completely quiet . . . they were "hooked."

T. BERRY BRAZELTON

even destructive models for living. Research bears out the negative consequences of television viewing among children. TV has been linked to declines in test scores, decreased literacy, increased aggression, reduced play activity, drug and alcohol abuse, and even heightened cholesterol levels. And given the choice, most children would rather watch a shoot-'em-up thriller or mindless Saturday morning cartoon than more edifying programs such as those on public television.

Yet TV has a bright side that many parents and educators overlook. It can teach, inspire, motivate, and enlighten children when it is used in the right way by teachers and parents. Although studies abound that detail the negative impact of television on the mental and emotional health of kids, other research suggests that TV can have a positive influence on learning. Television appears to be more powerful than books or audiotapes for teaching about subjects that involve dynamic processes like the growth of a seed or the eruption of a volcano. TV may also be superior to other media in illustrating tasks that involve physical demonstrations, such as putting together a puzzle or baking bread.

In addition, the medium by its very nature teaches children a host of visual skills. Through exposure to frequent use of camera zoom shots, for instance, children learn to see how individual details in a scene relate to the whole picture. In learning to follow and gain meaning from a series of edited camera shots, children exercise logical skills. And with TV's emphasis on stories and people, children have an opportunity to develop an understanding of plot and character.

Many educators have known about these positive factors for years and have been making use of television's potential in their teaching. Rosemary Lehman, a media specialist and consultant in southern Wisconsin and founder of Television Learning Ltd., has developed a curriculum based on helping children understand the aesthetics involved in television viewing. "When children were asked what they saw when they watched TV, they'd always describe the story line. None of them saw the other things going on that created the story. Then we began looking not at the story line, but at how light was used in the program they were watching." After being shown three-minute segments from commercial programs, children were asked simple questions about the use of light: Is it outdoor or indoor? Artificial or natural? Diffuse or direct? The kids were then encouraged to notice the use of light in the real world, and they studied the role of light in science, art, and other school subjects. They did the same thing for color, motion, and sound. Lehman says that as a result, the children who participated began to watch fewer high-action programs and more challenging programs, and they began to describe the programs they did watch more in terms of form than content.

Another approach to television literacy in the schools uses the medium to help teach the basic skills, especially reading. Rosemary Lee Potter, a reading specialist at a middle school in Safety Harbor, Florida, exposes children to books that have been made into television shows, such as *Little House on the Prairie*, and provides students with scripts adapted from the programs. Potter also uses captioned television programs with students who are reading below grade level. "We take a particular sitcom, like 'Head of the Class,' introduce it, and after five minutes we turn off the audio and they have to read the shows," Potter explains. Kids' interest in reading zooms when this approach is used.

Today's television child is attuned to up-to-the-minute "adult" news—inflation, rioting, war, taxes, crime . . . and is bewildered when he enters the nineteenth-century environment that still characterizes the educational establishment where information is scarce but ordered and structured by fragmented, classified patterns, subjects, and schedules.

MARSHALL MCLUHAN

☆ WHAT PARENTS CAN DO ☆ WITH TELEVISION

Even though some educators are doing innovative work with TV, parents need to serve as the primary guides to their children's television viewing. Without adult mediation, children would likely find their minds turned into pretzels through the clever media manipulations of unscrupulous advertisers and television executives. Here are some practical suggestions for taking a clear and guiding role in monitoring your child's television involvement.

Limit the amount of time your child spends watching television.
Children who watch television five or six hours a day are crowding out valuable time that should be used for other pursuits.

In the present video culture, with its emphasis on speed and ease, ideas have, it seems, become more fleeting and less valued. We are drawn toward those images that pack a bigger punch, provoke a more visceral reflex, or capture more cunningly our mercurial attentiveness. We have become the age of the flash and the zap, the hour-long epic, the thirty-minute encyclopedia, the five-minute explanation, the one-minute sell, the ten-second teaser.

ERNEST L. BOYER

Dorothy Singer, codirector of the Yale University Family Television Research and Consultation Center, recommends a maximum of one hour per day of television viewing for preschoolers and no more than two hours per day for children aged five to twelve, assuming that the time is spent watching programs that have been chosen with care. In addition, limit snacking during TV time and encourage your kids to get up and move around during commercials, as the sedentary life of TV viewing has recently been implicated in higher cholesterol levels (and risk of later heart problems) in children.

Watch television with your children. Parents should plan on being with kids as much as possible during TV watching to help explain and demystify what's happening on the screen. "Too often parents sit with kids, snacking together, responding unintelligently—'ooh that's awful' or 'Ooh that's good'—and not explaining or discussing what's going on," says Singer. "Parents have to ask themselves, 'Do I want TV filling my child's head with misconceptions, or do I want to be my child's teacher?'"

As you watch television with your children, think of questions you can pose to challenge their understanding of what they see. Use commercial time as an opportunity to turn down the volume and discuss the content of a TV show. A good starter might be, "Is this what goes on in real life?" Explain to your child what a stereotype is and then look for examples of distorted or exaggerated characterizations. Show your child how to talk back to the television. If you see something going on that seems immoral or inappropriate, let your child know that she can vent her feelings directly to the characters involved ("You shouldn't be smoking; it can make you very sick").

Take on the role of critic and examine the camera angles, lighting, set design, and costumes of a television program. Select programs that particularly interest your child and find books that go into greater depth on the subject. If your child is interested in superhero cartoons, for example, you might share some myths and legends of ancient Greek or Roman gods and goddesses. Since television can rob your child of his imagination by providing ready-made images, suggest that he take time during or after TV watching to close his eyes and imagine his own versions of the television shows. Ask him to tell you in detail about a recent show. This process of remembering a program can help activate his own natural visualization abilities.

Expose your child to the best that TV has to offer. Quality programming such as symphonies, operas, ballets, plays, classic movies, documentaries, and special news programs provides your child with an unparalleled opportunity to experience rich worlds of culture. Set aside some time at the beginning of each week to sit down as a family and go through the week's television guide. Together, select programs that reflect a high standard of excellence. Just as some communities have developed "pull the plug" programs that involve not watching television for a week or a month, you can pull the plug on bad TV by agreeing as a family to watch only public television or other quality programming for a specific period of time. Agree on a television schedule that will maximize quality and minimize trash TV.

Use alternative TV networks and a VCR to extend viewing possibilities. Current strides in technology provide even more ways for parents to enrich their children's television watching. The emergence of cable networks that cater to families and children represents one bright star in the TV wasteland. Networks such as the Disney Channel and Nickelodeon strive to provide movies and original programming that portray life from a child's point of view. Other networks such as the Public Broadcasting System and The Learning Channel also offer quality children's programming with shows like "Sesame Street," "Mr. Rogers' Neighborhood," and "Mr. Wizard."

Further, the presence of VCRs in over two-thirds of American households now makes it possible for parents to gain greater control over what their children watch. No longer are families at the mercy of the major network programmers' schedules. Patricia Greenfield, professor of psychology at the University of California at Los Angeles and author of *Mind and Media: The Effects of Television, Video Games, and Computers*, recommends that parents who have VCRs develop a library of favorite shows. "By watching a television program more than once, children can

All television, except in small doses, feeds children ready-made fantasy at a time when fantasy making is crucial for their development.

LAWRENCE J. FRIEDMAN

This instrument can teach, it can illuminate; yes, and it can even inspire. But it can do so only to the extent that humans are determined to use it to those ends. Otherwise, it is merely wires and lights in a box. There is a great, perhaps decisive battle to be fought, against ignorance, intolerance and indifference. This weapon of television can be useful.

EDWARD R. MURROW

dig more deeply into the show, just as they would with a favorite book." Parents can record favorite shows off the television, or rent and purchase quality programs such as Shari Lewis's one-minute tales, Raffi's musical concerts, or quality commercial movies like *The Little Mermaid*.

Everything the critics say about television is true. It clearly has misused its potential for expanding minds and enriching lives. Parents are entirely justified, in my view, in turning off the tube temporarily or permanently, freeing up family time for reading, singing, cooking, storytelling, drawing, and hundreds of other learning activities. However, for parents who see TV abstinence as an impractical alternative, the above suggestions should help make TV time a positive learning experience. By seeing TV for what it is—a tool that can be used for good or ill—parents might begin to reclaim it as a creative learning device and use it to unlock new doors of knowledge for their children.

RESOURCES

Greenfield, Patricia Marks. *Mind and Media: The Effects of Television, Video Games, and Computers*. Cambridge, MA: Harvard University Press, 1984. Excellent readable review of the research on the effects of television and other media on children, emphasizing their positive role in learning.

Lappé, Frances Moore. *What to Do After You Turn Off the TV*. New York: Ballantine, 1985. A practical book of activities families can engage in after making a conscious decision to limit or end television watching. Alternatives described include cooking, gardening, bird watching, games, trips, arts and crafts, storytelling, and much more.

Mander, Jerry. *Four Arguments for the Elimination of Television*. New York: Morrow Quill, 1978. Delivers substantially more than four arguments, including the negative impact of artificial light, suppression of the imagination, manipulation through advertising, program bias, sensory deprivation, and hypnotic effects.

Papert, Seymour. *Mindstorms: Children, Computers, and Powerful Ideas*. New York: Basic Books, 1980. Describes the development of Logo, a simple programming language used to introduce children to the world of computers and logical thought.

Schechter, Harold. *Kidvid: A Parents' Guide to Children's Videos.* New York: Pocket Books, 1986. Reviews over 300 programs (cartoons, old and new movies, stories, educational tapes, and other offerings) for kids from preschool to age ten. Useful in starting a home video library.

Singer, Dorothy G., Jerome L. Singer, and Daina M. Zuckerman. *Use TV to Your Child's Advantage: The Parent's Guide.* Washington, DC: Acropolis, 1990. Provides parents with answers to questions about the potentially damaging effects of television, as well as advice on how to use television to promote growth and understanding in children. By the directors of the Yale University Family Television Research and Consultation Center.

Winn, Marie. *The Plug-In Drug: Television, Children and the Family.* New York: Penguin, 1985. A classic on the dangers of television watching among children. See also her follow-up book, *Pulling the Plug on the Plug-In Drug: Helping Your Children Kick the TV Habit.*

Organizations

Action for Children's Television, 20 University Rd., Cambridge, MA 02138; (617) 876-6620. Advocacy group that encourages quality television for kids and works for the elimination of commercialism and exploitation in children's programming. Publishes books including *TV-Smart Book for Kids* and *How to Treat TV with TLC.*

CBS Television provides scripts adapted from selected television shows, and accompanying curriculum guides for use in the schools. Available for free from participating CBS affiliates, or by writing CBS Television Reading Program, 51 West 52 St., New York, NY 10019.

Center for Children and Technology, Bank Street College of Education, 610 West 112th St., New York, NY 10025. Major center for research on uses and effects of computers in elementary school classrooms.

Children's Television Workshop, One Lincoln Plaza, New York, NY 10023; (212) 595-3456. Supports research on new uses of television for educational and informational purposes. Developers of "Sesame Street," "Electric Company," and other educational programs for kids.

Educational Products Information Exchange, P.O. Box 839, Water Mill, NY 11976; (516) 283-4922. Information about the latest in software programs for children of all ages.

High/Scope Educational Research Foundation, 600 N. River St., Ypsilanti, MI 48198; (313) 485-2000. Puts out an annual review, *The Survey of Early Childhood Software,* which describes and rates over 400 computer software programs for children aged three to six ($19.95).

KIDSNET, 6856 Eastern Ave. NW, Suite 208, Washington, DC 20012. An up-to-the-minute subscriber-supporter computer database of comprehensive information on television programming for children.

National Coalition on Television Violence, P.O. Box 2157, Champaign, IL 61824; (217) 384-1920. Provides research updates, ratings of television programs, a newsletter, bibliographies, and other publications on television violence.

◆ ◆ ◆ ◆

Part Four

Preserving Your Child's Uniqueness in School

12. *Giftedness—Every Child's Birthright*

Every school day at eleven o'clock sharp, Jimmie leaves his regular fifth-grade class and goes to the gifted and talented room. There he designs futuristic model homes, builds complex geometric solids from cardboard, and brainstorms ways of solving the energy crisis. The reason for this classroom switch is that Jimmie was identified several years ago as a gifted child based on an IQ test he took that ranked him in the top 3 to 5 percent of the student population in the nation. Currently, nearly 2 million children in the United States are in gifted programs like Jimmie's that pull kids out of class for all or part of the school day. In addition to advanced level courses in basic academic subjects, these programs provide enrichment ranging from great-books discussion groups and critical-thinking seminars to courses in creative problem solving and philosophy.

Such programs are great, but unfortunately leave out a substantial proportion of schoolchildren who have equally strong talents and intelligences that deserve to be recognized and developed. That truth is that all children should be getting this

Each one of us has a gift. There is . . . the tortoise gift of the plodder, the fox gift of cunning, the dog gift of faithfulness, the song-sparrow gift of cheerfulness, the swan gift of beauty in motion.

HUGHES MEARNS

Gifted and talented children are those . . . who by virtue of outstanding abilities are capable of high performance. These . . . children . . . require differentiated educational programs and/or services beyond those normally provided by the regular school program in order to realize their [potential] contribution to self and society. Children capable of high performance include those who have demonstrated any of the following abilities or aptitudes, singly or in combination: 1) general intellectual ability, 2) specific academic aptitude, 3) creative or productive thinking, 4) leadership ability, 5) visual and performing arts aptitude, 6) psychomotor ability.

U.S. OFFICE OF
EDUCATION

quality of education in school. If we identified and treated each child as gifted, and provided all of them with the kinds of enriched programs described above, many of our educational problems would be resolved.

Every child is gifted in something. As we have seen throughout this book, each child is a natural genius. In this chapter we will look at some recent educational findings that broaden our conception of giftedness. You will learn how to think about your own child in terms of an expanded model of intelligence and how to use this information to work with your child's school system in recognizing and developing all children's talents and abilities.

THE MANY WAYS OF BEING GIFTED

The problem with the current conception of giftedness used in schools is that it is based primarily on tests—usually IQ tests— even though the U.S. Office of Education has defined giftedness more broadly. Joseph Renzulli, a leader in gifted education and professor of education at the University of Connecticut, calls this kind of intelligence *schoolhouse giftedness*. "Because it is the kind most easily measured by IQ or other cognitive-ability tests, it is also the type most often used to select students for entrance into gifted programs." This seriously limited definition of giftedness discriminates against kids who may be poor test-takers yet who possess other talents and traits such as creativity, curiosity, leadership, and problem-solving ability.

In contrast, one of the most flexible and useful models currently available for challenging the outmoded IQ concept of giftedness is the theory of multiple intelligences developed by Professor Howard Gardner at Harvard University. In his award-winning book *Frames of Mind*, Gardner suggests that there are at least seven basic intelligences that need to be addressed in any attempt to understand how the mind works: linguistic (verbal), logical-mathematical, spatial, bodily-kinesthetic, musical, interpersonal (social), and intrapersonal (highly developed sense of self).

◆ ◆ ◆ ◆

Seven Kinds of Smart

Children display at least seven basic ways of processing information at home and in school. These characteristic learning
styles represent fundamental intelligences that parents should
use in helping their children learn more effectively. The following descriptions of Howard Gardner's seven intelligences can
help you to identify your child's gifts and assist you and your
child's teachers in tailoring home learning and school-related
activities to his particular needs.

Linguistic. Children with high linguistic intelligence have a knack
for language and learn best by saying, hearing, and seeing words.
The best ways to motivate them include providing them with
books, records, and tapes, engaging them in discussions, and
creating opportunities for informal writing.

Spatial. Kids with spatial intelligence usually learn visually and
need to be taught through images, pictures, metaphor, and color.
Use films, slides, diagrams, maps, charts, art activities, visualization exercises, construction kits, and vivid stories to help them
learn.

Bodily-Kinesthetic. Children who excel in this area learn best
by moving their bodies and working with their hands. They need
learning activities that are kinetic, dynamic, and visceral—role-
playing, drama, creative movement, hands-on activities, and
sports of all types.

Musical. Musically gifted children learn best through rhythm
and melody. They can learn anything more easily if it is sung,
tapped out, or whistled. Provide music lessons (if the child wants
them), opportunities for music appreciation, rhythmic activities, and sing-along time.

Interpersonal. Youngsters with interpersonal inclinations learn
best by relating to and cooperating with people. Let them teach
other kids. Provide social games that emphasize important concepts and skills. Help them get involved in community projects,
school clubs, and volunteer organizations where they can learn
by doing things with others.

We are all so different largely because we all have different combinations of intelligences. If we recognize this, I think we will have at least a better chance of dealing appropriately with the many problems that we face in the world.

HOWARD GARDNER

Logical-Mathematical. Children who have logical proclivities often think in terms of concepts and look for abstract patterns and relationships. Provide them with materials they can experiment with, such as science resources as well as logic puzzles and games. Allow them plenty of time to explore new ideas, and offer rational explanations for their probing questions.

Intrapersonal. Children who lean in this direction frequently learn best when left to themselves. Let them develop their own learning activities, or give them self-correcting teaching materials they can use on their own.

◆　◆　◆　◆

Gardner's research indicates that every child has all seven types of intelligence in different combinations. One child may be weak in math, a whiz at spelling, a naturally social person, and a mediocre athlete; another might be a math genius, a tone-deaf singer, a brilliant reader, and a dud in the personality department. In Gardner's model, every child has a chance to be gifted in something. Even the so-called retarded child may demonstrate high levels of musical, interpersonal, or kinesthetic intelligence.

According to Gardner, each type of intelligence has its own particular neurological pattern; linguistic intelligence, for instance, is linked primarily with the brain's left hemisphere, spatial intelligence with the right. Each has its own course of development; for example, logical intelligence tends to peak early and decline in middle age, while musical intelligence often stays robust into old age. And the forms of intelligence enjoy varying prestige around the globe: Some African and South Sea Island cultures take pains to cultivate kinesthetic, musical, and spatial aptitudes in children at an early age, while American and European societies tend to value word and number skills more.

Regrettably, most of our nation's classrooms are set up for verbal and logical children. Kids with especially sharp reading, vocabulary, reasoning, and computational skills do well on tests and are most likely to end up in classes for the gifted. Children whose strengths lie elsewhere—in art, music, dance, mechanical reasoning, social savvy, intuitive perception, or sheer creative imagination—may perform poorly in school and not qualify for gifted education. According to Gardner's model, such children deserve to have their gifts acknowledged and developed. However, since schools focus most of their attention upon linguistic and logical-mathematical approaches to learning (lecturing, textbooks, worksheets, paper-and-pencil tests), the majority of talents among our nation's children simply never get a chance to be identified, let alone cultivated in the classroom.

FULL-SPECTRUM CLASSROOMS

Fortunately, a growing number of schools around the country use teaching methods that address the giftedness in all learners. At the Key School in Indianapolis, Indiana, children go through each school day engaged in activities touching upon all seven intelligences in Gardner's model. In addition to receiving instruction in the three Rs, they attend classes in art and music, physical education, and computers. Teachers place special emphasis upon social relationships and individualized projects as part of classwork. Separate *pods*, or learning centers, provide stimulation in specific intelligences. For example, a "young naturalists" area engages children in activities such as growing tomato plants from seeds and creating student-made books on endangered species.

Other teachers across the country have also applied Gardner's model to their own unique settings. At Cascade Elementary School in Marysville, Washington, for example, third-grade teacher Bruce Campbell has created seven distinct areas of his classroom to reflect the multiple-intelligences approach. Students study a common unit and then use the activity centers to help deepen their understanding in different ways.

In one recent unit on Planet Earth, students constructed a three-layer replica of the earth in the building center (kinesthetic intelligence), studied geometric concepts such as diameter and radius in the math center (logical-mathematical

The frustrated able child is likely to grow up with a conscious or unconscious resentment against the society that has done him an irreparable justice, and his repressed ability may be diverted from creation to retaliation. If and when this happens, it is likely to be a tragedy for the frustrated individual and for the repressive society alike.

ARNOLD TOYNBEE

*When I examined myself
and my methods of thought,
I came to the conclusion
that the gift of fantasy has
meant more to me than my
talent for absorbing positive
knowledge.*

ALBERT EINSTEIN

intelligence), and read a story about a group of schoolchildren exploring the center of the world in the reading center (linguistic intelligence). They also listened to music while spelling words such as *earth, crust,* and *mantle* in the musical center; cut out concentric circles reflecting the earth's different layers and pasted them onto construction paper in the art center (spatial intelligence); and cooperatively worked on a fact sheet in the working-together center (interpersonal intelligence). Finally, in the personal work center (intrapersonal intelligence), they wrote fantasy lists of things they would take with them on a journey to the center of the earth.

Parents and teachers can learn from these examples that virtually any skill or subject can be taught in several different ways so that every child's essential giftedness is recognized and utilized in the classroom. Multiplication tables and spelling lists can be illustrated, recited, sung, studied analytically, or traced in clay—either independently or in a group. Historical events can be read about, acted out in skits, rendered in artwork, critically assessed, or celebrated through song—again, either individually or with the entire class. Teachers should become familiar with their students' individual intelligence profiles (using the kinds of assessment approaches described in the next chapter) and vary the lesson plans accordingly; that way, all the children in the class can learn in ways that are most natural to them, and have equal opportunity to express their giftedness.

OTHER MODELS OF GIFTEDNESS

Gardner's theory of multiple intelligences represents only one way of expressing new conceptions of giftedness. Within the field of gifted education itself, there has been a reform movement seeking to develop programs that make the *gifted* definition available to a broader segment of the student population. One such program, at the Minter Bridge Elementary School in Hillsboro, Oregon, considers every student in the school eligible for the gifted and talented program. Using the Enrichment Triad/Revolving Door model developed by Joseph Renzulli and his colleagues at the University of Connecticut, teachers offer special learning activities to all the students. At the beginning of the school year, the staff polls students about their top ten interests, and their responses are stored in a computer database. Then, throughout the year, kids are informed of school activities that correspond to their chosen interests.

Recently, for instance, a graphic artist came to the school to talk about medical illustration, and all the children who had indicated an interest in drawing were invited to attend the presentation. Likewise, kids who had expressed an interest in pet care were assembled when a veterinarian brought a boa constrictor to school. Classroom teachers follow up these events with more advanced lessons for those students who show continued interest.

Although the school uses test scores and teacher recommendations to help determine eligibility for the more specialized components of the program, no student is turned away if he demonstrates ability to do the work. Stuart Omdal, enrichment coordinator at Minter Bridge, says,

> I don't want to be the one to say, "no, you can't learn about that; you don't have the test scores, you don't have the recommendations." One boy in a class for the learning disabled lectured other kids about shark habitats; his presentation was at a very advanced level. And a student we had considered "average" began doing work in astronomy that even I can't keep up with.

Another model that has assisted parents and teachers in going beyond the standard school definition of giftedness is the multiple-talent approach developed by Calvin Taylor, currently a researcher at the University of Utah College of Health in Salt Lake City and chairman of the World Conference of Gifted and Talented Children. Taylor says that besides traditional academic abilities, there are at least eight different talents worth developing in a classroom environment: productive or creative thought, planning, implementing a plan, decision making, forecasting, communication, human relations, and discerning opportunities. Taylor claims that if teachers would consider each of these talents in assessing their students, about 90 percent of all kids would be viewed as above average in at least one area.

Three out of five of the Four Hundred [eminent individuals of the twentieth century] had serious school problems. In order of importance, their dissatisfactions were: with the curriculum; with dull, irrational or cruel teachers; with other students who bullied, ignored, or bored them; and with school failure.

VICTOR AND
MILDRED GOERTZEL

When children know uniqueness is respected, they are more likely to put theirs to use.

DOROTHY CORKILLE BRIGGS

Using Taylor's approach, students at the Forbes School in Torrington, Connecticut, start identifying their own talents and those of their peers at the start of the school year, and they engage in activities designed to make full use of their abilities. Any child who wants to engage in an enriching experience, whether it be in dance, art, music, community affairs, environmental studies, or any other subject, simply needs to write up a plan and secure a mentor from the school or community to help implement it. "It doesn't take long before you see which youngsters are the productive thinkers, or the planners, or the decision makers," says Josephine Radocchio, principal at Forbes. Students love this approach to learning. Some students come to Forbes as early as seven in the morning to work on special projects and others stay until ten at night.

★ WHAT PARENTS CAN DO ★

Most schools, unfortunately, still do not provide the kind of breadth in their teaching methods that allows kids to take wing and develop their brightest potentials. It's regrettable but true that in many instances, and because of many problems, schools are locked into the perpetuation of mediocrity and conformity and not dedicated to the cultivation of creativity and giftedness. That often leaves it up to parents, in many cases, to champion their children's natural genius. Here are some positive steps that parents can take to help accomplish this goal.

Find out what your child shines in. The essential ingredient for success as a learner is self-esteem. Yet many parents seem more concerned about discovering what their children may be *at risk* for in today's crisis-ridden society. Instead, parents ought to begin thinking about what their children could be *at promise* to become. As Howard Gardner says, "The single most important thing in education is for each person to find at least *one* thing that he or she connects to, gets excited by, feels motivated to spend more time with." This one core interest can then serve as a trigger to stir other parts of the child's world into activity, so that eventually his whole life begins to resonate with a sense of mastery, accomplishment, and competence.

Observe and support your child when she is having a good time, when she is totally absorbed in a learning activity, or when she shows a real interest in some new subject or experience. Go through the list of seven intelligences described above and see which ones describe your child. Use some of the assessment techniques described in the next chapter to help gain a greater understanding of your child's natural talents and abilities.

Accept your child's gifts even if they are not abilities that you particularly prize. Oftentimes a child's greatest gifts will be in a parent's blind spot. I remember one student of mine who was a nationally acclaimed athlete but whose mother was an Evelyn Wood reading instructor. Her meetings with me focused much more on his reading difficulties than upon his sports accomplishments.

You may be musically illiterate and have a son whose guitar-playing gifts you can hardly appreciate, or be a businessman who cannot understand why his daughter wastes her time with artistic pursuits. It's important to recognize your own biases and not let them get in the way of your child's self-realization. Too many gifts and potentials lay discarded at the side of the road, victimized by a parent's neglect or overt hostility. Acknowledge and honor each and every gift you see in your child—no matter how far removed it may be from your own world. By doing this, you can help your child's abilities develop from fragile seeds into blossoming realities.

Draw out your child's gifts but don't pressure him to develop them. Howard Gardner suggests that children show inclinations to excel in specific intelligences at very early ages. It's important, according to Gardner, to recognize these gifts during their early stages so that they can be nurtured and developed as the child grows. However, the trick is to nurture the gifts in such a way that your child will not feel overwhelmed or pressured to grow in a certain direction, as this can result in imbalances later in life.

I often hear stories about parents who dedicated their lives

*Hide not your talents,
They for use were made.
What's a sundial in the shade?*

BEN FRANKLIN

People like me are aware of their so-called genius at ten, eight, nine. . . . I always wondered, "Why has nobody discovered me? In school didn't they see that I'm more clever than anybody in this school? That the teachers are stupid, too? That all they had was information that I didn't need." It was obvious to me. Why didn't they put me in art school? Why didn't they train me? I was different, I was always different. Why didn't anybody notice me?

JOHN LENNON

to the cultivation of a child's particular gift, only to see their prodigy later burn out because too much emphasis was placed on one specific area and not enough attention was given to the child's total development. Therefore, provide your child with resources that nourish all sides of his nature: artistic, verbal, logical, social, emotional, physical, spiritual, and moral. In areas of particular giftedness, simply be present to your child's accomplishments with a sense of interest, and provide him with one or two specific materials (a toy, a piece of music, a book, a game, or other learning tool) that can help him move to the next level of mastery. Allow yourself to be led by your child's own enthusiasm rather than pushing him in a direction you have chosen. Be careful not to overwhelm your child with lessons, kits, and tutors when what he really needs is someone who will simply acknowledge his gifts and provide him with appropriate tools to help him meet his *own* goals for success at his own pace.

Encourage your child's school to expand its own definition of giftedness and to honor your child's abilities in the classroom. Suggest to school officials that they look into one of the educational models described in this chapter (Gardner's theory of multiple intelligences, Renzulli's Enrichment Triad/Revolving Door model, the Taylor Talents approach) for use with a wider range of students than may be currently served in their gifted and talented program. Howard Gardner has suggested that in the ideal society, every school would have a *curriculum-broker* and a *community-broker* whose function would be to match every child's natural gifts to resources in the school and community. Until that time comes, you may have to function in this capacity for your child. For example, if your child is a gifted artist and is not getting the opportunity to express this intelligence in school, try to find an individual in the school or community (an artistically inclined teacher or a professional artist) who is willing to spend some time with your child helping her cultivate her aptitude for art. Or if your child is really excited about computer programming but doesn't get a chance to use this ability in class, try to locate a computer that she can use during recess or enroll her in an after-school program at a community center.

Finally, encourage your child's teacher to find ways in which specific talents can be expressed in class—through specific projects, show-and- tell activities, homework assignments, and volunteer tasks (a highly spatial child, for example, might enjoy helping the teacher run the audiovisual equipment).

Don't be discouraged if your child isn't chosen for the school's gifted program. "Giftedness isn't like an extra golden chromosome that you're born with," says Joseph Renzulli. "It's something that teachers and parents can help to nurture through the opportunities, resources, and encouragement they make available to kids." By focusing on your child's abilities at home and by encouraging the school to provide some kind of enriched education for all students, you can help your child develop the talents just waiting to be discovered within.

RESOURCES

Amabile, Teresa M. *Growing Up Creative.* New York: Crown, 1989. Written by a leading researcher in the field, an excellent resource for parents interested in nurturing their children's creativity.

Armstrong, Thomas. *In Their Own Way: Discovering and Encouraging Your Child's Personal Learning Style.* Los Angeles: Jeremy P. Tarcher, 1987. Helps parents and teachers use Gardner's theory of multiple intelligences to identify a child's unique qualities as a learner.

Bloom, Benjamin. *Developing Talent in Young People.* New York: Ballantine, 1985. Based upon Bloom's University of Chicago study of 120 highly accomplished scientists, musicians, and athletes. Underlines the importance of a supportive family environment.

Feldman, David Henry. *Nature's Gambit.* New York: Basic Books, 1986. A ten-year study of six child prodigies reveals much about the interaction of individual talent with family and cultural support systems.

Gardner, Howard. *Frames of Mind.* New York: Basic Books, 1985. Builds a case for the theory of multiple intelligences from several sources, including neuropsychology, developmental psychology, anthropology, cognitive psychology, and biographical studies. It is one of the most important books on learning of the past fifty years.

Goertzel, Victor and Mildred G. *Cradles of Eminence.* Boston: Little, Brown and Co., 1962. A fascinating study of 400 eminent men and

Three views of genius

Genius is one percent inspiration and ninety-nine percent perspiration.

THOMAS ALVA EDISON

Genius must be born, and never can be taught.

JOHN DRYDEN

Genius . . . means little more than the faculty of perceiving in an unhabitual way.

WILLIAM JAMES

193

women of the twentieth century. Sheds light on the formative forces that gave rise to their accomplishments.

Perry, Susan K. *Playing Smart: A Parent's Guide to Enriching Offbeat Learning Activities for Ages 4–14*. Minneapolis: Free Spirit Pub., 1990. Full of games, puzzles, and activities designed to stimulate your child's inquiring mind in areas such as logic, photography, psychology, cultural diversity, and scientific investigation.

Organizations

Creative Education Foundation, 1050 Union Rd., Buffalo, NY 14224; (716) 675-3181. Encourages research into creative processes of children and adults. Publishes *Journal of Creative Behavior.*

National Association for Creative Children and Adults, 8080 Springvalley Dr., Cincinnati, OH 45235; (513) 631-1777. Provides workshops and conferences on creativity, promotes the role of the arts in creative education, publishes quarterly *The Creative Child and Adult.*

National Association for Gifted Children, 4175 Lovell Rd., Suite 140, Circle Pines, MN 55014; (612) 784-3475. Distributes information to teachers and parents on the development of gifted children, conducts institutes, and publishes an academic journal, *Gifted Child Quarterly.*

Talents Unlimited, 1107 Arlington St., Mobile, AL 36605. Contact person: Deborah Hobbs. Disseminates information about the Taylor Talents approach to classroom learning.

Teaching the Talented Program, 231 Glenbrook Rd., Box U-7, University of Connecticut, Storrs, CT 06269. Source of information about the Renzulli Enrichment Triad/Revolving Door model of gifted education.

Workshop Way Inc., P.O. Box 850170, New Orleans, LA 70185-0170; (504) 486-7411. A system of education based on the inherent dignity and intelligence of all students.

Zephyr Press, 430 S. Essex Lane, Tucson, AZ 85711; (602) 745-9199. Mail-order distributor for many fine books and tapes on the topics of giftedness, creativity, and the education of multiple intelligences.

13. *The Rating Game— Alternatives to Standardized Testing*

"Should I have my child tested?" This is the question I have been asked most frequently in my work as a learning specialist. One parent wants to know if tests will show that her four-year-old is at risk for developing learning problems later in life; another wonders whether testing her first-grader will prove she is making satisfactory progress in reading; a third parent feels her eight-year-old son may be gifted in math, and wants verified results.

To be honest, I am tired of hearing this testing question over and over again. I simply don't understand why parents want more testing when their children are already being tested to death in the schools. Over 100 million standardized tests are administered to students every year, and the number continues to grow as pressure mounts for accountability in education. Concerned over commission reports suggesting we are a "nation at risk" in the educational marketplace, policy-makers continue to initiate reforms that place even greater emphasis upon standardized testing as a primary means of quality control.

This chapter will explore the limitations of standardized

Standardized testing has become the arbiter of social mobility, yet there is more regulation of the food we feed our pets than of the tests we give our kids.

ROBERT SCHAEFFER

testing in the schools and introduce parents to some alternative ways of evaluating their children's educational progress both at home and at school.

A BRIEF GUIDE TO STANDARDIZED TESTS

Many tests that students take in school are not standardized. These include the Friday spelling test, the end-of-unit history exam, the pop quiz in science, and other teacher-created or textbook-generated assessments. However, the most important tests—the ones that determine what kinds of programs your child will get into, whether he will receive special consideration, and even whether he will be allowed to graduate—are standardized.

In a standardized test, individual results are compared with a *norm* or *standard* that usually consists of a sample of individuals of the same age or grade level from around the country who took the same test when it was first developed. If your child scores at the 50th percentile on a test, he did better than about half the children in the original sample but not as well as the other half. Here is a summary of the types of tests that your child might be exposed to during his school career.

Academic screening tests. These are usually administered in kindergarten or at the beginning of first grade to determine a child's readiness for academic learning. Many of these tests attempt to determine a child's motor ability, eye-hand coordination, social maturity, vocabulary skills, and other indications of preparedness for school. Example: The Gesell developmental tests.

Achievement tests. Once or twice a year, your child and her classmates take a test that assesses their mastery of skills in math and reading. In addition, they may be tested for knowledge of other subjects, including social studies, science, spelling, and language arts. Test results are compared with a national average and are often used by a school district as a primary indication of students' general academic progress. Example: Iowa Test of Basic Skills.

Minimum competency tests. Many states have started using minimum competency tests at different grade levels to strengthen academic standards. These tests cover basic reading and math (and less often, writing) skills that students should have mastered by a given grade level. The most important of these tests occur during the last year or two of high school; in some states the tests determine whether a student will be allowed to graduate.

Ability or aptitude tests. These tests are also commonly referred to as intelligence tests. They attempt to determine a child's potential for learning as opposed to his actual achievement in school. These assessments can be given individually or in group settings and generally evaluate a child's verbal, logical, and (less often) spatial abilities. Example: Wechsler Intelligence Scale for Children, Revised (WISC-R).

Diagnostic tests. If your child has specific academic difficulties in school, you may be asked for permission for her to take a battery of diagnostic assessments to help determine the source of the problem. These can include individual reading tests (example: Gray Oral Reading Test), language tests (example: Illinois Test of Psycholinguistic Ability), tests of perceptual ability (example: Bender Visual-Motor Gestalt Test), projective tests (example: Rorschach test), and ability and achievement tests of the kinds listed above. Diagnostic tests are usually required before a child is allowed to receive special education help in school.

The basic idea behind standardized testing is that by comparing children to a given measure of achievement, the schools can obtain clear and concise records of academic progress. These statistics can then be used by teachers and administrators to improve instruction, and can be shared with parents and the public at large to prove that learning is taking place in the classroom. Testing also makes it possible for schools to identify

"Standardized tests" are the greatest single barrier to equal opportunity for disadvantaged groups, at least in the sphere of education. Minorities who get into higher education generally do so despite tests, not because of them, which is particularly ironic in light of the ostensible reason for the development of the tests themselves, to avoid petty prejudice and capricious or arbitrary rejections.

JAMES LOEWEN

Because the results are expressed in numbers, it is easy to make the mistake of thinking that the intelligence test is a measure like a foot ruler or a pair of scales. It is, of course, a quite different sort of measure. . . . Intelligence is not an abstraction like length and weight; it is an exceedingly complicated notion . . . which nobody has yet succeeded in defining.

WALTER LIPPMANN

children who stand out from the norm and provide them with appropriate instruction. As we shall see below, however, such benefits of testing, if they occur at all, often come at a heavy price.

THE TESTING MANIA

I consider that most standardized tests are poorly constructed, of questionable or unknown validity, pretentious in their claims, and likely to be misused more often than not.

OSCAR BUROS
FORMER EDITOR OF
MENTAL MEASUREMENTS
YEARBOOK

It might be said that everybody has something to lose in the new high-stakes testing climate that has developed over the last few years. Students can be kept back in school, even prevented from graduating, if they don't score high enough on minimum competency tests. In some areas of the country teachers may lose promotions or salary increases if their classes fail to achieve adequate test scores. School districts can have their budgets cut or fail to receive important grants or educational resources if their students don't achieve high enough test results. Administrators and school board members can even lose their jobs if their districts are not up to par in the testing arena.

It's not surprising, therefore, to realize that this kind of pressure may be creating some unintended side effects that are crippling the learning process instead of helping it along. Anxious teachers have turned their attention away from the broader task of motivating young minds and now spend increasing amounts of time prodding their students to pass tests through whatever means are at their disposal. According to recent news reports, teachers have occasionally helped students cheat on their exams by providing them with answers before the test or by changing their answers after the tests have been turned in. More commonly, teachers have been *teaching to the tests*—spending inordinate amounts of time instructing students on those skills that are likely to be covered in the tests. Test-makers assist in this process by creating special coaching programs that teachers can use to give their students an edge in the testing game.

Among administrators, student test scores have been reported "above average" in virtually every state of the union, despite the fact that the statistical rules of standardized testing demand that about half of all school districts be below average.

There is even a term for this phenomenon: the Lake Wobegon effect, named for Garrison Keillor's mythical town immortalized in the popular public radio program "Prairie Home Companion" ("where all the women are strong, all the men good-looking, and all the children are above average"). The reason so many schools are "above average" is that students are compared, not with their peers, but with the norm group who originally took the test—perhaps many years before. Furthermore, since teachers have been preparing students for these tests during the academic year, the scores invariably look better than those of the original sample of students who did not have a similar chance to prepare for the test. Meanwhile, administrators take turns publicly gloating over test results that were improperly obtained.

This testing mania seems to be having an overall effect of substantially narrowing the focus of classroom learning. As Arthur Wise, director of the Center for the Study of the Teaching Profession at the RAND Corporation, observes, the message to teachers seems to be: "Don't teach everything, just teach the basics. Don't teach children to read, just teach reading skills. Don't teach children to write, just teach them to fill in the blanks. Don't teach them to think, just teach them to give the right answers." The real tragedy of this testing craze is that standardized tests are ignoring 99 percent of the learning that children engage in during their young lives. Yet many parents and teachers seem to be treating test results as if they were the only way to evaluate a child's academic progress.

Our obsession with test scores has produced distorted curriculum, teaching, and educational policy. As long as it continues, we will get the dual phenomena of rising test scores and too many illiterate and innumerate citizens.

DEBORAH MEIER
PRINCIPAL OF CENTRAL
PARK EAST SECONDARY
SCHOOL, NEW YORK CITY

Testing is a way to short-circuit the discussion of what we want our schools to teach. We can agree more on our tests than on our goals.

ERNEST L. BOYER

BEYOND PAPER-AND-PENCIL TESTS

Fortunately, an increasing number of educators around the country are becoming uneasy with standardized tests and are experimenting with methods of assessing learning progress that go beyond fill-in-the-blank and multiple-choice. These alternative assessments examine a greater range of the child's abilities and reflect the kinds of real-life learning that parents see at home.

In the conventional [intelligence] test, the child is confronted by an adult who fires at him a rapid series of questions. The child is expected to give a single answer (or, when somewhat older, to write down his answer or to select it from a set of choices). A premium is placed on linguistic facility, on certain logical-mathematical abilities, and on a kind of social skill at negotiating the situation with an elder in one's presence. These factors can all intrude when one is trying to assess another kind of intelligence—say, musical, bodily-kinesthetic, or spatial.

HOWARD GARDNER

In New York, for example, 200,000 fourth-graders recently took a one-hour science exam that required them to sort seeds, determine a mystery sound in a closed box, and perform simple scientific experiments. In Massachusetts, 3,000 fourth- and eighth-graders were tested in their ability to apply math and science concepts to concrete situations. One problem required them to estimate the number of kernels of corn in a jar using a measuring cup and a scale. They were evaluated both on the answer they gave and on the methodology they developed for their solution. These examples suggest that innovative approaches to assessment can be developed to replace the standard pencil-and-paper tests routinely given to millions of schoolchildren across the country.

"Standardized testing is a confrontation with a child—not a confirmation of what children already know," says Brenda Engel, associate professor of education at Lesley College Graduate School in Cambridge, Massachusetts. Engel is working with teachers in the Cambridge public school system to develop alternative reading and writing tests that capitalize on children's existing literacy skills. In one such assessment, a child chooses from a selection of stories, reads the chosen tale, and then retells it in his own words—an activity that many children already engage in during regular class time and at home. The whole session is tape-recorded and transcribed, and a teacher then reviews the printed narrative, paying attention to how well the child has understood the story. The tapes, kept from year to year, show the child's reading progress much more clearly than a collection of standardized test scores.

At the Eliot-Pearson School in Medford, Massachusetts, preschoolers are taking part in another assessment experiment called Project Spectrum. David Feldman, codirector of the project, says its purpose is to make use of more diverse ways of measuring children's interests and abilities in music, dance, the arts, and social awareness, as well as in more traditional verbal and conceptual areas.

To assess storytelling skills and the imaginative use of language, for example, Spectrum instructors provide students with a storyboard on which miniature figures of people, houses, and animals can be placed. Teachers ask children to make up stories, using these objects as props. To test a child's logical abilities, Spectrum staff have developed a dinosaur board game that requires kids to roll dice and try to move their game pieces away from the dinosaur's mouth. By observing a child adding dice values and calculating moves, teachers can determine whether he is talented in the use of numbers and whether he reasons well.

Videotape is another dynamic tool that educators are beginning to use to show a child's scholastic progress. At the Key School in Indianapolis, Indiana, teachers keep video portfolios for each child. Throughout the year, children's projects and performances are videotaped and used, along with traditional test scores, to keep track of their achievements. Principal Pat Bolaños notes that "many accomplishments cannot be described in words, and so the only way to capture them is to use videotape."

Teachers at the Prospect School in North Bennington, Vermont, have developed yet another way of monitoring a pupil's progress: Schoolwork is saved and becomes part of the Prospect Archive of Children's Work. Pat Carini, director of the archive, says that a child who has attended Prospect for five or more years will typically have over 1,000 items in her personal file, including writing samples, artwork, and photos of three-dimensional projects. At fourteen, when a student is about to graduate, the principal helps her look through her archive file and assess her learning progress with an eye to the next stage of schooling.

While such collections may impress parents, one objection schools often raise about these and other alternatives to standardized tests is that they are cumbersome and time-consuming to evaluate. Yet it appears clear from the evidence that a little effort in record-keeping among teachers goes a long way toward profiling a child's learning performance. Teachers at the Prospect School write a mere four or five lines per week about each child's interests, accomplishments, and learning patterns. By the end of a child's five-year stay at Prospect, his file has accumulated about seventy-five single-spaced pages of text. This wealth of information contrasts sharply with the academic records of most children nationwide, which are heavy on test

Many of the important skills that children need to acquire in early childhood—self-esteem, social competence, desire to learn, self-discipline—are not easily measured by standardized tests. As a result, social, emotional, moral, and physical development and learning are virtually ignored or given minor importance in schools with mandated testing programs.

NATIONAL ASSOCIATION FOR THE EDUCATION OF YOUNG CHILDREN

Knowledge must come through action; you can have no test which is not fanciful; save by trial.

SOPHOCLES

Be patient . . . with the type of mind that cuts a poor figure in examinations. It may, in the long examination which life sets us, come out in the end in better shape than the glib and ready reproducer, its passions being deeper, its purposes more worthy, its combining power less commonplace, and its total mental output consequently more important.

WILLIAM JAMES

scores and light on concrete information about the child's actual experiences in school.

Despite the viability of these alternatives, though, standardized tests are likely to be a fixture in most schools for the foreseeable future. It is easier and more cost-efficient for educators to run a set of answer sheets through a computer than to sit down and truly assess the total learning performance of a child in the classroom. It is easier for many parents to understand their children's progress in school through scores or percentiles than by taking the time to discover what's really going on in the classroom. And it is easier for school officials to deceive themselves into thinking they have created improved learning among students through higher test scores, when in reality all they may have done is to create better test-takers. Yet by exploring alternative methods of describing achievement, we are giving kids who look bad statistically a chance to show their accomplishments in other ways, and we are giving *all* children the opportunity to demonstrate their learning progress in ways that reflect the richness of their individual lives.

✷ WHAT PARENTS CAN DO ✷

Parents may have to demand alternatives to standardized testing before schools will significantly change their approach, according to Vito Perrone, director of teacher education at the Harvard School of Education. "The schools," he points out, "have argued for a long time that standardized testing exists because the parents want it. Parents should say that what they *really* want is more information about their children's growth as learners—not just a numerical score." Here are some suggestions for improving the evaluation process.

Inform yourself of the kinds of tests being used at your child's school. Don't wait until the scores come home before finding out what tests your child is taking. Talk with school personnel and get the name of each standardized test your child's class will take during the year, as well as the names of diagnostic tests that might be required as part of an individual evaluation. Ask the school to describe the purpose of each test and explain how the scores will affect your child's school career. Consult the *Mental Measurement Yearbook* at a local library. This book provides critical reviews of most standardized tests and serves as a consumer's guide to tests for concerned parents and educators. Some questions to ask about each test: What specific abilities, skills, or domains is the test responsible for evaluating? Does the test actually evaluate what it claims to assess? Do test results remain consistent over repeated administrations? What are the minimum and maximum age levels for each test? This information can help you determine whether the tests are being used appropriately with your child.

Encourage your child's school to use nonstandardized assessments as much as possible in evaluating educational progress. Find out whether the school is using the kinds of alternative evaluation methods described in this chapter. The best teachers rely on much more than standardized tests for their knowledge of a child's learning progress, including some of the following: checklists or inventories of skills mastered, graphs and charts of academic progress, student work samples, interviews with students, student-kept journals or activity records, student questionnaires, and teacher journals or diaries.

At a bare minimum, the school should be engaged in performance-based or criterion-referenced testing at least part of the time. In these tests, results are not tied to a statistical sample of scores but to a specific set of skills or competencies a child must master. For example, if your child takes a criterion-referenced math test, results could indicate that he does not know how to subtract two-digit numbers that involve borrowing but does know how to add two-digit numbers that require carrying. Because criterion-referenced tests describe a child's actual mastery or nonmastery of a subject, they are superior to most standardized tests that simply compare the child's scores to those of other children without providing directions for how to improve in a given area.

Emile Zola was a poor student at his school at Aix, and he was no better at the Ecole Normale in Paris. . . . In his final examination he scored zero for literature.

R.S. AND C.M.
ILLINGWORTH

More and more of the imaginative work in the evaluation field is tending to forms of evaluation that are much closer to art and to literary criticism, to ethnography, and to cinema vérité than the older, quantitative, statistically based models of the past.

ELLIOT EISNER

Keep records of your child's learning activities at home. What parents typically know about their children is worth a thousand standardized tests. Parents are constantly observing their kids under a variety of changing conditions and over a period of years. Testers, on the other hand, see kids in only one setting: the school. Many parents have photos of their children working with blocks, dancing, playing, and helping around the house, as well as samples of their children's artwork, science projects, and homework. Testers have a measly collection of percentiles, decimals, and bar graphs. Parents, in short, see the real child, while testing reveals only the statistical ghost of a child.

The following are some specific techniques you can use to document informal learning that goes on at home. Bring this information into parent-teacher conferences to supplement school data and use it at home to keep track of your child's daily learning experiences.

- *Observe your child.* Your child is constantly providing you with diagnostic information that can help you understand her better as a learner, from the way she brushes her teeth in the morning to the books she selects to read at bedtime. Keep your eyes open, be nonjudgmental, and pay attention to things that seem to be interesting, unusual, or exceptional. Share your observations with your child, with your spouse, or with education professionals who can help you gain a more objective picture of your child's learning profile.
- *Keep a personal diary of after-school and weekend learning experiences.* Even simple notes of your child's activities ("drew picture," "played football," "wrote poem") can help you see patterns in your child's learning style that may be useful in planning future events or providing resources at home or at school. Make sure to share your notes with your child so that he doesn't feel he is being spied on.
- *Tape-record your child reading from her favorite books.* Do this at the beginning, middle, and end of each school year so that you can listen to the progress she has made. Label

each tape with your child's name, the date of each reading, and the selections read. Periodically go over the tapes with your child, if she's willing, and talk with her about how she experiences her reading evolving over time. Nonreaders can tell a story in their own words instead of reading from a book.

• *Take photographs of paintings, sculptures, and other projects your child creates.* Have a camera on hand to get a quick shot of any interesting activity that may be gone in the next instant (a sandcastle, a card house, a Lego spaceship). Pictures might also show the gradual evolution of a project from the beginning stages to the final product. Assemble photos in an album to represent a learning portfolio of your child's skill in one or more areas, much as art students keep portfolios to document their visual skills.

• *Keep a scrapbook of poems, stories, drawings, awards, and other important documents.* This can also include exceptional homework assignments, news items, and anything else that reflects in some way upon your child as a learner. Such a scrapbook will prove valuable during a parent-child conference in putting emphasis upon your child's strengths, especially if the teacher tends to be accentuating negative behaviors, poor grades, or low test results. It also makes a superb morale booster when your child is feeling anxious or depressed about school and learning.

• *Videotape your child demonstrating special skills.* Buy, rent, or borrow a camcorder to document events that cannot be easily communicated through words or still pictures. You'll want to have a record of your child's winning catch at a football game, his stirring dance number in a community musical, or his demonstration of first aid at a local Cub Scout meeting. These videos speak volumes about a child's expertise in a particular area and are often helpful in showing teachers a side of your child that they rarely get to see inside the classroom.

• *Engage your child in the process of self-assessment.* Invite your child to take a major part in documenting her learning experiences by suggesting that she keep her own journal, diary, or scrapbook of personal accomplishments and activities. This can serve to bolster her self-esteem and may also help to develop her powers of self-reflection.

RESOURCES

Gould, Stephen Jay. *The Mismeasure of Man*. New York: W. W. Norton, 1981. Chronicles the rise of intelligence tests in this country and describes their role in legitimizing racist policies (including the exclusion of immigrants from the United States). An eye-opening and well-documented study.

Mental Measurements Yearbook. Lincoln, NE: Buros Institute of Mental Measurements, University of Nebraska (135 Bancroft Hall, Lincoln, NB 68588-0348). A consumer's guide to standardized tests, now in its tenth edition. Includes reviews of recently released or updated tests from preschool to adult. See also their *Tests in Print*. Both resources are available in the reference sections of many public and university libraries.

Owen, David. *None of the Above: Behind the Myth of Scholastic Aptitude*. Boston: Houghton Mifflin Co., 1985. Focuses on the Scholastic Aptitude Test (SAT), a college admissions exam, but Owen's points about the difficulty of constructing a valid test will be of interest to parents of younger students as well.

Strenio, Andrew J., Jr. *The Testing Trap*. New York: Rawson, Wade Publishing Inc., 1981. Explores the limitations of standardized tests, describes how they pervade our lives, and examines what we can do to cope with them.

Organizations

Friends of Education, 600 Girard Blvd. NE, Albuquerque, NM 87106. Monitors test publishers and administrators. Distributes research findings, including "How Public Educators Cheat on Standardized Achievement Tests." Directed by John J. Cannell, a physician who coined the term *Lake Wobegon effect*.

National Center for Fair and Open Testing (FairTest), P.O. Box 1272, Harvard Square Station, Cambridge, MA 02238; (617) 864-4810. Works to eliminate bias in the testing industry. Publishes quarterly newsletter and other publications, including "Fallout from the Testing Explosion: How 100 Million Standardized Exams Undermine Equity and Excellence in America's Public Schools."

North Dakota Study Group on Evaluation, Center for Teaching and Learning, University of North Dakota, Box 8158, University Station, Grand Forks, ND 58202. Publishes several monographs on alternatives to standardized testing at the elementary school level, including "Informal Evaluation," "A Handbook on Documentation," and "The School Lives of Seven Children: A Five Year Study."

Prospect Archives and Center for Educational Research, North Bennington, VT 05257; (802) 442-8333. Includes one of the largest collections of children's schoolwork (writings, drawings, paintings, photos of three-dimensional work) in the world: an estimated quarter of a million items. Provides researchers with access to collection and conducts workshops and conferences for educators.

14. *School Labels—How They Can Hurt the Learning Process*

It can begin with a simple phone call: The school principal informs you that your child has learning difficulties and needs to take a series of educational and psychological tests. After the testing and several weeks of paperwork, an evaluation takes place, and finally one day you receive the results. Your child is no longer considered "normal," but now has a special classification. The label may be any of a number of currently fashionable terms: learning disabled (LD), attention deficit hyperactivity disorder (ADHD), educationally handicapped (EH), or even mildly retarded. Regardless of the term, there's no turning back from this new discovery. The label takes on a life of its own, and your child's world may never be the same again.

Currently there are almost 2 million public school children described as learning disabled, another million described as mentally retarded or emotionally disturbed, and over three-quarters of a million children taking medication for so-called attention deficit disorders. Millions of other children are informally labeled as problem learners or low achievers by parents, relatives, and school personnel.

Treat people as if they were what they ought to be and you help them to become what they're capable of being.

GOETHE

Such labels have devastating consequences on a child's life. They can secretly undermine a child's sense of self-worth and sabotage the unfolding of his natural genius. This chapter will explore the effects of these negative school labels. It will explain what you can do as a parent to avoid school labels or minimize their impact and show you how to get your learning-frustrated child the help he needs without stigmatizing him.

WHERE SCHOOL LABELS COME FROM AND WHY WE USE THEM

Educational labels have been around for a long time. As far back as 4,000 years ago, Sumerian scholars were describing each other as lazy and careless in their writing and computing skills. But only in the past hundred years or so has science given specialized names to identify an individual's learning problems. It's ironic, in fact, that many of the diagnostic terms used by physicians in the early part of this century to label children and adults have now passed into common usage as insults, including *imbecile*, *idiot*, and *moron*. Many other terms have gone in and out of fashion during this time describing a whole range of so-called learning diseases: *congenital word blindness* (1900), *strephosymbolia* (1930s), *Strauss syndrome* (1950s), and *minimal brain damage* (1960s).

More recently, parents have had to contend with two major educational diseases—learning disabilities and attention deficit hyperactivity disorder. These will be described in more detail later in this chapter. However, regardless of the specific school label, it is important to recognize that many labels are reflections of the culture in which they are used. Attention deficit hyperactivity disorder, for example, has become popular in recent years because of the emergence of cognitive psychology as a major field of study in our society, and because the study of attention is a central area of interest among cognitive psychologists. As psychology moves into other areas of study in the coming decades, we're likely to see a whole new brand of school labels invented and applied to children's lives.

You dolt, numbskull, school pest, you Sumerian ignoramus, your hand is terrible; it cannot even hold the stylus properly; it is unfit for writing and cannot even take dictation. Yet you say you are a scribe like me. . . . You are the laziest of scribes, the most careless of men. When you do multiplication, it is full of mistakes. In computing areas you confuse length with width. Squares, triangles, circles and sectors—you treat them all without understanding.

FOUR-THOUSAND-
YEAR-OLD SUMERIAN
TABLET

One major reason labeling of students is currently so popular is that parents often welcome it: It provides a deceptively clear definition of what's wrong with their child ("Oh, so *that's* why Mary can't read—she's LD."). This can bring a sense of relief to parents who may have blamed themselves for their child's failures. Schools, on the other hand, label children for more pragmatic reasons. The funds they receive are allocated by categories—for children meeting specific educational requirements—and labeling offers an efficient way of placing kids into the special programs that take advantage of those monies. To this extent, school labels are as much an economic and administrative convenience as they are descriptions of conditions existing within the child.

THE NEGATIVE EFFECTS OF LABELING

In spite of the clarity and convenience that labels provide, educational researchers have warned parents and teachers for years that labeling may carry with it a hefty price tag. Ever since the famous "Pygmalion in the classroom" experiments conducted by Robert Rosenthal at Harvard University in the late 1960s, psychologists have suspected that labels, and the expectations teachers and parents attach to them, are likely to be self-fulfilling. In those experiments, teachers were told that certain children would perform exceptionally well during the academic year, whereas in fact the kids had been randomly selected. When the children who had been predicted to perform well showed the greatest gains at year's end, researchers concluded it was the teachers' expectations for those children that fostered their academic success.

Other research has shown that teachers wait longer for an answer from a student they believe to be a high achiever than from a student they think is a lower achiever. In addition, some studies have suggested that teachers are more likely to give perceived high-achieving students a second chance to respond after an initial incorrect answer and are more likely to praise

One must remember that practically all of us have a significant number of special learning disabilities. For example, I am grossly unmusical and cannot carry a tune. We happen to live in a society in which the child who has trouble learning to read is in difficulty. Yet we have all seen dyslexic children who have either superior visual-perception or visual-motor skills. My suspicion would be that in an illiterate society such a child would be in little difficulty and might in fact do better because of his superior visual-perception talents, while many of us who function well here might do poorly in a society in which a quite different array of talents was needed in order to be successful. . . . As the demands of society change will we acquire a new group of "minimally brain damaged?"

NORMAN GESCHWIND

Honoré de Balzac was given up by his teachers as a failure, and abandoned to his dreams. One of them said: "This fat, little fellow goes around in a state of intellectual coma."

R. S. AND C. M.
ILLINGWORTH

It is among the commonplaces of education that we often first cut off the living root and then try to replace its natural functions by artificial means. Thus we suppress the child's curiosity . . . and then when he lacks a natural interest in learning he is offered special coaching for his scholastic difficulties.

ALICE MILLER

Woodrow [Wilson] did not learn his letters until he was nine or learn to read until he was eleven. There are letters from relatives who thought it odd that young Woodrow was so dull . . . and expressed sorrow for the parents.

LLOYD THOMPSON

these kids for their successes, while they are more inclined to be critical of students perceived as low achievers. In one experiment, two groups of teachers were shown a videotape of a fourth-grade boy engaged in various activities. Prior to viewing the tape, one group was informed that the boy was learning disabled, and the other group was told that he was a normal learner. After the presentation, the two groups filled out referral forms for the child based on what they had observed. The teachers who thought they were observing a learning disabled student rated the boy more negatively than did the group that was told he was normal.

In addition to the psychological damage inflicted by school labels, some educators have suggested that these labels have serious administrative consequences for many children. "I'm worried about what happens to a child after he gets labeled," says Margaret Dawson, a school psychologist in Exeter, New Hampshire, and president of the National Association of School Psychologists (NASP). "Once he has been labeled, the child is removed from the regular classroom for part of the school day to attend special programs, which causes the regular class teacher to see the child as no longer being her responsibility, even when he's back in her classroom part-time." Kids placed in special education classes often fall further behind their peers in the regular classroom, making it even more difficult for them to find their way back into the mainstream of school success.

LEARNING DISABILITIES:
THE MOST POPULAR SCHOOL LABEL

Twenty-five years ago the term *learning disabilities* represented an obscure concept in an educational psychology textbook. Today it is a household term. It has been the subject of novels, radio commercials, television specials, and full-length feature movies. In the thousands of books and magazine articles that have appeared over this period of time, parents have been alerted to some of the warning signs of this supposedly neurologically based condition, including reversal of letters and numbers, poor handwriting, awkwardness, difficulty reading, and scores of other symptoms. Along with the popularity of the concept, the number of kids identified as learning disabled has skyrocketed, up by more than a million students in the past decade.

However, despite the major attention the media have given to this popular learning disease, experts are still debating whether this term should be used at all to describe the learning difficulties of millions of American schoolchildren. Gerald Coles, associate professor of clinical psychiatry at Robert Wood Johnson Medical School, examined many of the theories and tests used to label children LD. In his book *The Learning Mystique: A Critical Look at "Learning Disabilities,"* Coles found most of these concepts and tools seriously lacking in validity: "The crux of my argument is that the very existence of this 'condition' has been virtually unproven, with only the shakiest of evidence reported. . . . After decades of research, it has still not been demonstrated that disabling neurological dysfunctions exist in more than a minuscule number of these children." Coles suggests that so-called learning disabilities are more a product of poor teaching, family psychological problems, and basic inequities in our social system than a result of some brain disorder.

My own experience as a learning disability specialist for five years in the United States and Canada taught me that this label is useless in helping children learn. It puts the emphasis on what these kids *can't* do at a time when they need to be around people who see the *best* within them. A growing body of research suggests that many kids who have been labeled learning disabled are actually superior to so-called normal children in certain types of nonverbal creative behavior, in three-dimensional visualization (the kind of ability that a good architect or mechanical engineer possesses), and in a host of other skills, talents, and abilities. While it's true that so-called LD children have difficulty with traditional school subjects, it appears that these kids are most gifted in precisely those abilities and skills that our schools place least emphasis on, including music, art, dance, drama, graphic design, mechanical repair, and other creative and hands-on pursuits. In short, a handicapping label such as *learning disabilities* may make it less likely that a parent or teacher will see a child's inner strengths and thus it can destroy a child's opportunity to develop his natural genius.

Ludwig von Beethoven had never mastered the elements of arithmetic beyond addition and subtraction. A thirteen-year-old boy whom he had befriended tried unsuccessfully to teach him simple multiplication and division.

JAN EHRENWALD

The term "learning disability" has appeal because it implies a specific neurological condition for which no one can be held particularly responsible, and yet it escapes the stigma of mental retardation. There is no implication of neglect, emotional disturbance, or improper training or education, nor does it imply a lack of motivation on the part of the child. For these cosmetic reasons, it is a rather nice term to have around.

U.S. GOVERNMENT STUDY
ON THE LABELING OF
CHILDREN

The horrifying truth is that in the four years I have been editor of the Learning Disability Quarterly, *only one article has been submitted that sought to elaborate on the talents of the learning disabled. . . . Why do we not know if our students are talented in art, music, dance, athletics, mechanical repair, computer programming, or are creative in other nontraditional ways? It is not for lack of assessment instruments. It is because, like regular educators, we care only about competence in its most traditional and bookish sense—reading, writing, spelling, science, social studies, and math in basal texts and worksheets.*

MARY POPLIN

THE LATEST LABEL:
ATTENTION DEFICIT HYPERACTIVITY DISORDER

The newest learning disease on the educational scene is something called attention deficit hyperactivity disorder (ADHD). Characterized by a wide range of symptoms, including fidgeting, distractibility, impulsivity, inattentiveness, and impatience, ADHD is said to affect around 5 percent of the school population. Yet experts are sharply divided over the legitimacy of this new label. While the American Psychiatric Association has included ADHD in its newly revised *Diagnostic and Statistical Manual of Mental Disorders*, some researchers are not sure that hyperactivity and attention deficits in children should be considered abnormal behavior. Diane McGuinness, professor of psychology at the University of South Florida and author of *When Children Don't Learn*, says that many of the behaviors attributed to attention disorders are actually the normal behaviors of highly active boys (the disorder is said to strike up to nine times as many males as females). Citing studies suggesting that young boys like to change activities frequently in the classroom, she also points to research showing that when so-called hyperactive children are allowed to regulate their own activities (something seldom allowed in many classrooms), they perform normally. Thus, attention deficit hyperactivity disorder in many cases may be more a function of the environment and the expectations that adults have for children's behavior, than a result of some intrinsic biological problem.

Because ADHD is seen primarily as a biological problem, however, medication has become the leading method of treating it. The most widely used medication for ADHD is methylphenidate hydrochloride (Ritalin), a stimulant drug that paradoxically calms down many children and adults. An estimated 800,000 children currently take Ritalin and other stimulant drugs (including Dexedrine and Cylert) to control their hyperactive behaviors. However, there is growing concern that doctors may be too eager to prescribe medication for these youngsters and may not be trying nondrug strategies such as modifying the classroom and home environments to accommodate these children's more active attentional and behavioral styles.

"We throw pills at everything for a quick fix," says Maryland psychologist Paul Lavin. "A lot of the parents I see are not aware of alternatives. They receive Ritalin from their doctors as the treatment of choice." Lavin's objections to the use of medication in treating hyperactive behavior stems in part from concerns about its potential side effects. Drugs such as Ritalin can produce a number of unpleasant symptoms, such as loss of appetite, abdominal pain, weight loss, insomnia, drowsiness, and tachycardia (rapid heartbeat), and have even been known to slow down a child's growth or trigger psychosis or Tourette's syndrome, a rare psychological disorder. There are also concerns that the use of medication may cause children to depend on the drug, rather than their own inner resources, for their sense of mastery. One study found that hyperactive children often disavowed responsibility for their behavior and claimed they needed a "good pill" to keep them under control.

◆　◆　◆　◆

Getting Your Child Out of a Negative Behavior-Learning Spiral Without Drugs

If you are the parent of a child who is receiving stimulant medication for hyperactivity, or have a child who has been diagnosed with ADHD, or are simply thinking of medication as a possible way to control your overactive child, here is a rundown of some of the major nondrug approaches that you ought to consider first. Many of these approaches are also appropriate for children who have been labeled learning disabled, educationally handicapped, emotionally disturbed, or who have been given other negative school labels.

Cognitive Therapy. Research suggests that children labeled LD and ADHD tend to attribute their failures to factors beyond their control ("I'm stupid," "I've got a mean teacher"). Cognitive therapy helps kids learn to change the way they think about themselves, teaching them sound strategies for learning and behaving. For example, children might be taught to rehearse out loud the steps they will go through to clean up their room. Or

The minister, of course, taught by rote, a method from which Alva [Thomas Edison] was inclined to disassociate himself. He alternated between letting his mind travel to distant places and putting his body in perpetual motion in his seat. The Reverend Eagle, finding him inattentive and unruly, swished his cane. Alva, afraid and out of place, held up a few weeks, then ran away from the school.

ROBERT CONOT

You care for nothing but shooting, dogs, and rat-catching. You will be a disgrace to yourself and all your family.

CHARLES DARWIN'S FATHER

they might be shown how to talk to themselves silently when they make a mistake ("It's not that I'm dumb, it's just that I forgot to carry the five on that math problem"). Most importantly, they are helped to see that their own personal efforts, and not some external factor, contribute the most to their failures and successes in life. Some clinical psychologists and psychotherapists provide training for parents in using cognitive therapy approaches with kids as part of their regular patient care. Teachers are increasingly using cognitive strategies in their work with children's special needs.

Psychotherapy. In some cases, a child's hyperactive behavior or learning failure may stem from emotional stress due to turmoil in the family, problems with peers, or internal conflicts. In these cases some form of psychotherapy, whether individual, group, or family, may be appropriate. In one long-term study conducted by James Satterfield, a psychiatrist and director of the Center for Hyperactive Children in Encino, California, rates of institutionalization and arrests among adults who had been treated for hyperactivity in childhood were 50 percent lower when these individuals had received psychotherapy as part of their treatment plan. If you choose this approach, make sure that you seek the services of a *state-licensed* psychotherapist (psychiatrist, psychologist, clinical social worker, or family counselor) with specific expertise in working with hyperactive children or learning difficulties.

Focusing Techniques. Children who are having trouble attending to work in school may benefit from any of a number of centering activities designed to help them concentrate. Studies suggest, for example, that the use of simple meditation and relaxation techniques, such as having a child focus on his breath or progressively relax the muscles of his body, may help decrease distractibility and improve academic achievement. Other approaches that have met with success include biofeedback, guided imagery, and the use of background music in learning (see the Resources section at the end of Chapter 16 for a list of organizations that use these approaches in education).

Diet. The impact of diet on learning and hyperactive behavior has been subject to conflicting interpretations. The most controversial approach is the Feingold diet, based on the work of the late California pediatrician Benjamin Feingold. In this regimen, artificial preservatives, colorings, and flavors are seen as the hidden culprits in stimulating hyperactive behavior. These and other offending substances are systematically removed from the child's diet.

While several controlled studies suggest that the influence of diet is without merit, a panel of thirteen experts assembled by the National Institute of Allergy and Infectious Diseases and the National Institute of Child Health and Human Development said that the behaviors of some hyperactive children improved when the kids were placed on a Feingold diet. They did suggest, however, that it was hard to predict which children would specifically benefit.

Similarly, methods that control for sugar intake and food allergies (such as sensitivities to milk, chocolate, and wheat) remain controversial as treatment methods, although a recent study did indicate that children tended to be less hyperactive when they ate a high-protein breakfast. Parents willing to put in the time and energy that such a dietary change involves may find that the positive attention their child receives in such a program, if nothing else, may help to remove unwanted behaviors and improve learning.

Educational Modifications. Many hyperactive children require medication only when they are in school. This suggests that their problem is situational: They may be responding to a specific classroom environment rather than suffering from a general disorder. When this is the case, good results can often be produced by changing the classroom environment in some way. Positive approaches include developing a more motivating curriculum to engage the child's personal interests and abilities, creating consistent classroom routines, providing one-to-one supervision as much as possible, offering a good physical education program, and establishing more flexible classroom expectations.

In one study, children labeled hyperactive were indistinguishable from so-called normal children in an open-classroom environment that allowed a greater range of activities and behaviors. Many kids labeled hyperactive and learning disabled are spatial and kinesthetic learners. They require innovative educational approaches that make use of art, music, movement, and hands-on opportunities for learning (building models, doing laboratory experiments, creating relief maps, using math manipulatives, and so forth).

Meet with your child's teacher and school officials and make sure the curriculum he is receiving is the best available for his specific needs. If it is not, then look for another educational setting for your child that allows him the opportunity to develop his natural genius. Options include placing him in another class in the school or in another school district where the teacher is more flexible, finding an appropriate private school, teaching him at home, or using existing special education laws to bring in a specialist to work one-to-one with your child in the regular classroom.

◆　◆　◆　◆

TRACKING: HOW SCHOOLS INFORMALLY LABEL CHILDREN

Ability grouping represents a broader institutional approach that schools have developed over the years to sort and label kids based upon learning potential. As early as kindergarten, children are placed in reading and math groups according to ability level. Teachers often give these groups euphemistic names like Bluebirds and Sparrows in the belief that children will develop a sense of group solidarity. Yet kids seem to have little trouble figuring out the pecking order in these academic aviaries. Ability groups in elementary school pave the way for a full-blown tracking system in junior and senior high school where each academic course has as many as four different versions. A literature course, for example, may have a basic (or local) track for the remedial students, an average track for the middle-of-the-road students, an accelerated track for the promising students, and an honors or advanced-placement track for the real stars of the school.

Proponents claim that tracking allows students of different ability levels to progress at their own rate without hampering the pace of others. In a heterogeneous (or multiple ability) classroom, according to this line of thinking, the "quicker" students are kept back by the "slower" students, and the "low achievers" are frustrated trying to keep up with the "talented" ones. By creating ability classes, teachers can prepare lessons directed to a specific academic level and therefore can efficiently teach students as a unified group rather than trying to reach every academic level.

The reality, however, is that many students end up being railroaded into failure under this system. Jeannie Oakes, a social scientist with the RAND Corporation in Santa Monica, California, suggests that the tracking system is particularly harmful to those students who end up in remedial programs with the *low achiever* label. Oakes's study of several thousand junior and senior high school students in ability groups around the country reveals several startling conclusions.

According to her research, students in remedial classes spend much of their time learning lower-order academic skills such as rote computation and grammar through commercially produced kits and workbooks. Students in the higher tracks, on the other hand, tend to be exposed to more complex (and more interesting) subjects in math and English, including probability theory and critical thinking skills. Teachers in lower track classrooms have lower expectations for success, tend to be less enthusiastic, and are more likely to ridicule students than teachers in higher track programs. In short, students in the lower tracks are more likely to receive the *worst* that the schools have to offer while kids in the advanced courses get the best.

The greatest problem with *any* school label, official or unofficial, is that the term will begin to take on an existence of its own and overshadow the actual needs of the child. If your child has been placed into a category such as learning disabled, attention deficit hyperactivity disorder, or remedial track, you'll need to talk with school officials and find out what these labels actually mean in terms of your child's school performance. More importantly, however, you'll need to fight to make sure that your child is seen first and foremost as a *person* and not as a label. By going beyond the limitations of the school label and encouraging teachers to see the best in your child, you can help your child realize his full potential in life.

Alpha children wear grey. They work harder than we do, because they're so frightfully clever. I'm really awfully glad I'm a Beta, because I don't work so hard. And then we are much better than the Gammas and Deltas.

ALDOUS HUXLEY'S
BRAVE NEW WORLD

★ WHAT PARENTS CAN DO ★

Since research suggests that labeling can be harmful to a child's educational health, parents should think twice before giving in to teacher and administrator recommendations that their children be placed in special classes and remedial programs. Here are some basic guidelines to follow.

Know your rights. If school officials inform you that your child needs to be tested for special learning or behavior problems, it is important for you to realize that you have several rights as a parent that are protected by federal law.

1. You have the right to be fully informed of the reasons for the evaluation, to contest it if necessary, and to have the results explained to you in nontechnical, straightforward language.

2. You have the right to have an independent evaluation of your child, paid for at public expense, if you disagree with the school's results.

3. You have the right to inspect your child's school records and contest any information in them that appears to be unwarranted or to include supplementary data that are more accurate.

4. You have the right to attend school meetings where your child's school placement is being decided on and to challenge any decisions you disagree with.

These rights apply only for decisions concerning placement in special education. Appeal procedures for tracking decisions are less clear-cut and may vary from district to district. The National Committee for Citizens in Education operates a toll-free hotline where you can receive more information about your rights as a parent: (800) 638-9675.

See that your child is in a normal classroom environment as much as possible. Programs that segregate a child from her peers and place her in part-time programs, special classes, or "dumb" tracks may cause her to lose out educationally and could lead to low self-esteem. The Office of Special Education and Rehabilitative Services in the U.S. Department of Education has strongly recommended that children placed in special learning disabilities classrooms be returned to the regular classroom and taught alongside their normally achieving peers. It has established several pilot projects around the country to achieve this objective. Check to see if your school district has programs like these where learning specialists come into the regular classroom to work with kids' special needs. Also, encourage your child's school to establish heterogeneous classrooms where kids of different ability levels can learn from each other.

Insure that your child receives an education based on his real learning needs and not on his label. Many children are placed in special classes that feed them prefabricated curriculum designed for the "learning disabled child" or the "remedial learner." As noted above, these programs are often less challenging and less interesting than the materials used in regular and gifted classes. Parents should demand that their learning-frustrated kids receive programs that motivate and excite them—otherwise, all the remedial workbooks in the world won't make a difference in their lives. The best educational approaches for children who have negative school labels are those that are successful with *all* children. These programs typically recognize individual learning styles, provide hands-on experiences, honor the value of cooperative learning, and encourage the development of responsibility and self-esteem. Meet with teachers and administrators to discuss a specific plan for getting your child out of the failure spiral through methods that honor and cultivate his own uniqueness and special strengths.

RESOURCES

Anderson, Winnifred, Stephen Chitwood, and Deidre Hayden. *Negotiating the Special Education Maze.* Englewood Cliffs, NJ: Prentice Hall, 1982. Practical guide for parents and teachers in becoming an effective advocate for a child who has special needs in the public schools.

Budd, Linda. *Living with the Active Alert Child: Groundbreaking Strategies for Parents.* New York: Prentice Hall, 1990. This book provides hundreds of practical ideas for coping with high-energy children (not specifically focused on ADHD).

Coles, Gerald. *The Learning Mystique: A Critical Look at "Learning Disabilities."* New York: Ballantine, 1989. A well-documented assault on many of the assumptions that have guided thinking about learning disabilities over the past twenty years.

Granger, Lori and Bill. *The Magic Feather: The Truth About "Special Education."* New York: Dutton, 1986. *Chicago Tribune* columnist Bill Granger and teacher/writer Lori Granger write passionately about the mislabeling of their six-year-old son, Alex.

Lavin, Paul. *Parenting the Overactive Child: Alternatives to Drug Therapy.* Lanham, MD: Madison Books, 1989. Describes some of the drawbacks of medication for hyperactivity and offers nondrug solutions, including behavior modification, cognitive therapy, and diet control.

McGuinness, Diane. *When Children Don't Learn.* New York: Basic Books, 1985. Reviews research suggesting that the concepts of hyperactivity and attention deficit disorder lack empirical support and tend to pathologize the normal behaviors of children (especially boys). Somewhat technical reading but worth it.

Oakes, Jeannie. *Keeping Track: How Schools Structure Inequality.* New Haven, CT: Yale University Press, 1985. This book discusses the history of tracking in America. Using data from the monumental "A Study in Schooling" (see Chapter 3 of this book), it provides the best picture available of the drawbacks of ability grouping.

Organizations

National Association of School Psychologists, 8544 Colesville Road, Ste. 1000, Silver Spring, MD 20910; (301) 608-0500. Advocates delabeling of children with special needs. Write for their "Rights without Labels" guidelines and information about alternatives to labeling.

Office of Special Education and Rehabilitative Services, U.S. Department of Education, Washington, DC 20202. The office's proposed Regular Education Initiative (REI) seeks to educate children with learning problems in normal classroom environments. Write for their free pamphlet "Educating Students with Learning Problems: A Shared Responsibility."

• • • •

Part Five

Educational Systems That Work

15. *Montessori and Waldorf Education*

After listening to my complaints about the worksheet wasteland in many public schools, parents often ask me at conferences what I think of private schools. Of course, there are many different kinds of private schools encompassing a broad range of programs and philosophies, from parent-run cooperatives and homespun free schools to highly competitive college preparatory schools and large urban parochial institutions, so it's really hard to generalize. But I feel that, in general, the majority of private schools suffer from the same sorts of pedagogical ills as public education—lifeless textbooks, stressful curricula, and few meaningful attempts to teach children the skills needed in real life. Some private schools are even more narrowly focused on straightjacket learning than public institutions.

However, I hasten to add that there are many *individual* private schools doing wonderful things with children. For example, at the Mead School for Human Development in Greenwich, Connecticut, creative arts are integrated with basic skills and students study with professionals in the community who are experts in oceanographic research, glassblowing, animal husbandry, architecture, and other practical skills. At the Peninsula School

In the progressive school that I attended a great deal of time was spent in study and discussion of social issues and moral values. Great emphasis was placed on our learning to work with others—to use our individual talents in such a way that we could enrich each other's experiences. We felt that it was just as important to learn to appreciate and respect each other, to live sensitively and compassionately and to take responsibility for our own behavior as it was to learn the multiplication tables or to memorize the capitals of each state.

EDA LESHAN

in Palo Alto, California, students have a chance every day, beginning in kindergarten and continuing through high school, to work on individual and group projects that address their deepest interests and to talk collectively about their feelings related to the learning process. These are only two of perhaps hundreds of independently based private schools around the country that are truly child-centered and empower students to take responsibility for their own learning.

Beyond such specific schools that I could mention, two private school movements have been around for over seventy years, doing an exemplary job of honoring and respecting the child's natural growth as a learner: Montessori and Waldorf education. Each of these systems works with the child in a very different way. Montessori emphasizes the child working alone or in small groups, tends to focus on the practical side of learning, and enthusiastically prepares children for reading and math as early as three or four years of age. Waldorf education, on the other hand, usually involves whole-class activities, embraces creativity and imagination as well as practical skills in learning, and avoids teaching the three Rs until children are six or seven.

Despite their differences, each of these systems embodies a similar philosophy that views the child as a natural genius deserving of deep respect from parents and teachers. It is because of their authentic child-centered perspective that I recommend Waldorf and Montessori schools to parents seeking private school alternatives.

At the same time, it is important to understand that there are many different kinds of Waldorf and Montessori schools. Their quality can vary greatly since they are usually independently operated. As a result, parents should shop around to find the best educational environment for their children. This chapter will help acquaint you with each system and provide you with guidelines for choosing a good private school based on one of these philosophies.

MONTESSORI: THE QUIET REVOLUTION

Seventy-five years ago, Montessori education was all the rage in the United States. Then it dropped out of sight in this country for fifty years, only to reemerge with renewed vigor in the 1960s. Montessori schools now seem to have found a solid place among quality daycare alternatives. Yet Montessori is more than simply daycare. It represents a way of looking at children according to their own unique learning and developmental needs. While 75 percent of the children in the estimated 4,000 Montessori schools in this country are preschoolers, the number of Montessori elementary schools is growing and there are even a few high schools. In addition, while this system has been considered to be a private school movement, more programs are being funded by public school districts. Over 100 public schools now offer Montessori programs, in cities such as Denver, Cincinnati, St. Louis, Indianapolis, and Houston.

Such popularity had very quiet beginnings. Maria Montessori liked to tell the story of how in Italy in the early part of this century, when she was just beginning to develop the teaching approach that would bear her name, she brought a four-month-old baby girl into her school to show to the three- to six-year-old students. Montessori, a physician-turned-educator, light-heartedly challenged the children to be as quiet as the infant. In just a few moments, the room became so hushed that everyone could hear the ticking of the clock and the chirping of a bird outside. The incident gave rise to what later became known as the silence game—a period of quiet listening that is still practiced in thousands of Montessori schools around the world.

Anyone who visits a Montessori school today is likely to be impressed by the quiet intensity that permeates its classrooms, even when the silence game is not being played. Children work individually and in small groups at a wide range of tasks specially designed by Montessori to develop specific skills. The teachers don't teach in the formal sense: They show the children how to use the hands-on Montessori learning materials correctly and how to follow the simple rules for courteous classroom behavior. Beyond this, children are largely on their own to work on the word puzzles, math manipulatives, science materials, and sensorimotor experiences that are so much a part of the Montessori school day.

Maria Montessori had a deep respect for the integrity of the child; she believed that children could be entrusted to choose their own materials to teach themselves and that they should

Children are innately honest, and they expect you to be the same way. It is one great thing about childhood. They are open and honest, and if allowed to experience freedom will remain this way all their lives without the shutting up of their feelings toward others.

A. S. NEILL

No one could have foreseen that children had concealed within themselves a vital secret capable of lifting the veil that covered the human soul, that they carried within themselves something which, if discovered, would help adults to solve their own individual and social problems.

MARIA MONTESSORI

be allowed to stay with an activity for as long as they remained interested in it. Thus, it is not uncommon for one child to spend an entire morning using a spoon to transfer dried peas from one jar to another, while a second child might use the same segment of time in many different ways: to play a color-matching game, build a tower of blocks, trace geometric shapes, and work with simple measuring sticks designed to teach the concept of number.

Parents who feel that this laissez-faire approach is too permissive may be surprised to learn that Montessori education has been criticized during much of its eighty-year history for being too rigid to suit children's creative nature. These two contradictory views of the Montessori program only highlight what may be its ultimate achievement: combining freedom and structure in a truly integrated way. Children are free to do what they want within the framework of the materials, which are themselves highly structured, self-correcting teaching tools. Critics often complain that these materials are *too* structured and that children are not allowed to use them in flexible, imaginative ways. In some schools there seems to be little room for a child to make a monster or a spaceship out of colorful blocks designed to teach him how to count. There are also concerns that in Montessori schools children spend too much time working in isolation, thus depriving them of the opportunity to develop important social skills.

TAPPING THE SENSES

Despite these criticisms, the Montessori method remains influential even in mainstream culture. Many of the materials that Maria Montessori developed during the first two decades of this century have been adapted by the greater educational community, and variations on Montessori materials can be found in any store that sells toys or early-childhood learning equipment. These include sets of colored cards to match and organize, pieces of cloth with different textures to feel, sets of bells to ring and arrange according to the musical scale, colored blocks of various shapes and sizes, wooden counting beads, maps of various geographic areas in puzzle form, and miniature brooms, chairs, and kitchen utensils.

Montessori designed these learning tools to lead children gradually, through a series of structured steps, to higher levels of competence. She believed that interacting with simple sensory materials could guide students from the concrete world of objects to the abstract world of numbers and letters. Preschoolers who spend time touching and feeling the difference between smooth surfaces and rough surfaces, for example, then proceed to more advanced materials, such as the sandpaper letter-cards she developed to help children learn writing. Students learn the alphabet in a tactile way by tracing with their fingers along the coarse contours of each letter's shape. Older kids similarly learn the essentials of fractions by working with square and round inset puzzles divided into thirds, fourths, fifths, and even tenths.

Purely academic achievement, though, is not the ultimate aim of a Montessori school. Although Montessori herself discovered preschool children "exploding" into reading and writing as early as four because of the preparatory methods she had devised, she still emphasized that the adult must be led by the child, not vice versa. "Children will read and write when they are ready to do it," says Bretta Weiss, national director of the American Montessori Society, the largest organization of Montessori educators in the country. "What's most important in the Montessori philosophy is that children be allowed to develop all of themselves—not simply their thinking skills."

To this end, Montessori schools include a rich diet of art, gymnastics, music, science, history, and geography, and involve children in learning personal hygiene and a host of real-life activities. Preschoolers sweep the floors with child-size brooms, practice pouring a glass of water without spilling, and engage in lacing and buttoning work on specially constructed frames in preparation for shoe-tying and dressing skills. Older kids help with gardening, cooking, cleaning, and other school maintenance tasks.

Maria Montessori's method continues to evolve as educators strive to adapt her teachings to the needs of a changing society. Regardless of the form this approach takes in the future, however, Montessori has left a legacy for all time. The list of historical figures influenced by Maria Montessori reads like a

One beautiful December day . . . I went up on the roof [terrace] with the children. . . . I was sitting near a chimney, and said to a little five-year-old boy who sat beside me, "draw me a picture of this chimney." . . . He got down obediently and made a rough sketch of the chimney. . . . The child looked at me, smiled, remained for a moment as if on the point of bursting into some joyous act, and then cried out, "I can write! I can write!" and kneeling down again he wrote on the pavement the word mano *(hand). . . . His cries of joy brought the other children. . . . Two or three of them said to me, trembling with excitement, "Give me the chalk. I can write too." And indeed, they began to write various words.*

MARIA MONTESSORI

The child is like a soul in a dark dungeon striving to come out into the light, to be born, to grow, and which slowly but surely animates the sluggish flesh, calling to it with the voice of its will. And, all the while, there is standing by a gigantic being of enormous power waiting to pounce upon it and crush it.

MARIA MONTESSORI

text in contemporary culture: Alexander Graham Bell, Sigmund Freud, Mohandas K. Gandhi, Jean Piaget, and many others. Her insights on the importance of early learning and her awareness of individual differences, at one time considered radical ideas, are now taken for granted by the vast majority of educators. She started the quiet learning revolution of this century, and her approach to educating children has shaped much of our thinking today.

WALDORF: LESSONS IN WONDER

Walking into a Waldorf kindergarten classroom is a little like entering a fairy-tale wonderland. The walls radiate with peach-toned pastels applied artistically in swirls. The fireplace, skylights, and kitchen nook all have a storybook look about them. The teacher assembles the children by sweetly singing their names ("*Na*-than!"), then leads them in simple movement activities where they become, for the moment, giants, pixies, and gnomes. During playtime, the children create fantasy worlds from tree stumps, brightly colored scarves, and homemade dolls shaped to look like little elves, fierce dragons, and brave knights.

This is a Waldorf classroom, the setting for one of the most innovative approaches to childhood education in practice today. Created more than sixty years ago by Rudolf Steiner, an Austrian philosopher, the method was named (ironically) after the Waldorf-Astoria cigarette factory in Stuttgart, Germany, where in 1919 Dr. Steiner developed a school for the employees' children. Currently there are at least 500 Waldorf schools in twenty-seven countries throughout the world (including over 125 in the United States and Canada). Programs range from simple kindergartens to full-scale K-12 facilities.

The Waldorf movement is still small, yet its philosophy is in harmony with some of the latest ideas in education. For example, Waldorf teachers share prominent educators' increasing alarm at the tendency in many schools to push young children to learn reading and other abstract skills before they're ready. A recent report issued jointly by the National Association for the Education of Young Children and the National Association of Elementary School Principals urges preschools to reduce their heavy emphasis on academic learning. While beginning reading is taught at many conventional preschools, Waldorf kindergartners—even the early readers among them—leave their books at home. Reading is not introduced until the end of first grade. "By not teaching reading, but instead giving them puppetry, stories, poems, verses, singing games, movement, and gesture, we're building a strong inner reservoir that children can later draw upon when they do learn to read," says Ann Pratt, founder of Pine Hill Waldorf School in Wilton, New Hampshire, and coordinator of the Antioch-Waldorf teacher-training center there.

While early reading is not stressed, *cultural* literacy is a key concern throughout a Waldorf program—and here Waldorf educators are in accord with other experts in the field. Best sellers such as *The Closing of the American Mind* and *Cultural Literacy* have pointed to the lack of meaningful content in American school curricula and to students' seeming ignorance of history, literature, and other important components of the legacy of civilization. By contrast, Waldorf schools make the study of human culture their central focus. From kindergarten through high school, students learn (and often memorize) poems, stories, and historical and cultural information from all over the world. Worksheets and textbooks are tossed out in favor of learning about Greek and Babylonian myths, Aesop's fables, Shakespeare, the Renaissance, botany, Arthurian legends, Hindu epic poetry, and the discovery of the New World, among a wealth of other subjects. The guiding premise is summed up by M. C. Richards, author of *Towards Wholeness: Rudolf Steiner Education in America:* "Childhood is the time to store the memory with cultural riches, which later can be conceptualized and subjected to independent judgement and criticism."

The Waldorf approach to the basics is also in keeping with current theory that early learning should be multisensory, acquired not only through sound and sight but also through imagination, touch, movement, and feeling. All the senses are engaged to teach the three Rs. Color plays a major role, and children do most academic writing with brightly hued pencils

Who can account by ordinary methods for a Shakespeare, a Beethoven, or a Michelangelo and for all the wonder and renewal of culture such men bring into human life, so that history advances and never does in fact repeat itself? Yet even men of their stature were small children once—they did not know but had first to discover their faculties as they grew up. So it is in some degree with every human being. Every child is on a similar voyage of discovery; as a child, no matter what he may become later, he is in our responsible care, to help or hinder the latent genius of his being. Childhood is an awakening as well as a growing process: it leads from the "sleep" of infancy, through the "dream" of the childhood years, to the "waking to selfhood" of the adult.

FRANCIS EDMUNDS

and crayons. Art and movement activities are integrated with mathematics and reading. To learn the times tables, students march around the room clapping and counting out loud. They act out the week's reading in skits. Students also sculpt in beeswax, knit and crochet, paint with watercolors, and engage in many other highly sensory tasks.

EDUCATING HEAD, HEART, AND HAND

The structure of the classroom day in a typical Waldorf elementary school reflects Rudolf Steiner's threefold philosophy of educating the intellect (head), the emotional life (heart), and the will or physical nature (hand). The first part of the school day addresses the needs of the intellect through what is called the Main Lesson. This is a ninety-minute block of time devoted to a single subject, such as animal study, grammar, geography, or Norse myths. Students study a single topic for a period of three to five weeks before moving on to a new field of investigation. This is in contrast to most traditional public school classrooms where students are required to shift their attention from one subject to another every forty-five minutes all day long. In a Waldorf classroom, students listen to a spirited teacher presentation, engage in dialogue, and then write or draw in Main Lesson books that record their learning experiences in each subject.

During the second part of the day, students exercise the feeling or heart dimension of their lives through such activities as singing, dancing, drama, and playing the recorder or other musical instruments. Finally, the last portion of the classroom day is given over to the *hand*, and students engage in physical experiences such as woodworking, gardening, gymnastics, and games.

Teachers stay with the same students as they move from first to eighth grade. This gives them an opportunity to get to know students more deeply, and allows each student the chance to proceed at his own pace, since work not done by the end of the term can be taken up with the same teacher at the beginning of the new school year. As children move through the grades, they are introduced to subjects that parallel their own increasing levels of understanding. Thus, primary school stu-

Vague and general phrases—"the harmonious development of all the powers and talents in the child," and so forth—cannot provide the basis for a genuine art of education. Such an art of education can only be built upon a real knowledge of the human being.

RUDOLF STEINER

dents learn about culture through fairy tales, myths, and legends while older students are introduced to actual historical events and facts. The emphasis is upon learning subject matter in an integrated fashion. For example, children are often introduced to the letter *s* in first grade through the metaphor of a snake. The children might hear a story about a snake, put on a play about it, paint a picture of it, and mold a snake out of beeswax—and in the process they would see that a snake can assume the shape of an *s* and that it also makes a similar sound.

This integrated approach seems to pay off. Despite some parents' fears that Waldorf programs spend too much time teaching the arts, standardized test scores for academic achievement among Waldorf elementary and high school students compare favorably with the national average. In addition, a study conducted in Europe showed that Waldorf students score above average on verbal and nonverbal creativity tests.

Waldorf schools in the United States have doubled in number in the past decade, with supply falling behind demand. More than 100 Waldorf teaching positions nationwide remain unfilled due to a shortage of trained Waldorf teachers. It seems many parents are discovering that Waldorf education fills a need for a creative and artistic approach to learning that is hard to find elsewhere. In a society that may be nudging its children prematurely into adulthood, Waldorf schools try to preserve the magic and fairy-tale wonder of being a child.

The teacher must be a person of initiative in everything that he does, great and small. . . . The teacher must be one who never makes a compromise in his heart and mind with what is untrue. . . . The teacher must never get stale or grow sour.

RUDOLF STEINER

★ WHAT PARENTS CAN DO ★

Parents interested in Montessori or Waldorf education for their children should be aware that these names are not registered trademarks. Any program, regardless of its educational standards, can call itself a Montessori or Waldorf school. "The word *Montessori* doesn't guarantee a high-quality education," says Barbara Willer, director of information services at the National Association for the Education of Young Children in Washington, D.C. "It's more important to look at the nature of an individual program—its philosophy, materials, methods; the interactions between children; and the quality of its teachers." Here are

There is one type of feeling which is above all important to foster in childhood. Children have naturally an abundant faculty for wonder and reverence. . . . There are so many books, so many radio and television hours, so many encyclopedias and, alas, so many teachers whose aim is to impart knowledge quickly and easily without any element of that faculty which the Greeks said was the beginning of philosophy—Wonder. It is a strange thing that an age which has discovered so many marvels in the universe should be so conspicuously lacking in the sense of wonder.

A. C. HARWOOD

some guidelines to follow that can help ensure your child will receive a quality education with either of these approaches.

Visit one or more Montessori and/or Waldorf schools in your community. Check the yellow pages of your phone book or write the organizations mentioned at the end of this chapter for a list of schools in your area. Spend at least an hour at each school observing classroom activities. Ask yourself questions such as: Why is that child doing this task? What is the purpose of the materials being used? What is the role of the teacher? Do the children seem involved and interested? How does the teacher deal with discipline? If your child accompanies you (make sure she wants to and check to see that it's okay with the school), ask her what she thinks about the school and whether she'd like to attend.

Before you leave, share any concerns you have about the program with the teacher or other school personnel and ask for some literature about the school's philosophy—any good school should be able to provide it. Find out what national or international organization the school is affiliated with and whether the teachers were formally trained in Montessori or Waldorf techniques. The best schools should have most or all of their teachers certified by one of the major Montessori or Waldorf teacher training programs. Give yourself some time to think about the program before deciding whether to enroll your child (although you may want to put her name on a waiting list while you're making the decision).

Encourage your child's public school to integrate Montessori and/or Waldorf principles into the curriculum. This suggestion applies to parents who can't afford private schools and to those who live in areas where there are no Waldorf or Montessori schools. Find out if there are teachers within your child's present school who have been influenced by either Rudolf Steiner or Maria Montessori and who use their principles and materials at least part of the time in their curriculum. If so, see if you can get your child into one of these classrooms. On a larger scale, encourage your school district to transform a school or classroom into a magnet program based on one of these philosophies. As mentioned earlier in the chapter, several public school districts have created Montessori programs over the past few years, and the board of education in Milwaukee, Wisconsin, recently passed a resolution to open a Waldorf school within the Milwaukee public system. These efforts demonstrate that good public schools are often interested in providing parents with quality alternatives in educating their children and that such programs are therefore worth pursuing.

Use Waldorf and/or Montessori principles and methods with your child at home. Even if there are no Waldorf or Montessori programs of any kind in your area and school officials resist your pleas for change, you can still integrate one or both of these philosophies into your child's home life. Begin by reading material written by Montessori, Steiner, and their followers so that you gain a sense of their underlying faith in the learning processes of the child. Then, purchase special materials based on either of these methods to use in helping your child learn (a list of books and suppliers is included in the Resources section at the end of the chapter). General activities that help integrate Montessori into the home include showing your child how to use math manipulatives, buying child-sized kitchen utensils and cleaning equipment, and having plenty of sensory materials available for exploration, including things to touch, smell, taste, hear, and see. To integrate Waldorf education into the home, begin by encouraging storytelling of myths and legends, memorizing of favorite poems, engaging in crafts like knitting and weaving, and providing opportunities for free play with simple wooden toys. Since Montessori and Waldorf approaches are much more than their materials and activities, however, make sure to spend time thinking about the deeper message that each of these philosophies provides concerning the natural genius residing within the soul of every child.

My meeting with Rudolf Steiner led me to occupy myself with him from that time forth and to remain always aware of his significance. We both felt the same obligation to lead men once again to true inner culture.

ALBERT SCHWEITZER

The advent of the Waldorf schools was in my opinion the greatest contribution to world peace and understanding in the century.

WILLY BRANDT

RESOURCES

Hainstock, Elizabeth G. *Teaching Montessori in the Home: The Pre-School Years.* New York: New American Library/Plume, 1978. Provides instructions for making Montessori materials and using them in clearly described exercises for promoting sensory awareness, practical life tasks, and beginning reading, writing, and arithmetic skills. See also a companion volume, *Teaching Montessori in the Home: The School Years*, focusing on language and math activities.

Montessori, Maria. *The Secret of Childhood.* New York: Ballantine, 1973. One of Montessori's clearest expositions of her philosophy and method. See also her books *The Absorbent Child* and *The Discovery of the Child.*

Richards, M. C. *Toward Wholeness: Rudolf Steiner Education in America.* Middletown, CT: Wesleyan University Press, 1980. An excellent introduction to Waldorf education. Includes a directory of major Waldorf schools and teacher training programs around the country.

Steiner, Rudolf. *The Four Temperaments.* New York: Anthroposophic Press, Inc., 1971. Outlines Steiner's theory of four behavior styles (choleric, phlegmatic, sanguine, melancholic) and how they manifest in children's lives. Other books by Steiner on children and education include *The Kingdom of Childhood* and *Education as an Art.*

Organizations

American Montessori Society (AMS), 150 Fifth Ave., New York, NY 10011; (212) 924-3209. Professional association that certifies teachers in the Montessori method. This organization has tended to modernize Montessori's approach so that it is in line with contemporary American educational philosophy.

Association Montessori International—USA, P.O. Box 421390, San Francisco, CA 94102-1390; (415) 861-7113. Like the AMS, this is a professional association that trains and certifies Montessori teachers. Its philosophy has been considered to be the more traditional of the two major Montessori associations.

Association of Waldorf Schools of North America, 17 Hemlock Hill Rd., Great Barrington, MA 01230; (413) 528-3455. A loose affiliation of Waldorf schools. This association does not train teachers but provides information about different teacher training programs and Waldorf schools around the country.

Hearthsong, P.O. Box B, Sebastopol, CA 95472; (800) 325-2502. Mailorder supplier of Waldorf-oriented books, toys, art supplies, games, musical instruments, and other family resources. Free catalog.

Nienhuis-Montessori USA, 320 Pioneer Way, Mountain View, CA 94040; (415) 964-2735. Mail-order supplier of Montessori materials for use at home or school. Free catalog.

North American Montessori Teacher's Association, 2859 Scarborough Rd., Cleveland Heights, OH 44118; (216) 371-1566. Publishes directory of Montessori schools nationwide.

St. George Book Service, P.O. Box 225, Spring Valley, NY 10977. Books on Waldorf education available by mail, including *The Waldorf Parenting Handbook.*

16. *Super-Learning— Education for the Natural Mind*

Kids look forward to Wednesdays in Pamela Thornburg's fourth-grade classroom at John Gill Elementary School in Redwood City, California. That's the day they learn vocabulary skills through music and drama. Using Pachelbel's famous Baroque masterpiece Canon in D as a background, Pamela leads the class in a rhythmic reading of the day's lesson: "aqua–water–aqua," "derm–skin–derm," "geo–earth–geo." Students then close their eyes and relax while she repeats the material they've just recited, also in time to the music. Later in the day the children look up words that contain these Latin or Greek roots and put on little skits that might portray a *derm*atologist taking his *aqua*plane to a *geo*logy class.

These children are involved in an innovative educational approach frequently referred to as super-learning. Based upon the work of Bulgarian psychiatrist Georgi Lozanov, super-learning consists of a loose collection of techniques and educational principles designed to activate high levels of ability, motivation, and memory in learning. Originally developed in the 1960s in Eastern Europe, imported to the United States in the 1970s and popularized in the 1980s with the publication of the

The ultimate creative capacity of the brain may be, for all practical purposes, infinite.

GEORGE LEONARD

Although Dr. Lozanov was interested in human potentials generally, it was something that happened in his psychiatric practice that led him to concentrate increasingly on supermemory. People were consulting him who suffered from what he came to realize was apparently a common, but unnamed, disease. After dealing with numerous cases, Lozanov gave it a "proper" name: didactogeny, *illness caused by poor teaching methods.*

SHEILA OSTRANDER
AND LYNN SCHROEDER

book *Superlearning* by Sheila Ostrander and Lynn Schroeder, super-learning recognizes what psychologists have known for decades: that much of what we learn in our lives is a result, not of hard concentrated effort, but of relaxing and enjoyable experiences. "Most conventional teaching goes inside a student's brain and is lost in the hinterlands," says Charles Gritton, a junior high school teacher in Des Moines, Iowa, who has used super-learning techniques for the past fifteen years. "The knowledge is still there somewhere, but it's in a nonusable form. Super-learning teaches students how to process this information in a recallable, usable way."

HOW SUPER-LEARNING WORKS

The basis of super-learning is the development of a classroom environment that motivates children to get involved in academic learning without strain or stress. The teacher plays a central role in orchestrating class lessons that inspire students to learn in a relaxed and informal way. Through varying intonations of voice, the spirited use of gestures, and a highly positive demeanor, the teacher communicates an underlying message to students that learning is fun and easy. "If the teacher feels depressed, or thinks the students are stupid, or that the method won't work, students will realize it, and this will affect performance," observes Lozanov. A teacher who invokes enthusiasm and admiration from the class creates a positive classroom climate that allows all the other elements of the super-learning method to work more effectively.

Music represents one key component in this process. Lozanov discovered that certain forms of Baroque and classical music, particularly pieces that are slow and steady in tempo and rhythm, tend to be both physically relaxing and mentally stimulating. By playing this music as a background while the teacher rhythmically repeats the information to be learned—whether it be history facts, math formulas, vocabulary words, or a literature passage—Lozanov discovered that students can assimilate the material more quickly and remember it more effectively than if they had simply listened to the teacher without music.

Similarly, Lozanov found that students could acquire a great deal of information in a short period of time if they used that knowledge in the course of a simple role-play or skit, or by carrying on impromptu dialogues with each other about the subject to be learned. At the Guggenheim Elementary School in Chicago, which has used Lozanov's techniques for years, there is a super-learning lab where students regularly use role-play and drama as a way of mastering basic subjects. For a unit on science, teacher Nancy Ellis hands out signs for students to wear with famous scientists' names written on them, including Galileo, Kepler, Einstein, Madame Curie, and George Washington Carver. During the forty-five-minute class period, students take on the personalities of these historical figures. Nancy throws a ball to students in turn asking them to provide information about their lives as astronomers, physicists, and chemists. Later, they drop their scientist roles and put on a play about the growth of a seed to demonstrate certain principles of plant physiology. These techniques help students integrate knowledge directly into their lives through a lively and playful attitude toward learning.

Perhaps the most important feature of super-learning involves the use of verbal and nonverbal suggestion (the original name given to super-learning in Bulgaria actually translates into English as *suggestopedia*, meaning "learning by suggestion"). Lozanov observes, "We're all bombarded constantly from the day we're born, with limiting suggestions." Comments from parents such as "Peter's lazy," or "Our family's never been very good at math," as well as assumptions by educators that "learning requires great effort" and "only the talented student can truly succeed," secretly undermine the learning potential of millions of children, says Lozanov.

To replace this, the super-learning teacher focuses on sending positive, supportive messages to her class about learning. Pamela Thornburg has a "sunshine thought" at the front of the classroom that changes every week (for example, "Learning comes easily and naturally to me"). During her music super-learning sessions, she precedes the vocabulary lessons with affirming statements to her students that they will find the words easy and fun to learn.

The kids dislike the Baroque music at the beginning of the year, but after I play it in class for a few weeks, they like it and before the end of the school year, they're wanting to purchase recordings like this. Many kids come back saying "I need to take those tapes back to college with me."

CHARLES GRITTON

Suggestion is the most simplified and the most typical conditioned reflex in man.

I. P. PAVLOV

SUPER RESULTS

While some of the claims for super-learning have been extravagant and thus far unsupported—that it could achieve results as much as 50 times greater than that of a normal classroom, for example—research indicates that it often does promote greater gains in learning when compared to control groups receiving conventional instruction. One study that was generally critical of newer educational technologies, commissioned by the U.S. Army and conducted by the National Academy of Sciences, found evidence to warrant further investigation into the use of relaxation exercises and background music in learning. Other studies conducted at several American universities have shown that super-learning techniques have been successful in teaching math, science, foreign languages, and literature, useful in remedial reading classes, and helpful with special education populations. While it appears that super-learning techniques have been particularly successful in helping students master rote learning tasks such as foreign language vocabulary or math facts, studies suggest that the techniques may also promote more complex forms of learning, including creative writing, concept formation, and problem solving.

Super-learning seems to work because students absorb knowledge much as they did when they were infants: easily, naturally, and without being conscious of how much they are actually learning. "The human mind remembers a colossal quantity of information: the number of buttons on a suit, steps on a staircase, panes in a window, footsteps to the bus stop. These 'unknown perceptions' show us the subconscious has startling powers," says Lozanov. The role of the educator is to use this marvelous power of the mind in helping students activate the natural genius that lies within each of them.

UNBRAINWASHING STUDENTS

One major limitation of the super-learning approach may be its demands upon the teacher. "Not every teacher is going to be capable of doing this," notes Donald Schuster, professor of psychology at Iowa State University, "because it requires being able to project a charismatic personality so as to inspire the kids and make them want to learn." In addition, the method demands that teachers go beyond the typical textbook curriculum of most American schools in preparing their own creative learning methods and materials. To help train teachers to use super-learning techniques and principles, Schuster has co-founded the Society for Accelerative Learning and Teaching (S.A.L.T.), which offers teacher training workshops around the country and conducts conferences where educators can trade new ideas about the method.

Another concern that some parents and educators have about this approach is that it may be subtly coercive to children—brainwashing or hypnotizing them into learning whatever the teacher wants them to learn. However, according to its proponents, Lozanov's philosophy represents just the reverse. "We're so brainwashed already with our present educational system," says Charles Schmidt, a former student of Lozanov's and director of Learning in New Dimensions in San Francisco, "that our job is to unbrainwash you—to get you back to the enormous potential you have for learning." Junior high school teacher Charles Gritton is more blunt: "I'm paid to manipulate my kids in math—I'm trying to manipulate my students to become good mathematicians, to love math, to pursue it in itself—that's the role that a teacher has."

Super-learning is not so much a coherent philosophy of education as it is a collection of quality learning ideas and activities. In the final analysis, super-learning is not really all that new and revolutionary. Rather, it is the application of educational ideas and techniques that good teachers have always used in their instruction. Those who are familiar with recent movies on the teaching profession will recognize how super-learning techniques formed an integral part of these master teachers' instructional methods. For example, Jaime Escalante's poster at the back of the room in *Stand and Deliver* proclaimed, "Calculus cannot be made easy. It already is easy." And John Keating (portrayed by Robin Williams) played background classical music in *Dead Poets Society* while each student

If the human brain were so simple that we could understand it, we would be so simple that we couldn't.

RELATED BY
MICHAEL GRINDER

From many years of observation I have found that I have rarely met a stupid child, but I have met many stupid and debilitating, and yes, even brain-damaging systems of education. As we subsequently discovered, a child can learn math as a rhythmic dance and learn it well. . . . He can learn almost anything and pass the standard tests if he is dancing, tasting, touching, hearing, seeing, and feeling information. He can delight in doing so because he is using much more of his mind-brain-body system than conventional teaching generally permits. So much of the failure in school comes directly out of boredom, which itself comes directly out of the larger failure to stimulate all those areas in the child's brain which could give him so many more ways of responding to his world.

JEAN HOUSTON

read a quotation from English literature and simultaneously kicked a soccer ball.

Innovative teachers have always known that it usually takes something *super* or out of the ordinary to break down barriers that stand in the way of a child's natural learning potential. By taking a fresh look at the learning process through the super-learning method, parents and teachers can discover innovative ways of relating to what Lozanov called the "hidden reserves of the mind" in the child and thereby help unlock new potentials just below the surface of awareness waiting to be explored and used.

★ WHAT PARENTS CAN DO ★

Super-learning is essentially a way of helping children learn in ways that are most easy and natural for them. Unfortunately, some parents and teachers have gotten on the "better baby" bandwagon and are using these techniques to push children into learning academic material much too early in life and to pressure older children into mastering school subjects more quickly. Ivan Barzakov, an early student of Lozanov who went on to develop his own super-learning method called Optima-Learning, paraphrases Epictetus in saying: "No great thing is created suddenly any more than is a bunch of grapes or a fig. If you tell me that you desire a fig, I answer you that there must be time. Let it first bloom, then become fruit, then ripen." In the same way, parents should employ super-learning principles and techniques with sensitivity so that they are not used to accelerate a child into learning skills before he is ready for them. Honor your child's right to learn at his own pace, and regard superlearning not as a way to speed up the process but as a means to make it more enjoyable and relaxing. Here are some general guidelines.

Send positive messages to your child that affirm her ability to learn. We've already explored in a previous chapter the negative consequences on a child's self-esteem of school labels like *learning disabled* and *attention deficit disorder.* Perhaps even more devastating are the informal ways in which parents and other adults sabotage a child's natural genius with comments like "You'll never be the student your Uncle Albert was," or "Why don't you use your brains—if you have any!" Steer clear of statements that begin "You can't . . . ," "You never . . . ," and "You don't . . . ." Instead, use positive statements that reinforce your child's strengths and abilities ("We're lucky to have an expert like you around to give us advice." "I loved that poem you just wrote." "I'd like you to teach me how to throw a ball like that."). Even errors can be turned into positive statements that promote the learning process. Barzakov points out that if a child answers the question, "Who was the first president of the United States?" with "Abraham Lincoln," a teacher can always ask, "What did George Washington and Abraham Lincoln have in common that makes it easy to confuse them?" In this way, the child's ability to learn is affirmed.

Put on background music when your child is studying or learning something new. Advertisers have recognized for decades the importance of music in creating a mood that can motivate consumers to remember and buy their products. Parents and teachers can take a cue from these entrepreneurs and explore ways music might be used to create a mood for remembering and learning academic material. In line with Lozanov's recommendations, select a piece of Baroque or classical music with a slow and even pace to use as a background while your child studies at home. Examples of appropriate composers include Corelli, Teleman, Haydn, Bach, Albinoni, Vivaldi, Pachelbel, Beethoven, and Mozart. The organizations listed at the end of this chapter sell cassettes specifically designed to evoke a super-learning response. However, you can also purchase tapes of these composers at a good music store that will achieve the same effect. Engage your child in the process of selecting the music. If he wants to listen to rap or rock music while he studies, suggest that you conduct an experiment, trying the classical or Baroque music some of the time and his music at other times, and then compare the results.

A mind stretched to a new idea never returns to its original dimensions.

OLIVER WENDELL
HOLMES

We are only now on the threshold of knowing the range of the educability of man—the perfectibility of man. We have never addressed ourselves to this problem before.

JEROME BRUNER

Use drama to spice up your child's homework sessions. Instead of sitting hunched up at the kitchen table trying to prod your child into doing the next worksheet or textbook page, consider warming things up a bit with some improvisation that can reinforce what she's been assigned to do in class. Suggest that your child take on the role of the character in a story or a historical figure in a textbook and then carry on a conversation with her while she acts out the part. For example, in a geography lesson where the explorers of the new world are the focus, she might become Vasco da Gama or Ferdinand Magellan and explain to you all that she's experienced during her travels. You can ask for clarification or raise questions that may cause her to think more deeply about her role ("Did you ever feel like turning the ship around and going back home?"). She will have to use what she's learned in the book in order to create a good dramatic part for herself. Younger kids may want to do their role-playing with puppets or in costumes.

✎ STARTING POINTS ✎

Subliminal posters. Select material that your child may be having particular difficulty with and put the information on colorful posters that you and your child design. The words or numbers should be integrated in some interesting way with colors and pictures—just as advertisers combine images and words in their trademarks and commercials. For example, if your child is learning French, draw a picture of a dog or paste several pictures of dogs cut from old magazines on a piece of construction paper and write the word *chien* in large letters across the drawing or collage. Then place the poster on a wall near your child's study area. Mention to him that he doesn't need to study the material—he'll absorb it naturally over a period of time.

Positive seed thoughts. Spend some time with your child creating positive statements about learning ("Learning comes easily to me," "I love to learn," "I'm a great student,"). Make sure the words come from your child's own language. Then together create little "seed cards" or more elaborate posters to place near your child's study area. Alternatively, your child can record positive thoughts on a cassette tape to listen to whenever he needs a boost in his self-esteem.

Relaxation routine. Before your child is about to study, or during a study break, suggest that she lie on the floor and relax with her eyes closed. Guide her through a simple relaxation procedure by suggesting that her head feels like a marshmallow, her eyes feel like Nerf balls, her arms and legs feel like spaghetti, and her whole body feels like it's sinking into the floor. Play relaxing music (super-learning music, recordings of nature, or slow and mellow jazz pieces are particularly effective). This relaxation period can be used as a preparation for the rhythmic recitation or positive seed thought exercises, or it can function simply as a stress reduction technique to promote effective learning in general.

Visualizing success. While your child is in a state of relaxation (after doing the relaxation routine above or at any other time of day), suggest that he form an image of himself as a successful learner. Ask him to think about a time when he learned something new and exciting. Suggest that he experience the event vividly through all of his senses—picturing it, feeling it in his body, hearing sounds, and even tasting or smelling it. If he wants to, he can later draw a picture of the experience and put it up in his room as a reminder of his natural genius.

Rhythmic recitation. Use the relaxation routine before starting this activity. Then, take a portion of material that your child needs to memorize or comprehend—spelling words, math facts, foreign language vocabulary, historical dates, or a textbook passage, for example—and repeat the material to your child in rhythm to a piece of slow, regularly paced Baroque or classical music (four-four time is recommended by some). Try varying the pitch of your voice, saying certain words or portions of the text softly, other segments loudly, and still other sections in a medium tone. After your child has returned to a normal state of alertness, suggest that she read the material out loud in rhythm to the same music.

RESOURCES

Buzan, Tony. *Use Both Sides of Your Brain*. New York: E. P. Dutton, 1974. Numerous techniques for improving reading speed, study skills, and notetaking ability. Most helpful for older students in assisting with traditional lecture and textbook type learning.

Hendricks, Gay, and Russel Wills. *The Centering Book*. Englewood Cliffs, NJ: Prentice Hall, 1975. A well-organized and practical guide to relaxation exercises and other activities designed to enhance learning. See also the *Family Centering Book*.

Kline, Peter. *The Everyday Genius: Restoring Children's Natural Joy of Learning*. Arlington, VA: Great Ocean Publishers (1823 North Lincoln St., Arlington, VA 22207), 1988. Personal account of the author's experience with super-learning methods. Includes many excellent suggestions for making learning come alive in the home and classroom.

McCarthy, Michael. *Mastering the Information Age*. Los Angeles: Jeremy P. Tarcher, 1991. For older students and working professionals. A guide to accelerated learning based on Lozanov's techniques and the author's own system.

Ostrander, Sheila, and Lynn Schroeder. *Superlearning*. New York: Delta, 1979. The best-selling introduction to Lozanov's method. Includes lists of musical selections and practical exercises.

Rose, Colin. *Accelerated Learning*. New York: Dell, 1985. Another book that combines Lozanov's approach with other educational technologies, such as neurolinguistic programing and guided imagery. Generally written for the adult learner but includes sections specially designed to be used with children.

Vitale, Barbara Meister. *Unicorns Are Real: A Right-Brained Approach to Learning*. New York: Warner, 1985. A varied collection of multisensory strategies for teaching math, reading, and study skills at home and school.

Periodicals

Brain-Mind Bulletin, P.O. Box 42211, Los Angeles, CA 90042. Newsletter published every three weeks that reports on the latest developments in brain research as they impact on psychology, behavior, and education. Includes frequent articles on super-learning approaches.

Holistic Education Review, 39 Pearl Street, Brandon, VT 05733-1007; (802) 247-8312. Quarterly publication that covers innovative methods in teaching and learning as well as broader educational issues.

Organizations

Barzak Educational Institute Inc., 88D Belvedere, San Rafael, CA 94901; (800) 672-1717; in California (415) 459-4474. Conducts seminars for educators and other professionals in OptimaLearning,™ an adaptation of Lozanov's suggestopedia. Mail-order service for super-learning cassettes and foreign language instruction for children.

Learning in New Dimensions, P.O.Box 14487, San Francisco, CA 94114. Conducts trainings for educators and foreign language seminars for adults. Has mail-order service for educational materials and super-learning music cassettes.

New Horizons for Learning, 4649 Sunnyside N, Seattle, WA 98103; (206) 547-7936. An international clearinghouse for information about new strategies in learning. Publishes newsletter, *On The Beam,* three times a year.

Society for Accelerative Learning and Teaching (S.A.L.T.), Box 1216, Welch Station, Ames, IA 50010. Professional association of educators concerned with applying super-learning insights to classroom environments and other formal learning settings. Conducts research, sponsors conferences, and publishes a periodical and several books and pamphlets.

Superlearning™ Inc., 450 7th Ave., New York, NY 10123; (212) 279-8450. Sells tapes and resource materials based on the book *Superlearning* by Sheila Ostrander and Lynn Schroeder.

17. *Cheers for Peers— The Value of Cooperative Learning*

It was lunchtime at Swasey Central School in Brentwood, New Hampshire, and first-grade teacher Gail Stevens had reached her limit. She'd worked long and hard with one student, Andrea, who still failed to grasp the concept of regrouping in subtraction. What would it take to help her comprehend? Stevens discovered the answer after lunch, when Andrea came running up to her with a friend. They had been writing in sand out on the playground, doing little math problems. Andrea's friend proudly proclaimed, "Mrs. Stevens, you don't have to worry anymore because during recess I taught Andrea how to regroup."

Such peer tutoring represents a powerful but neglected instructional tool that has strong historical roots and is making something of a comeback in educational circles. Back in the days of the one-room schoolhouse, older or more advanced kids routinely worked one-on-one or in small groups with younger or less knowledgeable students. Teachers needed all the help they could get with children of so many different ages represented in one classroom. As far back as the early 1800s, a man named Joseph Lancaster achieved fame by claiming it was possible to teach one thousand children at a time using a complex tutoring system in which students were put in charge of training each other. Over the past few decades, though, the instructional methods of peer tutoring fell into disuse in schools, perhaps partly because they challenge the concept of the adult teacher as the holder of all knowledge in the classroom.

Yet in an era of growing classroom size and overburdened teachers, peer teaching can help ease a teacher's load by making children instructors. The economics of peer teaching also make sense. According to a recent study conducted at Stanford University in California, peer tutoring is more cost-effective in terms of instructional gains than computer-assisted instruction, small class size, or a lengthened school year.

TRAINING THE TUTORS

A large body of research suggests that peer teaching provides solid academic gains for the children being taught. But what is even more remarkable is that in many studies, the tutors themselves appeared to make strong academic gains by teaching what they already knew—often improving as much as the tutees themselves. This result seems to affirm the old Latin saying *Qui docet discet*: One who teaches, learns.

According to Helen Featherstone, former editor of the *Harvard Education Letter*, "Tutoring gives children an excuse to review the basics; it also forces them to think about how they learn." In line with these observations, an increasing number of tutoring programs are being created in which kids who have trouble reading, who are potential dropouts, and who have disabilities are asked to serve as tutors. One program turned the tables on the usual learning expectations and had twelve behaviorally disabled students teaching sign language to twenty-four gifted students twice a week. Such programs boost self-esteem as well as academic performance by empowering learners to become teachers.

Peer teaching, however, is not without its drawbacks. Although children informally teach each other all the time, creating a formal tutoring program in school presents a major challenge. Robert S. Feldman, professor of social and educational psychology at the University of Massachusets at Amherst, says, "We put teachers in school for four years to learn how to teach. We can't expect students to teach without some extensive training." Untrained student tutors may ridicule other students' mistakes, overly control the teaching session, or simply give up on students who aren't making much progress.

When educators are committed to a well-structured program, however, peer tutoring can be a success. One such effort, called Companion Reading, was developed by Grant von Harrison, professor of educational psychology at Brigham Young University in Provo, Utah, for kids in the first grade and up. First, teachers provide reading lessons for the whole class. Then they train students to work in pairs with classmates for ten-minute review sessions in which they help each other read selected words and phonetic patterns, or concentrate on reading comprehension or writing tasks.

The training procedure is relatively simple: The teacher shows students how to place their finger under a word and ask their partner to say the word. If the partner reads the word correctly, they're instructed to say "good" or offer other praise and go on to the next word. The teacher circulates among the children to make sure that the procedure is followed and that the tutors are providing accurate feedback. Children also read and write stories together. Bobbie Talbert, a Russelville, Arkansas, first-grade teacher, reports that this system has revolutionized her classroom. "People wouldn't believe it if they didn't see what happens to the whole child. We don't have discipline problems. No kids teasing others . . . those things come from low self-esteem and we don't have that anymore." In addition, reading achievement rates have almost doubled since the implementation of the program.

Other peer and cross-age tutoring programs have had similar success stories. In San Antonio, Texas, high school students on the verge of dropping out are paired with elementary school students in a tutorial program that takes place eight hours each week. Tutors are paid the minimum wage for their efforts.

For the most part Thoreau made little impression on his schoolmates—and they little on him. One thought Thoreau "an odd stick, not very studious or devoted in his lessons, but a thoughtful youth and very fond of reading . . . not given to play or to fellowship with the boys; but shy and silent." On the other hand, it has been reported that the boys used to assemble about Thoreau as he sat on the school fence to hear him talk.

WALTER HARDING

What children can do with the assistance of others might be . . . even more indicative of their mental development than what they can do alone.

LEV VYGOTSKY

One high school student reflected on her tutoring experience: "Right now I feel very good about school and would give it an eight out of ten . . . when I was a freshman I would have given it a one."

In a tutoring program where fourth- through sixth-graders tutored kids in the primary grades in Boise, Idaho, peer teaching has been shown to be even more effective than conventional teacher-directed instruction. One reason for this amazing result seems to be the sensitivity many children have to the needs of their peers. In a study done at the University of Wisconsin, experienced teachers, sixth-graders, and third-graders watched a film of a group of eight-year-olds who were studying material that was sometimes very hard and at other times quite simple. Researchers discovered that the adults often overestimated how much the students in the film actually comprehended. The third- and sixth-grade observers, on the other hand, were better able to tune into the students' real needs. Peer tutoring, then, seems to tap into the intuitive genius that children have as natural teachers.

COOPERATIVE LEARNING: AN EXPANDED CONCEPTION OF PEER TEACHING

At the heart of the peer-tutoring approach is the notion that children learn best by learning together. This fundamental idea serves as the foundation for an approach to instruction closely allied to peer teaching: cooperative learning. Largely guided over the past twenty-five years by the efforts of two University of Minnesota psychologists, David and Roger Johnson, cooperative learning seeks to draw out the social nature that thrives inside every child.

According to the Johnsons, schools have typically organized classroom activities primarily on the basis of competition. Students vie with each other for the "right" answer, are graded on a statistical curve that requires a certain number of students to fail, and compete for less tangible rewards like the teacher's praise. Partly in reaction to the disadvantages of this system,

Boris had trouble reducing "12/16" to the lowest terms, and could only get as far as "6/8." The teacher asked him quietly if that was as far as he could reduce it . . . Much heaving up and down and waving of hands by the other children, all frantic to correct him. Boris pretty unhappy, probably mentally paralyzed. . . . She then turns to the class and says, "Well, who can tell Boris what the number is?" A forest of hands appears, and the teacher calls Peggy. . . . Boris' failure has made it possible for Peggy to succeed, his depression is the price of her exhilaration; his misery the occasion for her rejoicing. This is the standard condition of the American elementary school . . . To a Zuni, Hopi, or Dakota Indian, Peggy's performance would seem cruel beyond belief.

ANTHROPOLOGIST
JULES HENRY

many educators switched to a system of individualization, where students work in isolation from each other at their own pace. But while individualization avoids the survival-of-the-fittest mentality of the competitive approach, it tends to cut students off from their social instincts.

Cooperative learning avoids the problems inherent in both these approaches to learning. Instead of the teacher constantly having to admonish students with comments like, "Sally, turn around and don't talk to Joe," or "Do your socializing during recess, young man!," interpersonal contact becomes the vehicle through which knowledge is mastered in the classroom.

In cooperative learning, groups collectively pool their ideas for a single project—for example, writing a composition. They might begin by discussing their story ideas, brainstorm key words or elements of the plot, and then write the story line by line, modifying it as they go along—much as screenwriters work in preparing a television episode for production. Or, they might divide the work into segments, with one student responsible for the introduction, another student taking care of the middle part, and a third member in charge of the conclusion. Alternatively, they could assign different roles among group members, so that one person might do the writing, another might go over the composition for spelling and punctuation, and a third could be responsible for reading it to the class and leading a discussion.

The guiding principle in cooperative learning is that the group cannot reach its assigned goal until *all* members of the group reach their own personal goals. Individuals who shirk their responsibilities in the group (a phenomenon David and Roger Johnson have termed "the free rider effect") can be subjected to some intense peer pressure. In addition, the teacher might call on potential "hitchhikers" at any time to report on their individual contributions. Yet, in most cases, teacher monitoring isn't even necessary. "There is a strong sense of positive interdependence among group members," say the Johnsons. Some teachers require groups to merge their individual homework or classroom assignments into one single paper to be handed in and evaluated. The teacher then gives each individual a grade based on the achievement of the whole group.

None of us is as smart as all of us.

DAVID AND
ROGER JOHNSON

Competition, which is the instinct of selfishness, is another word for dissipation of energy, while combination is the secret of efficient production.

EDWARD BELLAMY

Research on cooperative learning suggests overwhelmingly that when children are allowed to work in collaboration with each other, rather than separately or in competition, their learning significantly improves, they feel better about themselves and their peers, their problem-solving skills are enhanced, and they generally have a better attitude about school. "You know where self-esteem comes from?" Roger Johnson asks. "It comes from peers, from being liked, accepted, connected." On the other hand, points out David Johnson, the message of competitive approaches tends to be quite different: "The minute you lose, your value ends. That's a terrible thing to tell a kid."

Peer tutoring and cooperative learning acknowledge and make use of the natural abilities that many children bring to the learning process. Cross-age teaching in particular creates important educational and emotional links between children of different ages, allowing the knowledge of one person to illuminate the innocence of another. Cooperative learning provides many kids with a sense of pride and accomplishment that they might not experience in any other way. It creates an atmosphere in which any child can be a teacher, no matter how rudimentary the skill level, since there is always something of value that a child can contribute to another person or to a group.

We destroy the . . . love of learning in children, which is so strong when they are small, by encouraging and compelling them to work for petty and contemptible rewards—gold stars, or papers marked 100 and tacked to the wall, or A's on report cards, or honor rolls, or dean's list, or Phi Beta Kappa keys—in short, for the ignoble satisfaction of feeling that they are better than someone else.

JOHN HOLT

Everybody has won, and all must have prizes.

FROM LEWIS CARROLL'S
*ALICE'S ADVENTURES IN
WONDERLAND*

★ WHAT PARENTS CAN DO ★

Parents who understand the value of peer teaching and cooperative learning will find the rewards to be well worth the effort invested. Here are some suggestions for supporting cooperative learning in your child's educational life.

Encourage teachers and administrators to build cooperative learning into school programs. Cooperative learning is used only about 20 percent of the time in American classrooms despite its highly successful track record. If your child's school is not using cooperative learning, or not using it enough, set up a meeting with school officials to discuss the effectiveness of these methods and suggest that they work out a strategy for implementing at least some features of this philosophy in your child's classroom. In addition to the approaches discussed above, there are a number of ways to do this. One school has developed a method called *ripple tutoring* where one student teaches another, then both go off to teach additional students. This "each one, teach one" system has maximum benefits at a minimum cost. Other approaches include setting up combination classes where teachers work with children of two or more grade levels who can then informally teach each other; mixed-age school activities (such as extracurricular clubs); and buddy systems or *adopt-a-class* programs where older kids provide informal assistance for their younger charges, teaching them how to take out library books, how to use the school computer, how to play games in physical education, and how to do a number of other school-related tasks.

Suggest that your child do homework with a sibling or friend. You can avoid power struggles during homework time by encouraging your child to collaborate with a brother, sister, or neighborhood friend on homework assignments. Research suggests that siblings who are widely spaced in age tend to work together better than those close in age. Provide the youngsters with some simple guidelines in helping each other, including avoiding criticism, making tasks specific ("Let's focus on writing one paragraph tonight"), giving immediate feedback, and arranging in advance to limit the session to a set amount of time.

Have family meetings on a regular basis. You may want to pattern your meetings after the family council model of psychiatrist Rudolf Dreikurs, who proposed these conferences back in the 1950s as a way of effectively dealing with problems and conflicts among family members. Dreikurs' rules were simple: Meet at a regular time every week. Anyone can bring up any sort of issue and everyone has the right to be heard. Sample topics might include setting television hours, negotiating household chores, dealing with privacy issues, arranging family outings, and deciding how to handle inappropriate behaviors.

Certainly, aggressiveness exists in nature, but there is also a healthy nonruthless competition, and there exist very strong drives toward social and cooperative behavior. These forces do not operate independently but together as a whole, and the evidence strongly indicates that, in the social and biological development of all living creatures, of all these drives, the drive to cooperation is the most dominant, and biologically the most important. . . . It is probable that man owes more to the operation of this principle than to any other in his own biological and social evolution.

ASHLEY MONTAGU

Two are better than one, because they have a good reward for their toil. For if they fall, one will lift up his fellow; but woe to him who is alone when he falls and has not another to lift him up. . . . And though a man might prevail against one who is alone, two will withstand him. A threefold cord is not quickly broken.

ECCLESIASTES 4:9–13

The majority opinion rules (you might need to modify this in households with two parents and one child, and decide how to break ties—some experts suggest the decision should be by unanimous consent). Decisions made by the group are in force for one week. No discussion is allowed on the decisions until the next meeting time. If the proposed solution to the problem did not work during the week, a fresh solution can be sought at the new meeting.

These rules can be modified to suit your own family structure. However, it's important that the meeting be truly democratic and that parents not seek to control, either overtly or subtly, the decisions made. These meetings provide a way for a family to govern itself cooperatively and maintain a sense of openness and fairness in the course of everyday life.

Plan collaborative family projects. The possibilities for growth are tremendous if you begin to think about your family as a learning unit that can collectively accomplish more than any member within it could individually. Ask family members to think of things they would like to learn more about (examples: the stars, ecology, dinosaurs, the Vietnam war, weaving). Arrive at a consensus for one major topic of interest. Don't force an early decision on this; make sure each family member feels satisfied with the result before proceeding. Then divide up the responsibilities for obtaining information about the chosen topic. One person might go to the library and get books, another might write to organizations for information, a third person might get materials necessary for learning more about or practicing certain aspects of the topic. Make sure everyone has an activity he or she feels good about. Then carry out the learning project and meet periodically to share information.

Turn family outings into collaborative learning experiences. Think about family vacations and trips as cooperative educational events. Whether you go to a museum, a park, a historical site, or take a trip to a neighboring state or another country, plan on documenting your experience as fully as possible. Determine in advance the roles each family member will take: who will take photographs, who will collect souvenirs, who will keep a diary of events, who will bring along an audio tape to interview individuals or record animal sounds. Each person is then responsible for producing a finished product (photo album, audio tape, written description, scrapbook) of the outing. Package the items in a large folio to represent a complete family record of the experience.

Play cooperative family games together. Many popular games pit one person against another. However, you can modify just about any game structure so that the goal becomes a collective one. Play a board game such as Scrabble, Monopoly, or Trivial Pursuit, or a physical game like volleyball, badminton, or softball. Instead of having individual players or teams compete against each other, work to achieve the highest score possible as a whole unit by pooling your individual or group points. Rather than trying to outwit your opponents, your strategy should involve helping others as well as yourself. In addition, play games specifically designed to stimulate cooperative feeling between individuals. (The Resources section below includes suppliers of noncompetitive games as well as titles of several books filled with cooperative play activities.)

RESOURCES

Johnson, David W., Roger T. Johnson, and Edythe Johnson Holubec. *Circles of Learning: Cooperation in the Classroom.* Edina, MN: Interaction Book Company (7208 Cornelia Dr., Edina, MN 55435), 1986. An introduction to cooperative learning for parents, teachers, and administrators. Contrasts cooperative learning with competitive and individualistic approaches.

Kohn, Alfie. *No Contest: The Case Against Competition.* Boston: Houghton Mifflin, 1987. Describes the harmful effects of competition in business, sports, school, and society in general. Well-documented argument for cooperative learning.

Orlick, Terry. *The Cooperative Sports and Games Book.* New York: Pantheon, 1978. Hundreds of noncompetitive activities invented or discovered by the author. See also his *The Second Cooperative Sports and Games Book.*

Organizations

Animal Town, P.O. Box 485, Healdsburg, CA 95448; (800) 445-8642. Family-owned mail-order business specializing in noncompetitive board games, outdoor play things, and children's tapes and books.

Cooperative Learning Center, University of Minnesota, 202 Patte Hall, 150 Pillsbury Dr. SE, Minneapolis, MN 55455. Major center for research in cooperative learning (Roger and David Johnson, directors). Write for available materials.

Family Pastimes, R.R. 4, Perth, Ontario, K7H 3C8, Canada. Manufactures and distributes more than fifty indoor games for adults and children, including cooperative versions of backgammon, Scrabble, and Monopoly. Free catalog.

International Association for the Study of Cooperation in Education, 136 Liberty St., Santa Cruz, CA 95060; (408) 429-6550. Promotes the study of cooperative learning at all levels of education. Maintains databases, publishes annual *Cooperative Learning: A Resource Guide*, a quarterly newsletter, and other materials.

Conclusion

We've come to the end of our journey into the child's natural genius. But I hope that for many of you who have made it this far, it will be only the beginning of a new adventure in learning that will take you and your children into exciting new territory. I realize there are probably still a few of you who resist my suggestion that all children are natural geniuses. Perhaps you're thinking that genetics places limitations upon what a child can achieve. Of course this is true to some extent. However, when one considers that every child has 100 billion brain cells to work with, and that only a small fraction of these cells may have been called into action thus far, those constraints seem comparatively insignificant. Moreover, we've learned a great deal in the past thirty years about how the brain expands its capacity to learn as a result of contact with the environment. In other words, the more a child learns, the more capable he becomes of learning even more. Consequently, a child's neurological makeup may well be subject to expansion as a result of the kinds of interventions made by parents, teachers, peers, and other segments of the child's world.

We do not really know what the parameters for genius are in children. As we've seen in this book, educational structures too often strangle children's natural genius before they have even had a chance to express it. Yet we have also seen many examples of instances when the child has been given a chance to express himself as an inventor, musician, linguist, artist, scientist, historian, or creator of culture in many other ways. We have caught a glimpse of what children can become when they are allowed to function at their best.

I believe that we have simply scratched the surface. Ultimately, children may represent the capacity within civilization itself to evolve into a more integrated whole. If our world is to survive, it will be imperative that the creativity of childhood be allowed to filter up through the dense layers of rigidity and ignorance in society and transform it from the inside out. This can only happen when we start to acknowledge the intrinsic genius of each and every child, and educate the child in such a way as to bring forth his riches into the world. The root definition of *education* is "to draw out" (not "to pound in," as some parents and educators believe). Its meaning is therefore inextricably linked to that of *genius*, whose definition as you will recall from Chapter 1 is "to give birth." Education is thus a process of giving birth to the natual genius within each person.

You may feel that your child is already destined for some fixed position in life or has her potentials limited in some other way. I'd like to invite you to let go of these limiting ideas and see your child's unknown possibilities. Antoine de Saint Exupéry provided a lovely metaphor of the child's potential in his book *Wind, Sand, and Stars*. Traveling through war-torn Europe, he encountered a child sleeping in his mother's arms in a crowded railroad car one day: "I bent over the smooth brow, over those mildly pouting lips, and I said to myself: This is a musician's face. This is the child Mozart. This is a life full of beautiful promise. Little princes in legends are not different from this. Protected, sheltered, cultivated, what could not this child become?" I'd like to leave you with the same question: What could not *your* child become?

Index

Organizations interested in scheduling Dr.
Armstrong for a presentation on the material
in this book can contact him at:

Thomas Armstrong, Ph.D.
MindStyles Consulting Services
P.O. Box 548
Cloverdale, CA 95425
707-894-4646